JAMES CONAWAY

THE KINGDOM IN THE COUNTRY

FOXNETWORKS.COM
the WINE SHOW.COM

AVON BOOKS ◆ NEW YORK

AVON BOOKS
A division of
The Hearst Corporation
1350 Avenue of the Americas
New York, New York 10019

Copyright © 1987 by James Conaway
Cover photo by Jerry Sieve
Map by George Ward
Published by arrangement with Houghton Mifflin Company
Library of Congress Catalog Card Number: 87-10035
ISBN: 0-380-71613-5

The Houghton Mifflin Company edition contains the following Library of Congress Catalog-
ing in Publication Data:

Conaway, James.
  The kingdom in the country.
  "A Richard Todd book."
    Bibliography: p.
1. West   (U.S.)—Social   life   and   customs.   2. West   (U.S.)—Public   lands.
3. West (U.S.)—Description and travel—1951–   . I. Conaway, James—Journeys—West
(U.S.) II. Title.
F595.3.C66 1987   978'.03   87-10035

First Avon Books Trade Printing: April 1993

AVON TRADEMARK REG. U.S. PAT. OFF. AND IN OTHER COUNTRIES, MARCA REGISTRADA,
HECHO EN U.S.A.

Printed in the U.S.A.

OPM   10   9   8   7   6   5   4   3   2   1

For Jessica
and
For Nona Lane Alley Jackson, *in memoriam*

Everywhere men feel the discrepancy between the faulty present and their vision of a golden past.

Thomas King Whipple
Study Out the Land

Enjoy the land, but own it not.

Henry David Thoreau
Walden

Contents

THE
KINGDOM
IN THE
COUNTRY

MILES   0   50   100   200
KILOMETERS   0   50   100   200

•••••••••• State Boundaries
∿∿∿∿∿ Route Traveled
▨▨▨▨▨ Indian Reservations
░░░░░ National Forests, Parks
▒▒▒▒▒ BLM Lands

N

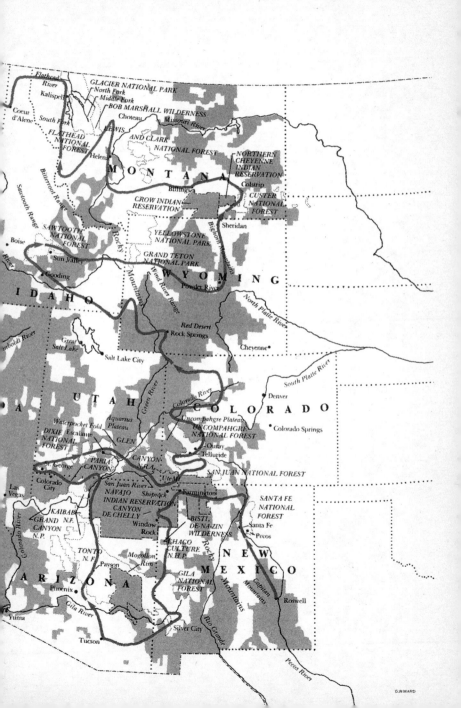

Vamos . . .

I FIRST HEARD about the West—the West as experience—from my grandmother. In 1900, when she was thirteen, she traveled from Arkansas to California in a covered wagon. Her mother had tuberculosis, and the doctor had prescribed a slow transition from humidity to drier climes. At night the girl slept under the wagon, and during the day she shot jack rabbits from the hard plank seat. Her father had taught her to use a rifle and once convinced her to shoot a cigar out of his mouth in an audacious display of marksmanship, or so she claimed.

My parents took the same route, to Tucson, in the early thirties, from Memphis, their Chevy convertible packed with everything they owned. They had just married and were avoiding hometown rules and expectations. The West was dry and distant, and imbued with exotic promise. They rented a stone house in the Sonoran Desert, and for a season my father chased cows for a rancher while my mother filled up canvas with paintings of ocotillo and red rock. They returned home two years later, to the prospect of children, a world war, and endless responsibility. But the photographs of them in the West show an unencumbered man and woman, touched with radiance, standing amidst the spectacular geologic rubble of high, arid ranges.

My father's spurs became the legacy of a man interested in escape, not horses. They hung on our wall in Memphis as life went on, the big Mexican rowels rusting, the hand-tooled leather going to dust. Memphis in the fifties claimed to have more churches than gas stations, and I grew up yearning for a glimpse of all that land beyond the Mississippi, and the freedom it implied. Memphis had served as a jumping-off point for west-ward migration a hundred years before, as important in its way as St. Louis. Travelers who were not "GTT"—Gone to Texas—angled up through Fort Smith, Arkansas, and then headed southwestward to their real or imagined destinies. Walter Pres-cott Webb compared the South and the West in *The Great Plains.* Both, he said, were exploited by the more powerful Northeast, both "tributary to the masters of the Industrial Revolution. Both kingdoms produced what promised to be a distinctive civiliza-tion, a thing apart in American life."

I finally got that glimpse of the West while in college. I worked one summer as a hotel desk clerk in Central City, Colorado, and another summer harvesting peas in Washington State. I rode the Greyhound across miles of apparent emptiness between home and what amounted to another country. I often told my-self that someday I would really get to know the West.

In the early 1980s I lived in Washington, D.C., about as far from those open spaces as I could get and still be in the republic. I worked for the *Washington Post,* writing profiles of various characters who washed up on the shores of Ronald Reagan's Potomac. They were an intriguing lot—the White House chief of staff, the director of Central Intelligence, the secretary of defense, the ambassador to the United Nations—all housed in buildings much like the *Post*'s, with security guards and windows that didn't open. I also performed, for the Style section, what were referred to as "day hits"—shorter pieces about prominent visitors as various as the Dalai Lama and a rising actress who had tied up Jerry Lewis in a film about urban obsessions.

One day, at the office of the secretary of the interior, in a gray edifice seemingly built to confirm every prejudice about federal architecture, I met James Watt, the secretary of the interior. Watt viewed the American West as an economic opportunity and an ideological battleground. His contentiousness and politi-cal zeal made him popular among developers and unpopular with conservationists. He had become the most controversial of all the interior secretaries, including Harold Ickes, who had used his friendship with Franklin Roosevelt to transform the department into a real power base. Ickes had a bedroom at Interior because he spent so much time there. He reportedly used it for his liaisons as well as for sleeping. He suffered a heart attack in 1937 and insisted upon recuperating there. Watt had the bedroom transformed into his executive suite, and used the expansive westward-facing office—the most impressive in town—only for ceremony.

I eventually found myself sitting with Watt in his limousine, in the basement of Interior, while the secretary denounced environmentalists and the Eastern press as tacit conspirators in an attempt to overthrow the democracy. He seemed oddly vulnerable, with his Coke-bottle glasses, high domed forehead, and ideological fervor. "The battle's not over the environment," he said. "They want to change our form of government."

It was a preposterous view, but unequivocally held and unequivocally stated—a rarity in Washington. Watt was dismantling Interior's influence, and some of its prime country as well, in the name of God and progress. But the controversy wasn't what interested me. I couldn't forget the epiphany I had experienced when I first walked into Secretary Watt's outer office, or the sense of possibility it entailed. In the deep russet carpet, the wood paneling, and the portraits of former secretaries lay the intimation of distant peaks, desert rock, and riverine lands. Congress and the Supreme Court had the law, the Pentagon had the power of destruction, but Interior had *real estate*—millions of prime acres in the West.

Later, I spread a map of America's public lands on my living room floor. Great gold-colored swaths represented Interior's land, most of it the responsibility of the Bureau of Land Management; green represented land administered by the U.S. Forest Service, the sister agency within the Department of Agriculture. Green and gold overlay much of the states between the Rockies and the Pacific—a federal domain of staggering immensity.

The two agencies—the Bureau of Land Management and the Forest Service—can be seen as a monolith. Both grew out of the

old General Land Office, which was set up to deal with the
remnants of western expansion. The BLM and the Forest Service control close to half of the intermountain West, a domain
almost as large as western Europe, but relatively unpopulated.
Surveying my map, it occurred to me that a person could travel
this federal kingdom from the Mexican border to Canada and
seldom leave it, and never lose sight of it.

Over the months I returned on my own behalf to the gray
buildings of Interior and Agriculture to talk to BLM and Forest
Service career officers and resource specialists. Many of them
seemed out of place in Washington with their wide ties and
sideburns, talking in accents from the far side of the Mississippi,
and trying to manage more than 300 million acres in the Lower
Forty-eight. Their kingdom, spread with some of the most beautiful and terrifying terrain on Earth, seems endless; but for many
people it has little meaning. To most Easterners, for instance,
public lands are parks—which actually represent just a tiny fraction of the whole—or worthless pieces of desolation left over
from an age of scalps flapping on lodge poles.

Meanwhile, like a lot of other males in their forties, I was
developing physical abilities beyond those required for a merely
urban existence. Weightlifting was an unacknowledged prepara-
tion for a fantasy beginning to take shape. I ran daily in Rock
Creek Park, a fugitive in shoes designed for the briefly unencumbered, and reflective garb more appropriate on an astronaut.
The park cuts through the city like a verdant wedge and offers
in its approximation of wildness one of the boons of Washington
life. On otherwise deserted trails, far from quarrelsome traffic,
I could envision bigger country where less rain fell; in miniature
chasms I saw the origins of a grander, broader landscape.

I began to collect maps as a lifer collects law manuals. They
provided detail about the national forests in the West and about
remote areas run by the BLM, forlorn and therefore alluring,
where roads and towns are pathetically overwhelmed by the
country.

I decided to head west, without a salary or the need for day
hits, and took a year's leave of absence from Style, knowing I
wouldn't return. I told myself that I was obeying the same im-

pulse that had drawn people out of fields and factories a century before; I had to admit that an adolescent urge had become a middle-aged preoccupation. Giving way to it was chancy and painful but irresistible. I said goodbye to my wife and children, knowing I wouldn't see them for months, and left in a van packed to the windowsills with camping gear, books, a typewriter, and oil company credit cards.

Every day travelers in station wagons and five-axle semis look out their windows at the West and think that all that alternately inspiring and godawful stuff belongs to the descendant of some titled lord or to some son of a bitch too tough or too dumb to up and leave. Most of us travel it for days without knowing that it belongs to *us.* People living there lease parts of the West and turn their animals or their clients loose on it. They dig holes in it, dynamite it, mine it, cut timber from it, steal parts of it to build their patios, grow dope on it, hunt on it, drive machines of fantastic aspect across it, get drunk on it, make love and sleep on it.

I left Washington to look at federal real estate. What I discovered was people—repositories of a national myth. Cowboys, Indians, gold miners, mountain men, and hustlers you might expect; but I also found some I couldn't have foreseen: a gunfighter holding sway over a remote part of Wyoming at the end of the twentieth century, for instance, and men still taking multiple wives in the shadow of flaming sandstone cliffs. I found defenders of a mythic place, abusers of the same, some ordinary and many extraordinary men and women. Where they fit in the larger scheme did not become clear to me until much later, after the bits of experience had been scattered. In the pages that follow, these people appear, not according to my itinerary, but in deference to their purposes in the land that supposedly belongs to no one.

· I ·
THE RANGE

I had driven for two days across the plains of Oklahoma and Texas, seeing redbud blooming on the streambanks and smelling manure and diesel fumes, when suddenly the West began. Huge country rises from the Pecos River toward a lost, rocky upthrust known as the Capitan Mountains, in southeast New Mexico. In April, antelope clover turns whole sections an electric yellow, and the long straight road mounts and dips among the thermals.

This rising plateau country is the range, the most salient aspect of the West, and the most evocative. Walter Prescott Webb wrote of the range, "There you will see action, experience adventure, hear strange new words, and see a relationship between man and man, man and horses, man and cattle, man and woman, that you will find nowhere else in America."

When I thought of the range I thought of sweeping country altered by cows and sheep; of men on horseback, remote settlements in difficult places; of gorgeous scenery in which you could become lost; of self-sufficiency and hardship and raucous good times. All of those images inform the notion of Western character so important to our national myths, an idea still vigorously mined by cigarette advertisers and scriptwriters.

In that notion of superior Western character, the range is ruled by individualists—ranchers bound by the wisdom and audacity of their own decisions. But what they think about this view, and how they actually do what they do in this era of feedlots and the disappearing beef-eater remained a mystery to me. I often wondered exactly who these people were and why they kept at it.

· · · · ·

THAT FIRST DAY in the West, as I approached the junction of the narrow highway and a dusty track without a sign, mailboxes came into view. They sat on a pipe frame that had been welded in someone's barn, proof of life beyond mirage; they were full of bullet holes. For the first time in hours I got out of my steel box, with its cushiony tires, vibrant electronics, and all the insulation of the contemporary voyager. The bright colors of mail-order catalogues gleamed in shafts of sunlight; I heard the wind whisper through the ventilated names of strangers.

One of those mailboxes belonged to Bud Eppers, who owned land in the last unbroken string of ranches in New Mexico, extending a hundred miles south from Vaughn to Roswell and sixty miles west to Ruidoso. This part of the state, close to the Texas Panhandle, had been the scene of big cattle drives the century before and now was home to more sheep than cows. They foraged and birthed on Bud Eppers's thirty thousand lean acres, the lambs and calves standing up on wobbly legs amidst sacaton grass and dried mud left by rare rainstorms, gawking at big open country between the high plains and the Chihuahuan Desert.

Eppers's was the first wire fence I came to west of the Pecos, and the first stop on my journey. I had met him at a stockmen's convocation in Denver the autumn before; he was expecting me. Bud owned cows and sheep but was identified as a sheepman, an ongoing bit of cultural segregation as old as the West. As soon as a cattleman acquires a sheep he loses a century's worth of social superiority. The sheepmen have the reticence of any minority but tend to open up more than cattlemen once you get to know them. Bud talked in unabashedly countrified locutions about yoyos who worked for the federal government, and the deficiencies of the Federal Land Policy and Management Act, which forced the BLM to actively manage the land. He had a boxer's two-tiered nose, and when he took off his hat he revealed the white head that is the hallmark of ranchers.

I assumed that a man with thirty thousand acres lived in relative splendor, with a green lawn and a servant or two. But Bud lived in a whitewashed stone house that had a corrugated iron roof and was surrounded by piles of rock, at the end of a sixteen-mile dirt road. A string of bright red chiles hung from the eaves. A cow skull sat on the ground next to a metal screen door that would have been more appropriate on a penal institution than a ranch house.

Bud came out to greet me in faded Levi's and pointy-toed boots that were split up the seams and covered with a patina of dried mud and sheep dung. A cracked leather belt with a silver buckle held up a middle-age spread. On his Cat hat—one of those billed, slogan-bearing caps made stylish by the drivers of Caterpillar tractors—was an advertisement for a feedlot in Roswell, the closest town. As he showed me around his place he pointed out a ramada he had built of pipe to shelter the geraniums from the sun. When we passed an old Chevy pickup sitting in the grass, a bullet hole in the windshield, Bud said affectionately, "Kids."

His three sons and a daughter all lived in distant towns. They preferred life on the ranch, but thirty thousand acres would not support more than one family, not when you needed forty acres to run five sheep or one cow. Fewer people were eating beef and lamb, and paying less for the privilege. And the federal government wanted to raise grazing fees, with the livestock industry already ailing.

The Epperses' house had been built in 1850 and patched and painted over the years by Bud and his wife, Alice, a sturdy woman who in a pinch could do any work required of her husband. Now she put on stockings and make-up every morning and went to work for the local congressman in Roswell, an eighty-six-mile round trip. Some days she and Bud talked more by CB radio than face to face, while she drove back and forth over the blacktop and he traveled the back roads in his pickup. Often he had to make dinner himself.

"And he gets to make up his side of the bed," Alice said.

"Women's lib," said Bud.

His CB handle was Redman, after the brand of chewing tobacco; hers was Padrona. They had been born within three months of one another, and delivered in Roswell by the same general practitioner. Both were accustomed to ranch life, however. She carried a .38 Smith & Wesson in the front seat of her car, mostly for shooting rattlesnakes, and he carried a .357 magnum.

We ate dinner prepared from cans. Bud had bought a secondhand pool table for $150, balls and cues included, and a beer tap where he drew a single ice-cold mugful each evening after work. There was plenty still to do on the house, but the Epperses didn't have the time or the money. Ranching wasn't the moneymaker it had once been. Bud's secondhand Cessna sat on a sage flat above the house, unused in more than a year.

His stepfather had come to New Mexico from Missouri in a covered wagon and lived to see space shuttles hurtled into the atmosphere on the screen of the Zenith color set in Bud and Alice's living room. He died at eighty, after that same general practitioner who had delivered Bud and Alice removed a piece of his intestine. He had seen some of the range wars in what became Chaves County. Water, not land, was the power base. Once you understood that, Bud said, you could understand the West.

Bud ran three hundred mother cows and sixteen hundred ewes on land not designed for such an industry. Now he could barely make ends meet. His ranch was part his and part the government's, although he didn't think of it that way. He had inherited the land and water, and grazing rights on government land that went with the water rights he owned, all from his stepfather. He treated all the land as his own, but in fact he paid grazing fees to the Bureau of Land Management for much of it.

The measurement of use was something called an Animal Unit Month, or AUM, a complicated formula that boiled down to $1.35 a month per cow, or 27 cents per sheep. That seemed cheap to me, but Bud recalled the time before the passage of the Taylor Grazing Act in 1934 when the range was free. It would be free again if he had anything to say about it. The range, in his view, had become the province of the politicians and bureaucrats. They had tried to force him to adapt his fences to let antelope through. Bud had always objected to the federal government telling him how to ranch, but this was the last straw. And he was willing to go to extremes to preserve what he saw as his rights.

Although he owned and carried several guns, Bud had never used one on a human being. Instead, he registered his protest to government interference by going to Rock Springs, Wyoming, to testify before the Senate Subcommittee on Administrative Practice and Procedure. The only other time he had stood up before a group of people was to call a square dance at the Roswell high school. Bud told the senators, "I resent statements by bureau personnel that all or the majority of public lands are being considerably abused by the livestock permittees."

Asked by a senator about BLM agents' knowledge of ranching, Bud had said, "They lack strongly in that area."

"His voice shook," Alice said.

"I was scared," Bud admitted, "but the force of what I wanted to say helped me overcome it."

He was invited to the nation's capital to testify again, and he took along a .38 revolver, as he always did when traveling. When he was finished on the Hill he dropped the pistol into the pocket of his suit jacket, which he left hanging in the lobby of the Hyatt Regency while he had a drink with another rancher. He didn't discover that the gun had been stolen until he got back to New Mexico. "I almost went back and found the bastard," he said. "If there's anything I hate, it's a thief."

I went to bed in their spare room and propped the pillows up against the whitewashed wall. Stuffed animals sat in old milk crates, waiting for the Epperses' grandchildren. Beyond the window I could see hills flushed with the yellow light of a westward-trending moon and the dark crease of the Macho Draw, which ran through the ranch, dry now. Bud had called this land "right rough ole country." I thought of the Anglos who settled here in the early nineteenth century; they had contended with the Spanish for what they considered *theirs*. In 1845 a magazine editor named John L. Sullivan excoriated foreign countries for "limiting our greatness and checking the fulfillment of our manifest destiny to overspread the continent allotted by Providence for the free development of our yearly multiplying millions."

Those multiplying millions were at first reluctant to die at the hands of savages, or to starve in country rough beyond their imagining; they had to be oratorically prodded out of Eastern cities. By the time of the Civil War most land in the West not too rough or dry to be plowed had come into private ownership, much of it through fraud. The Homestead acts and a string of uncommonly wet years moved nesters into places normally unfit for farming or other human sustenance. Boosters like William Gilpin, the territorial governor of Colorado, proclaimed that moisture followed the plow and that firewood lay under the sand and that, in short, agrarian culture could modify the West's aridity and transform the landscape. It was a cruelly deceptive claim.

Tenacious dirt plowers and their suppliers, including disgruntled Southerners fleeing the aftermath of the Civil War, settled by the dozens along the Macho, where no families live today. Three derelict schoolhouses are testimony to the homesteaders' optimism. Eighteen inches of annual rain at the end of the last century had meant flowing streams year round, and flourishing grain; but that precipitation proved to be a fluke, and widespread disaster followed in the drier years. Bud himself had been raised in one of the settlers' dugouts, a one-room house with a dirt floor, but he belonged to a very different tradition—that of the stockman, fencer of the range. His stepfather had bought up a number of homesteads early in the century, after extended drought ended the squatters' dreams.

John Wesley Powell, the first runner of the Colorado River and visionary of the settled arid West, advocated more land for homesteaders, to be sold or given to them according to the amount of available water. Where water was scarce, more land would help overcome the shortage of moisture and so of crops. But Congress stuck with its policy; too little land for homesteads created cemeteries in country where individual families could not make a living on a quarter-section or a half-section or even a whole section. Before the end of the century, cattle and sheep had come to dominate the West.

In 1890 the U.S. Bureau of the Census announced that for the first time it had been unable to discover a clear boundary between wild and settled areas. Officially, there was no longer a frontier. But the West as a state of mind remained important to Americans, whether or not they intended to go there. "American social development has been continually beginning over again on the frontier," Frederick Jackson Turner said in 1893, in a speech before the American Historical Association that left a lasting impression. Free land, he said, had made our unique democracy possible. "This perennial rebirth, this fluidity of American life, this expansion westward with its new opportunities . . . furnish the forces dominating American character."

The evolution of public lands could be seen from the window of Bud's spare room. The homesteads had clung to the river, where low meadows received water at least some of the year. They could be plowed, and wells dug, and a house built like this one, within sight if not the shade of cottonwoods. The higher country, away from water—the land nobody wanted—touched and mingled with the private holdings, but its ownership had been ignored or taken for granted. No one wanted to buy this land when it was for sale. It had been free for the use up until the passage of the Taylor Grazing Act. Now the government leased it for far less than the cost of grazing rights on similar private land, but ranchers had always considered the public land theirs. They still did.

Bud had not saddled a horse in two years. Dirt bikes were faster than a horse, he told me, and cheaper. "When my Honda's settin' there, it ain't eatin'," he liked to say.

He and another rancher were getting ready to round up sheep to be tagged, a cooperative process known as neighboring.

Bud's neighbor straddled a new candy-apple-red Honda, much brighter than Bud's mud-splattered two-year-old. The rancher's jeans were unfaded, his shirt pressed, his Cat hat spotless. He wore a .38 revolver in a new nylon holster—protection, he called it—tied down to one thick thigh. He sold real estate in Roswell and had decided to take up ranching in one of the worst years in fifty.

They waited for the third member of the party to catch up, a Mexican who worked for Bud. He feared his dirt bike and rode it badly. Now the shriek of his engine carried up from the dry bed of the Macho, out of sight below the steep-cut bank.

"Watch it," said Bud.

The Mexican vaulted into view, legs dangling like wet linguine, and landed in a cloud of dust. He almost went over the handlebars but regained his balance and bravely smiled.

"You can't get good wets anymore," the real estate agent said, unperturbed by the presence of the Mexican, who spoke no English. "They used to walk up here from the border and hang around the barn, to see if you'd give 'em food. If you didn't need 'em, they'd move on."

"Now they walk right up to the house," said Bud.

"Or drive up."

All three men sputtered off in search of ewes, across land severely grazed for a century or more. I waited in the shadow of the barn. Half an hour later, forty sheep came down from the hills, made skittish by the dirt bikes. The men herded them into the corral and dismounted.

I joined them, as did a Mexican who worked for the real estate agent; we all waded in with pliers and blue plastic tags, grasping handfuls of wool and punching holes in the ears of the animals. The ears bled, and the sheep lunged and bleated, raising dust that drifted across the yard and the dry Macho and the arching, lemony sweep of country.

After the tagging was done, conversation turned to predators. Coyotes were the worst, Bud said. They crawled through holes in the net wire fences strung for sheep, and preyed on lambs. "It's damn near impossible for a coyote to get away from a dirt bike," he said. He carried a .22-250 rifle on the Honda, between his legs, fitted with an eight-power Leopold scope, the bluing long since worn away by the machine's vibration. Sometimes he just ran over the coyotes.

Eagles were also a problem. In the old days ranchers killed them, but that was illegal now. The real estate agent remembered checking snares with a dog, which killed most of the predators on the spot, but not the eagles: "We had to beat 'em off that dog."

The sheep were to be trucked to spring pasture. The men loaded them into a trailer and then put the dirt bikes into the pickups, just like horses. Bud said goodbye to his neighbor and climbed into his pickup with his Mexican, Abel, and me. Abel's clothes were grease-stained and smelled of wood smoke. As Bud drove toward home, Abel jumped out of the truck to open gates, the real measure of distance and proprietorship on land with few natural barriers.

Abel got out for good at the tin-roofed shack where Bud allowed him to live and unloaded the hated dirt bike. He had wrecked it once and broken his wrist, but biking went with the job. I felt sorry for him.

"Hope we get some wind," Bud said. "I want to burn that old sacaton in the bottoms, so the new grass'll grow."

Bud went out to the machine shed before supper, to change the oil seal in the Honda. Alice, sitting on the sofa and combing out her freshly washed hair, told me something of his past. The conversation was accompanied by the sound of the television set.

Bud's real father had left his mother while Bud was an infant, Alice said. "He never knew why his father left, he never asked his mother. He thought if she'd wanted him to know, she would have told him." She tugged the comb through a tangle. "His father didn't go far, just down into Texas. We pass the town all the time, on the way to El Paso. Once I said, 'Why don't we get off the Interstate and go look up your father?' Bud said, 'I don't care to meet him.'

"Bud can't tell even a little lie. It's what gets him, gets all the ranchers, into trouble. Their individuality."

He came in and washed his hands. He sat down with the newspaper. "I've never seen so many ranches for sale," he said.

The next morning the Epperses' oldest boy, Tom, called to ask if he could drop the kids off for the weekend. He ran a feedlot in the Texas Panhandle; he and his wife were headed for the Albuquerque Marriott for a brief vacation.

Bud and I drove out after lunch to meet them. "My forebears made all the improvements here," he said, pointing to a stand of grama grass. "They made the pastures and drilled the wells and put the water around. But the BLM don't think ranchers are worthy. They don't know anything about ranching. They're bureaucrats. They sit around that Roswell office with all their vehicles and their feet up on the desk, and try to tell us what to do."

We sat next to the highway, facing east. Thermals on the horizon gave the impression of rampaging herds. Antelope strolled across the foreground, with mulish faces and white rumps. A station wagon sailed up on the far side of the road, and Tom and his wife and children got out. Tom wore a new Stetson, his wife a new blue pantsuit. The towheaded boy rose in his grandfather's arms, followed by his sister. They were Kirk and Lisa, six and seven, minted in the Panhandle and soft as her Cabbage Patch doll.

A rancher cruised past in a pickup, finger raised in greeting.

"They foreclosed on him," Bud said, of the rancher.

"The heck!" said Tom.

Tom and his wife went on to Albuquerque; Bud and I drove back to the ranch, with Kirk and Lisa on the seat between us, sitting contentedly on the tools of their grandfather's trade— baling wire, a Phillips screwdriver, a chisel, and a .357 Ruger.

Bud looked down at Kirk. "Now what's this I hear about you being in *love*?"

Bud turned in past the riddled mailboxes; he fished his CB microphone down from the sun visor and thumbed the button. "How 'bout it, Padrona?"

Nothing but static came back. He tried it again, and put the mike away. "I was lucky to get the gal I got," he said. "She's town-raised but moved out here and learned to like it. It's not something everyone would enjoy. You learn to tough it out, to pull together. Our lifestyle's changed," he added, "with Alice working and me on all these boards."

He was chairman of the Public Lands Committee of the New Mexico Woolgrowers Association and a similar committee of the New Mexico Cattlegrowers; president of the New Mexico Public Lands Council; and vice chairman of the Public Lands Council of the National Cattlemen's Association. Now Bud wanted to run for the New Mexico legislature. He hated government so much he was about to become a politician.

Spending time with Bud, I had learned that the range is an intensely public affair and that ranchers depend heavily upon the system, like everybody else. They have to pay rent, obey rules, fill out forms, and tolerate the presence of government specialists in water, grass, and livestock on "their" ranches.

Alice had beaten us home. She was watching television, shoes off, stocking feet up on the couch. Lisa and Kirk changed into their bathing suits but Alice wouldn't let them swim in the water tank, it being only April. Bud took them out into the dust and spent an hour tossing a softball while they cut at it with an old hickory bat. Then he drew us both a beer. Alice served enchiladas and sat off to one side, dieting, while the men ate.

That night Bud stood in the front yard next to his Honda, watching thunderheads build in the north. The unused Cessna sat forlornly against the gray backdrop. The wind had come up; the sky, spectacular even by Bud's standards, held a burnt ocher sun and purple wisps of moisture riding down toward Mexico.

Spidery lightning spooked the kids, promising rain.

"We won't catch it," Bud said. "Not when the fire stays in the clouds."

Big drops drummed on the tin roof but, sure enough, the rain moved on.

"Oh, it's good ole country when you can get some water on it," he said. "Maybe this wind'll hold. I've got some grass that needs a-burning."

▪ 2 ▪

I HEADED NORTH, toward Santa Fe. I had seen rangeland as it is popularly envisioned, too dry and difficult for anything but livestock, and often too dry for that. There are 300 million acres of public range in the West. Slightly more than half of that domain is administered by the BLM and supports 4 million head of livestock. In fiscal 1985 the BLM took in about $15 million in grazing fees. That is a fraction of what the land would generate if competitive rates were charged, but the range has other functions, some of them subtle. Much of America's breeding stock is not confined to feedlots but roams the range instead; and there are people who depend upon the vastness of the range to support ways of life that would otherwise evaporate—some of them distinctly odd by urban standards.

The Forest Service is also in the range business. Some people in the West think the heifer is a more fitting symbol of the FS than the black bear. Bud Eppers had shown me BLM range, and now I wanted to see some belonging to its sister agency.

The land rose gently, the emerging mesas promising bigger things to come. Outside Vaughn ("Home of the Mattaburger") I passed a boy wobbling along on a ten-speed beside the highway, reminding me of home. Sundays in strange places inspire a peculiar sort of loneliness. I stopped at an isolated gas station where a woman sold Coors to men in pickups, on their way to somewhere else. I wanted a beer, but she couldn't change my hundred-dollar bill—Washington money. In the van I had nothing stronger than chicory coffee and some garlic hanging in a mesh bag from the roof, so I had to settle for water from my tin Sierra cup.

To the north I could make out the tail end of the high Rockies, what early explorers had called the Shining Mountains, snow-drenched and too distant to be real. Blue sky lay flat against the western horizon. Islands of juniper and piñon pine lay beneath flat-bottomed cumulus kiting at the end of high-tension wires, in a clarity that destroyed all depth perception. This part of New Mexico had linked the plains and the mountain West since prehistory. Cíbola, the mythical cities of gold, had brought the conquest through. "Romantic, histrionic, cruel, and trance-bound," Bernard De Voto wrote of the Spanish in *The Course of Empire*, "they marched in rusty medieval armor toward the nonexistent." This portion of New Mexico had been a trading route for Indians, home to Spanish settlers, and later became part of the Santa Fe Trail.

The Santa Fe National Forest is the source not only of recreation but also of forage, firewood, and old blood claims. I could see that much of this national "forest" was in fact high, open range. It surrounded whole towns, among them Pecos, which was older than nearby Santa Fe and had been bypassed by the picture framers and blue corn tortilla entrepreneurs who had turned Santa Fe into another tourist stop.

Pecos lay a few miles off the Interstate. I passed through after everyone had gone to sleep and drove on up the canyon. The Pecos River rose in the wilderness not far away, fat with snow melt, roaring in the darkness. I spent the night in a Forest Service picnic area and the next day returned to town. Pecos's little rancheros were planted with overturned jalopies preserved in the clear mountain air. The eaves of the houses were hung with strings of chiles. Two girls in tight jeans waved at backfiring low-riders passing on the main street. There were a post office, a dry goods store, two bars, including one with a sign, "No knives allowed on premises."

"Pecos had more than its share of dark legends," Willa Cather wrote in *Death Comes for the Archbishop*. Coronado came through in the sixteenth century. At the Pecos pueblo he picked up the Turk, an artful Indian liar later garroted in what is now Kansas for failing to produce cities of gold. Before the Plains Indians had horses, they came to Pecos on foot to trade with the Indians of the desert West and with Spanish settlers out of Mexico. They had alternately violent and affectionate relationships, the latter apparent in most of the faces on Pecos's main drag.

The Pecos pueblo had moved en masse to Jemez, about fifty miles west, in 1837, leaving the land to the Spanish settlers. The Indians had also left an old masterpiece given to them by the viceroy; it still hangs in the church, La Iglesia de San Antonio de los Pecos. Supposedly it's a Caravaggio.

I walked past the open windows of the parochial school, where a confirmation class was in progress. Young voices sang hallelujah while birds piped in the fallow field opposite. Catkins had appeared on the willows. Inside the church, the lacquered white altar seemed to glow. Elaborate carved *santos* offered an abbreviated religious and secular history: Christ with a crown of thorns, an hidalgo, and what I presumed was a Franciscan friar. High above the altar, suspended by chains, hung an oil painting of Christ with angels at his feet, and a firmament of gold and gorgeous blues.

I found the young priest in a room with whitewashed walls, his black beard neatly trimmed, on his way to visit shut-ins. "I don't know if it's a Caravaggio," he said. The painting, he noted, represented one of the few material possessions the descendants of the original settlers had managed to keep. "After the Mexican-American war, New Mexico became independent. The treaty said the property of settlers would remain theirs. Much of it was communal and that's anathema in the United States."

The government said they had to fence the land. Most refused. Many people moved into town to live, still considering the outlying land theirs. But it was later confiscated by the U.S. government and put into the national forest.

The priest said, "These people have been living off what they consider theirs ever since."

The headquarters for the Pecos District of the Santa Fe National Forest was an amalgam of concrete and glass recently sunk in the red earth and ringed by green pickups. There I met a large and friendly range conservation officer—"range con"—named Pete. He explained that the Pecos District consisted of 350,000 acres out of 1.5 million acres in the Santa Fe National Forest and included the Pecos Wilderness and the snowy peak of Pecos Baldy, visible from the main street.

Two thousand souls lived in Pecos, according to Pete, most of them dependent in some way on *La Foresta,* as the Forest Service was known in those parts, and occasionally at war with it. The forest was used for grazing only from spring through early autumn; permittees were at that moment preparing to drive their herds onto public pasture. Two thousand cattle ran on the Pecos District, owned by fifty-six permittees, most of them of Spanish descent, some owning only a few animals. "There are lots of petty rivalries," he said. "They're always trying to get permission to run more cows on the forest. They've got problems, mind you. There's no protection on government land. People will kill one of their cows, throw it into a pickup, and butcher it at home. Somebody just stole a permittee's new corral. The whole damn thing!"

Most were poor, but not all. "I've got a rich one who lives in a penthouse on Fifth Avenue and comes out for a month every summer. He's not a rancher—it's a tax deduction. He wants Uncle Sugar to take a little less of his daddy's money. When he's out here he buys up every cow in sight and then lets somebody else take care of them. He wears a safari jacket and little khaki shorts, but he's good people."

The Forest Service and the Bureau of Land Management share a common mandate and common problems, although the Forest Service's 130 million acres of graze are comparatively well watered, and their use is more restricted. Both agencies grew out of the old General Land Office set up in 1812 to deal with federal lands. Settlers and others got their land free—or almost free—but the most valuable parcels often went to those with the best political connections. By the turn of the century fraud was so pervasive in the GLO that Gifford Pinchot, founder of the modern Forest Service, convinced his friend Theodore Roosevelt, who was then the U.S. president, to move the forest reserves out of the GLO and into the Department of Agriculture. That is where they have remained.

For almost thirty years after the breakup, the GLO functioned defensively, a paradigm of inefficient bureaucracy. The Taylor Grazing Act, written under the guidance of Secretary of the Interior Ickes, put an end to what was known as the "public domain" by assigning exclusive rights and creating grazing districts administered by the Grazing Service—and later the BLM—which issued permits to users of record. The act favored ranchers who owned some land and already had the habit of using public land. It eliminated itinerant sheepherders and limited the entry of new ranchers in an attempt to correct overgrazing, which has not abated in more than a century.

The Forest Service, insulated and politically nurtured in Agriculture, became a more professional agency, complete with uniforms and rule books. FS grazing allotments aren't interspersed with private or state land, as BLM parcels are, so FS lands can be more effectively supervised. FS grazing regulations are stricter than those on BLM land, and the FS doesn't have to face grazing advisory boards made up of local ranchers like Bud Eppers.

I rode to Santa Fe with Pete and his boss, the district ranger, to attend a wildlife and grazing workshop. To the left of the highway lay the high, dry P-J (piñon-juniper) country, which would eventually peter out in desert, and to the right, the narrow, parched defiles and arching headlands of the Santa Fe National Forest. It is divided up among the Pecos, Coyote, Cuba, Jemez, Las Vegas, Tesuque, and Espanola districts. Each reports to the forest supervisor, who in turn reports to the regional director, who in turn consults with Washington.

Each level has a certain amount of autonomy. District rangers are linchpins between users and the government and take heat from both sides. This district ranger lived in the FS village and occasionally went jogging, curious behavior in Pecos. His greatest responsibilities were evenly divided, he said, between grazing and the cutting of timber. Recreation, however, was gaining.

Pete said, "Recreationists are just like cows. They shit where they sleep."

The previous year, fifteen thousand cords of firewood had been cut on the Pecos District, including two thousand cords of green piñon posts. But most of it was "dead and down," meaning expendable. Cutters came from as far away as Albuquerque, annoying the Pecosans. "They tend to think of it as theirs," said the ranger.

In Santa Fe two dozen range cons and the range technicians had gathered in a modern office building beside the highway, most of them with the telltale disk of Skoal or Copenhagen in their hip pockets. They discussed a controversial new grazing procedure known as the Savory method, after a Rhodesian expatriate whose holistic approach to resource management had swept through the ranching establishment. The Savory method contradicted exponents of the old rotation system upon which many a federal program and reputation had been built. The rotation system, which called for short periods of disuse so the range could recuperate, though never fully, was to the West what the V-eight once was to Detroit. It had been used for so long that no one wanted to change it.

Savory advocated "time-control" grazing instead. Simply put, that meant moving cows regularly, rather than allowing them to stand and eat most of the ground cover at any given place. Savory's controversial wagon-wheel fencing allowed cows to gradually circle a water source like the hands of a clock, macerating the soil with their hooves and increasing seed germination, and then moving on.

It was difficult to see how the Savory method or the rotation system related to the small ranches near the rugged Pecos District. There wasn't enough grass, period, to justify the academics or the cows. I wondered how a rancher with a handful of cows and no trust fund could make it, when big operations were going bust.

Driving back to Pecos, the irrepressible Pete said, "We're supporting a huge infrastructure by spending taxpayers' money on 'management.' Range management has turned into producing grass for livestock. That's ass-backwards. We should be using livestock as a tool to create the landscape we want."

* * *

I told Pete I was looking for a small ranch, to check out the economics of the small-scale operation firsthand. He knew of what was surely one of the smallest in the West; it belonged to an old Spanish rancher named Juan, who owned nineteen cows. He was nicknamed Sapanda—a Spanish word meaning a car with a broken spring—because he had injured a leg in a riding accident and walked with a limp.

Juan's cows used the grazing allotment known as the San Luis–El Barro, forty thousand acres of steep P-J country with a rough dirt road crawling the ridges. The San Luis–El Barro supports the grand total of eighty-three cows. They feed in tiny, well-watered valleys that in April collect the sun like quicksilver and only then are lush with Kentucky bluegrass, redtop, grama, and crested wheat grass.

I rode out the next morning in the FS pickup with a range technician named Gonzalo, and Juan, a taciturn old man with a long, mournful face who was working temporarily for the FS. His gray hair was mashed flat by a straw cowboy hat, and his Levi's were worn almost to transparency. The faded denim jacket was buttoned to the neck. He carried a black lunch bucket, and when he spoke it was with a slight stutter.

"There's no future in cows," Juan said, soon after we had set out. "The government controls our land."

Gonzalo, the agent of that government, drove with great intimacy, massaging the steering wheel, fondling the gearshift lever, raising and lowering the window in an ever-changing accommodation of dust and fresh air. He was a GS 9, a low-ranking civil servant. The silver conchos on his hatband had been made by a lady friend, he said. Another lady friend had made the silver watchband. Gonzalo had the reputation as Pecos's local stud. He pastured two Arabians and an appaloosa higher up and used them occasionally to chase other men's cattle trespassing on La Foresta.

Gonzalo ran the show, but Juan and ranchers like him were the reason jobs such as range technician existed. Together the two men—rancher and regulator—were after a bull that had wandered onto Forest Service land before grazing season officially began. We passed the tiny hamlet of Colonias, where Juan lived—all dust and rock and three-legged dogs. He paid the U.S. government $1.35 per month for each of his nineteen cows grazing on public land. That amounted to a total of $149.34 for the approximately six months a year that the range was open to grazing.

I asked if he made money on cattle. Juan said, "I hope to break even."

The total of eighty-three cattle on the San Luis–El Barro had brought the Forest Service the grand sum of $650 in grazing fees the year before. Ten percent of that went to the county. When all administrative costs were tallied, the federal government estimated that it lost an average of $2.29 a month for every cow on public land. Grazing fees were too low, but raising them would cause a war, according to Juan.

Ten years before, he had served as a lieutenant for a radical Chicano named Tijerina, who had tried to claim large chunks of New Mexico for the descendants of Indians and Spanish settlers. Juan had taken part in the occupation of Echo Amphitheater campground and had traveled with a contingent of protesters to Mexico City, to plead with the Mexican president for support of claims based on old Spanish grants. Juan seemed an unlikely revolutionary, working part-time as he did in the Forest Service's Older Americans Program, cleaning up campsites and doing odd chores with Gonzalo.

Our road climbed into ponderosa pine, crossing and recrossing a broad avenue left by fire. The country greened up with aspen, the leaves quaking in the breeze—good cover for elk and deer. Grass clung to the exposed slopes, where the cows had to work to get it. A red-tailed hawk broke from a snag above the road, and wild turkeys scratched on the far hillside, moving warily up among the trees. An old ranch house sat abandoned. Gonzalo looked after the place and brought his sons up weekends to work on the fences. They regularly ran off motorcyclists from Santa Fe, who had torched one of the outbuildings and performed wheelies all over the lot.

Gonzalo honked his horn; the horses came running. We could see the bull standing unpleasantly among the willows, up to its knees in water. It had been captured twice and twice escaped.

Gonzalo saddled the appaloosa, tossed a braided lariat over the horn, and strapped on silver spurs. "I'm going to drive him through the gate," he said, "and into the paddock by the barn."

"I doubt it seriously," said Juan.

After Gonzalo had cantered off, Juan added, "I knew that bull's daddy. He was one mean son of a bitch."

The bull was a black Angus, hornless but large. Gonzalo approached it from behind, whistling and beating the lariat against the saddle. The bull turned on horse and rider, then changed its mind and lumbered across the meadow and into the trees. The sound of breaking timber suggested a marauding tank. The bull re-emerged, trailing a foot of slobber, and was skillfully driven into the paddock by Gonzalo.

"These young bulls won't stay with the cows," he said. "They wander. *No sabe.*"

We sat down next to the house, in the sun. Juan opened his black box and ceremoniously removed a bologna sandwich; Gonzalo contented himself with a cigarette. He didn't use chewing tobacco, he said, because the ladies didn't like the taste.

A handful of FS men stood outside the Pecos headquarters when we returned. Juan got out of the truck and asked the Anglo range con for a chew of tobacco. "You been pulling afterbirth with that old hand?" the range con asked, but gave him the packet anyway. Juan stuffed a bird's nest of tobacco into his mouth, and carried his lunch bucket off toward the post office, on his way home. He could have gotten out of Gonzalo's truck when we passed through Colonias, but he would have lost two extra dollars in pay and an opportunity to visit in town. He didn't say goodbye.

We had covered one hundred miles of dirt road to put a bull in a paddock so a distant permittee could come and claim it. The cost for the day's work would include Gonzalo's salary and Juan's minimum wage; also gasoline, and vehicular wear and tear. The government would lose more than $2.29 on that little bull.

I joined Gonzalo at his favorite saloon, appropriately named the Casanova. It had high ceilings, dark beams called vigas, rough-hewn tables, and a phalanx of Boone's Farm Wild Mountain Wine bottles behind the long wooden bar. Gonzalo stood at one end of the bar, facing the door, pouring beer into his leather-girded bulk with a facility I couldn't match. He and the big Anglo range con were a team, he said, but they never drank together. "He's a good man. He's respected around here because he stays. He can communicate," he added, "but he can't negotiate."

The phone on the wall rang. *"No aquí,"* Gonzalo said, without looking at it.

The bartender answered and, sure enough, it was a woman calling for Gonzalo.

"No aquí," said the bartender.

I said I couldn't understand how Juan made a living, with his tiny bit of land and a few cows; Gonzalo said he knew ranchers in worse shape. "I know one whose wife died in childbirth. He's trying to raise seven kids. Some of them are illiterate. The father's had a couple of strokes, and an operation. There's a big lump on his neck. He's trying to hold things together, to cook and get these kids thirty-five miles to school every day. When his ten-year renewal came up I went to see him, and I could see the fear on his face. I explained that I had to see his ownership papers. He went up in the attic and brought down a box full of deeds, some of them in Spanish. He said, 'Here, take what you need.' I could have taken his land and nobody would have known the difference. It's a big responsibility."

The phone rang. This female caller had seen Gonzalo's pickup out front.

"No aquí!"

"The ladies," Gonzalo said wearily.

"You always hurt the one you love," said the bartender, and a dozen men nodded assent without taking their eyes from the rerun of the 1973 Ali-Norton fight.

I was introduced to a bearded young Easterner, the only other Anglo in the Casanova. His hands were black from loading piñon. He had dropped out of school in New Jersey and was a self-confessed *raquitaria la Foresta*—a wood poacher.

"Everybody does it," he said, of poaching. "You get a permit to cut a cord, and you cut six cords. You're not going to get checked. Everybody knows there's not a Forest Service employee up on that mesa between four-thirty in the afternoon and eight in the morning."

Gonzalo looked uncomfortable. "We're putting sensors up there," he said. "Infrared, and magnetic. From now on we'll know who's trespassing where."

"But who's going to catch them? You don't have the manpower." The raquitaria turned to me. "You notice that the Forest Service never uses the word 'steal'? It's 'trespass' or 'violation,' but not stealing. At night, there's everything from firewood to cedar posts coming off the mesa."

"I could go up and bust somebody right now," Gonzalo said, "if that was part of my job. But I have to live here, too."

When the woodcutter had left, Gonzalo said, "I know that boy's mother real well."

The telephone was ringing.

The way to Colonias angled steeply up from the San Luis–El Barro road. I drove it the next day, to see Juan's ranch. I had no way of calling him since there were no telephones in Colonias. Half a dozen log and adobe structures stood out starkly against the wasted hillside. Ancient deadwood corrals leaned in various directions, empty, surrounded by the most spectacularly wrecked cars I had ever seen. More wrecks than dogs, although several of the latter came to look me over. A spotted dingo, accustomed to trouble, jumped when I slammed the van door.

I had no idea which house was Juan's. Nothing human moved on Colonias's littered plain; the entrance to the tin-roofed church had been nailed shut. A dust-shrouded compact with an open hatch stood outside a tiny house. Goats escorted me to the gate; inside, the packed dirt looked hard as brick. Deep shadow lay beneath the porch eaves, half the posts rotten and dangling in the wind. I called out and a woman answered. She stepped out into the sunlight, tall and dingy blond, wearing jeans and a blue T-shirt that displayed a surprising amount of Anglo amplitude.

"Who are you?" she asked.

I started to tell her, but she interrupted, "Juan's gone after the cows. Help me bring in these baby chicks."

She brushed past and took a carton of mail-order chicks from the car. She handed it to me and picked up another. I obediently followed her into the house, under low eaves. The kitchen had a dirt floor covered with flagstones. There was no electricity or plumbing, and basic supplies stood in disarray on shelves made of crates. "I ordered *araucanas* from South America, but they sent me Rhode Island reds, too." She placed a pan of water among the crying chicks. "Araucanas lay green eggs. Aren't they cute? My name's Brigitta."

Her accent belonged in Scandinavia. Before I could ask, she was telling me that she came from a family of distinguished Stockholm architects, that she was an artist, a photographer, a crocheter of avant-garde women's clothes, and a wardrobe person for a crew that filmed television commercials. The rest of the time she milked goats, read Louis L'Amour, and talked to her neighbor Juan.

"What brought you here?" I asked.

"A car wreck." It was a joke. "I lived in Santa Fe for years. It never occurred to me that the city would turn into one big boutique. My rent there went from two hundred and fifty dollars a month to six-fifty. I had to sublet. I advertised it as an adobe with a Swedish maid and got somebody right away, but I still couldn't take living there."

A friend with a contract to cut shingles on the forest had hired her. She drove past Colonias every day with the crew. Then she met Rodolfo, and independent contractor who built houses with materials harvested on the forest. He bought the house and an acre for nine thousand dollars, she said. "He could have gotten it for six. They won't bargain here, it's considered undignified."

He also owned the peeling yellow Lincoln outside, a yardful of pullets, and the stove into which Brigitta shoved butt ends of juniper. Rodolfo was presently gathering stone on public lands to build a client's house. Like Juan, he depended upon La Foresta, and so did Brigitta—for inspiration.

We went back outside. "It's beautiful," she said, "but by classical European standards this place is a dump. Chicano wind chimes"—she nodded toward discarded beer cans. "They leave their garbage down below, on the edge of the forest. The public land is the public dump—it's heartbreaking."

Juan appeared, leading a bay mare with a rope bridle. The collar of his Levi's jacket had been turned up, and he wore wrangler's gloves. "Did you see the water running in the arroyo, Juan?" she called. "It's so beautiful to see. I want to build a little dam there, Juan, and plant potatoes."

A grin broke that long, mournful face. He clicked at the horse like a young vaquero as we walked down to view the prospective potato field. Grass had sprouted among the Chicano wind chimes, and the water ran clear. "If I plant potatoes, Juan, they won't steal them." *They* were the neighbors, although Brigitta and Juan looked to be the only people in Colonias. "They don't know what potatoes are, Juan. They're ignorant," she told me. "They don't read anything here but license plates, and the obituaries, to see who killed who, and if they're related. They're obsessed with death."

Juan put the horse in his dilapidated corral and secured the gate with a discarded tire. The bleached barn siding looked ancient. He had grown up in the little adobe and was the only family member left. No chiles hung from the eaves, and the crumbling clay *horno* had roasted no corn in years.

Juan had delivered mail in Colonias on horseback, one of the last mounted postmen in the country, but now there were not enough people to justify it. He invited us into his house. Mexican coronets blared and skittered on the radio, one of his few possessions. A saddle sat on the floor at the foot of his frame bed—sign of a true cowboy. He owned a bit of land south of town where the cows wintered. The year before he had grossed twelve hundred dollars by selling beef to some friends and neighbors, and working in the Older Americans Program.

He had no coffee to offer, so we walked back to Brigitta's, where she stoked up the stove and moved blocks of government surplus cheese from the one chair, so Juan could sit. He watched her, transfixed.

"Now what shall I do?" she asked, hands on hips, taking in her jumbled domain. "Ah, yes, feed the goat."

"Wonderful woman," Juan said.

I thought he had a crush on her, and couldn't blame him. Brigitta liked hearing about his civil disobedience of twenty years before, he told me. The rumor in town had it that she was after his land and grazing permit, and they laughed together about that. I noticed that when Brigitta was present, Juan didn't stutter.

She returned and laded our coffee with mocha chocolate; then she led me into the back room. An album lay spread on a card table. In the photographs I saw Brigitta in elaborately crocheted shawls, bonnets, and gowns, leaping through the sunlit streets of Paris and Ibiza. "I used to think that was the normal way to dress. I sold it all with no effort. I came up here to start again, but now there's no reason to *do* anything."

A wild-eyed man with a bandana tied round his head stared out of a Polaroid. "Rodolfo," she said. "My wild Apache. He calls himself Spanish, but he's got to be a Jicarilla Apache. They all are around here. He and his so-called friends get drunk and he passes out and then they steal from us. When I go to California on a shoot I have to lock up all my stuff. I always come back, though. He'll do anything to keep me here."

Juan stood up when she returned to the kitchen. She folded down the old man's collar and smoothed the faded denim tips—the wardrobe mistress. Then she flipped the collar up again.

"Continuity," she said.

Pickups crowded the lot outside the Pecos high school the next morning, a Saturday. Weatherworn men gathered in the refectory to hear about an FS study to raise grazing fees. There was not a pair of tie shoes among them, and not much spoken English. Gonzalo and his colleagues moved gingerly among the ranchers and officials, "being responsive"—FS argot for politicking.

The range con told the mayor of Pecos, "The forest and the people have to be friends," to which the mayor responded, "They should be family."

The day before, I had asked his opinion of grazing fee increases and enforced quotas on woodcutting, which would mean fewer sales of Skoal, baking powder, and salsa. The mayor had said, *"Chinga la Foresta,"* a less delicate sentiment.

Juan arrived late, wearing his best wrangler's jacket and two-tone boots. He sat at the back of the room, alone, the picture of skepticism. He might own the smallest ranch in the West, and what seemed to be the least profitable one, but his passion for range and his "rights" was as great as that of the patriarchs of the big spreads, and their corporate equivalents. Juan Sapanda's connection to the land was considerably more solid than that of the administrators or, for that matter, most ranchers. It went back to the conquest.

The president of the cattlemen's association, an Anglo, stood up to address the group. His belt buckle was engraved "'73 Tri-State Rodeo Steer Wrestling Champion." He held aloft a copy of the FS grazing study and said in a modest drawl, "This is four million dollars' worth of mush. It looks like Greek. They spent five years to produce a political document. The assumption that you can stand an eight-to-ten-dollar increase is not correct, as we all know. Basically they decided they were going to raise fees and then backed the data out to justify it."

Gonzalo, the district ranger, and the range con sat shoulder to shoulder in silence. The president of the cattlemen's association asked the ranchers to write to their congressmen, then handed out demo response forms. None of them had spoken.

I asked the district ranger why the FS didn't respond to the rancher's criticism. "We're not here to defend the study," he said. "Grazing fees are too low. If we advertised tomorrow that we had land available for a dollar thirty-five an AUM, we'd have a line of applicants from here to Albuquerque."

"This is informational only," said the range con. "When it gets down to choices over exactly how the fees will be raised, then we'll hear from these guys. Well, I guess we'd better socialize."

Juan Sapanda was leaving. "They just held this meeting to be safe," he said of the FS. The president of the cattlemen's organization, Juan added, "should have said, 'Nobody leaves this room without signing a piece of paper and giving his address.' Then they could have shoved it under the noses of Congress, the BLM, and the Foresta."

Even if the ranchers signed such a petition, it would be filtered through the local FS office, the forest supervisor, and eventually the regional office in Albuquerque. In some altered form it might find its way to a management orifice in the Department of Agriculture, and maybe in yet another form to an undersecretary. Legislation might eventually be written that contained some kernel of the ranchers' opinions and might or might not be considered by Congress in a city far away. The chances of the studies, meetings, workshops, reports, and deliberations significantly improving Juan's fortunes were exceedingly thin.

There was something pathetic about the whole business: insufficient grass; insufficient cows to make a decent living; small ranchers at the mercy of the system and their own history. At the same time, they had the use of the land, and a shadow government in the guise of the Forest Service for recourse. Juan was making a living, such as it was.

I watched him limp out into the sunlight. He and Brigitta were going for tortillas and green chiles at the bus station, in splendid view of Pecos Baldy.

Small mercies, I thought.

∎ 3 ∎

THE COW MAY BE the symbol of the range, but in a curious way the sheep represents the stockman's collective conscience. Traditionally sheep have been kept from public view in the least accessible portions of the federal kingdom, but they contributed as much to wrecking the range as did cows. What cattlemen criticized sheep and herders for—overgrazing and independence—they encouraged in their own business. Cattlemen are still intolerant of sheep. They once thought sheep poisoned the streams, and many a sheep and herder were gunned down by hired thugs.

Lamb still suffers in the West from old prejudices, as a visit to a meat rack in most Western supermarkets proves. The number of sheep on the public range was greatly reduced by the Taylor Grazing Act, but it is still impressive. For a portion of each year Forest Service lands alone support a million sheep, most of them in the West. Ironically, sheepherding has improved in reputation since the partitioning of the range, which reduced the size of herds and confined them to higher, wetter country, where the grass has an equal chance.

Sheepherders are shadowy figures in our Western mythology, lonely aliens wandering a huge land. It is a tradition in the West to use Basque herders from the Spanish Pyrenees. Some of the richest sheep country still lies in Idaho, where the Basques, speaking a language stranger than Spanish, first arrived on railroad crews. Out of "Basco" boarding houses at the turn of the century emerged men looking for other work. They took up herding as a career choice, rather than as a continuation of some European pastoral habit.

I had been told that the sheepman with the most Basque herders was John Faulkner, in Gooding, Idaho. He lives just north of the Snake River where the road runs across cracked and bedded lava, past gigantic cinder piles with green pasture in the moist parts. I had no trouble finding the Faulkner Land and Livestock Company. It consists of twenty-five thousand sheep, sixteen hundred cows, sixty horses, about forty dogs—kelpies, Border collies, and Australian shepherds—a permanent payroll of forty people, and several hundred acres of alfalfa, beets, corn, and onions. Faulkner and his brother run it. John lives in a house with a neat white fence, with big hay barns out back.

He seemed bookish when we met, with glasses and a red beard shot through with white. When he laughed his eyebrows levitated in wild, adolescent delight, but his voice had gravel in it. He was fifty-two years old, with Scots ancestors on both sides. One grandfather had ridden with Teddy Roosevelt up San Juan Hill and later went off to Alaska at the president's behest with four hundred mules for the army. He was told to shoot them at summer's end, but the elder Faulkner disobeyed. He successfully wintered over the mules in the Yukon Valley and earned lasting notoriety. The other grandfather ran away from home in Missouri at an early age and ended up stoking fireboxes on the Union Pacific in Wyoming. He quit after a friend was killed in a head-on collision, and came west to Idaho, to raise sheep. He made and lost a couple of big herds, and Faulkner's father had to start his own business anew with only thirty-five head.

The average Faulkner sheep, John said, walked four hundred miles a year, not counting the browsing. They started on the desert southwest of Gooding, in winter, and after shearing and lambing moved north toward the Sawtooth Range.

The country was brown and sere when we set out to retrace that migratory route in summer, he in his battered red pickup, I following in my van. Faulkner's bumper sticker said "Sheepherding—the World's Second Oldest Profession." His public grazing allotments included some of the most gorgeous country in a state full of it and touched the borders of several towns and one of the world's renowned resorts, Sun Valley. To Faulkner, it was one long sheep run. "The woollies get fat on the grass," he had said, adding, "They're beautiful."

I liked the curious syllabic clusters in sheep talk, full of woollies and wethers, smutties and ewes. The wethers—gelded sheep—were castrated early to keep them from humping the ewes as they traveled and upsetting Faulkner's carefully worked-out system. He put black-faced Suffolk rams on white-faced Panama ewes in September, producing smutties in January that became fat lambs by August. The ewes were sheared in early November. A dozen men could handle fifteen hundred a day. The smutties were born in "jugs"—lambing sheds close to Faulkner's house—and the ewes moved into the "sunny pens." They ate hay moved on a horse-drawn sleigh.

On the far side of the hills the valley lay under silvery brush strokes of giant sprinklers moving crabwise across the arable stuff. Faulkner pulled off the road and stood waiting.

"The sheep move across those big flats," he said, when I had joined him. He pointed east. "They break through snowbanks left in May, and head up toward Kelly Mountain."

Vegetation had a tough time surviving in those granitic soils. The federal government owned most of the view. "We had real battles with the Forest Service in the fifties and sixties," he said. "We had to take a lot of sheep off. Then they decided we were doing some good higher up," in the lusher valleys, keeping willow and other browse under control.

Beyond the valley the Pioneer Mountains rose like thunderheads against a sky hazed with smoke from distant forest fires. "We used to go up on Soldier Mountain and clean out the bears before grazing season," he said. Each year Faulkner lost 4 percent of his woollies to bears and coyotes, and an equal number to poisonous plants and natural deaths in the sheds—two thousand a year, more or less. The number of sheepmen abroad on the land was a tenth what it used to be. He pointed to a spread at the western end of the valley. "That old Basco's in Chapter Eleven. Everybody borrowed too much money against their allotments, and the banks decided all of a sudden that they weren't good collateral."

His Basques moved woollies in "bands"—groups of about two thousand, although numbers, like sheepherding, were extremely fluid. Spooked sheep often got into pileups in narrow canyons and smothered. Faulkner had lost five hundred in a single pileup the previous year, although a Basco spent a solid hour trying to pull them apart. Faulkner liked Basco herders because they were physically strong, politically conservative, and "working fools."

They cost him $750 a month, plus room and board. What sounded like the indenturing of defenseless aliens was really a bureaucratic tour de force involving seventeen different agencies, including the BLM, FS, Immigration, Internal Revenue, Social Security, Fish and Wildlife, and the state and federal labor departments. It took a year to hire a Basco, on average. Faulkner had to advertise for qualified Americans first, on both coasts, a process that had brought a hippie or two to Gooding, and a few Indians. They didn't care for the weather. Most of his Bascos had been with the company for more than a decade. They got two weeks' vacation, and once a year a priest came to the Gooding cookhouse and said mass for the whole bunch.

I asked what they did for women.

"Camp followers, mostly Mexican. I don't know how those girls find 'em up in the mountains, or how they get up there, but they do."

Once, taking food to a sheep camp, Faulkner came around a curve and saw two Peruvian sheepherders trying to get a large woman into the wagon. One held her arms; the other had a shoulder beneath her haunches. At that moment she squeezed through the narrow doorway and the herder went down beneath her. Faulkner had put his pickup in reverse and backed down the road, where he waited for an hour before delivering the grub.

We drove on, through buckbrush and high sedge meadows. Conical mountains, brown on the tops, green in the valleys, marched north toward Ketchum. I left the van in the town of Hailey and got into Faulkner's pickup. "It's all big money from here on," he said, but when he looked out the window he didn't see the new condos now confronting us. He saw BLM land on one side of the valley and FS land on the other, and a county road in between that sheep had as much right to as sports cars.

Fifteen years before, the mayor of Ketchum had tried to keep Faulkner Land and Livestock from bringing its sheep through town, the only route to the Sawtooths, and a legal one. "It was a nasty time. Women sicced their dogs on us, people called us names." He had brought many herders with him, ready for a fight. The highway patrol knew it, and convinced the mayor to back down. Things had since changed, and relations were relatively good between herder and townie.

"Sheepmen have a lot to answer for," he said, after a bit. "Herders figured they got there first and could do what they wanted. They used to leave their sheep in the graveyard, the best fence in town, while they went to the whorehouse. But they policed themselves, too." When there was a dispute between bands, each would send out its best fighter to settle things.

Ketchum has its cunning specialty shops, a golf course, and $250,000 lots, but the straitjacket of public lands has kept the development frenzy in check. Sun Valley lies a mile to the east, nestled among those glaciated breasts that have made skiing famous in America.

"That's old Jack Lane's store," Faulkner said, indicating a renovated corner that now housed a bank. "Hemingway used to sit out there on a bench and whittle and watch dogs fight in the street. That was Ketchum."

Faulkner was nine or ten in those days. He took part in the drives, and slept against the gates in the stockyards down by the river, which had since been replaced by an industrial park. "We didn't want anybody stealing our sheep. Hemingway would come down and talk to us. He liked the kids but was pretty sarcastic with the old-timers."

Hemingway walked up every day and had a drink of rye in the Pioneer, Faulkner said. "It was a good ole saloon. Now it's got wine by the glass, and foxy cocktail waitresses."

We parked and went in. The dark walls still sagged beneath the weight of game heads, but the place had been spiffed up since Hemingway's day. The big color screen was alive with the rock music telethon for the aid of Ethiopian refugees. We drank draft Bass ale, feeling conspicuous among the ripped pastel sweatshirts and punk hairdos.

"Hemingway was already sick when he came here," Faulkner said. "He had stomach cancer, you know."

I asked if Faulkner blamed him for committing suicide.

"Hell no. Why sit up there and suffer?" He took another swig. "I guess you get a little callous," he added, "being a stockman. If something falls behind on a drive, you slit its throat."

We resumed our journey. Handy fly-fishing on the Big Wood River seemed to satisfy some of the same needs as Nautilus in the cities. A dozen men in pristine waders and tailored leather vests posed against the FS backdrop on the outskirts of town. "Most of these new people are all right," said Faulkner. "But they don't know much about the country. They used to think we were destroying it. Hell, we've been here a hundred years. We pass on, we avoid the overgrazed areas."

Environmentalists refer to sheep as hooved locusts, echoing John Muir; the restful sight of moving sheep means little to developers, or movie producers. The previous year, Faulkner said, his herders had had to detour around the hills north of town because Clint Eastwood was filming *Pale Rider* and didn't want woollies in his frames.

"I remember when Dad got his first Forest Service permit," Faulkner said. "For a thousand sheep, in 'forty-one. We bought another band after the war. In 'fifty-seven we bought another. Eventually we bought out thirteen outfits. It's not all that hard to get together a million-dollar sheep outfit. We'd be better off if we put it in the bank and lived off the interest, but it's a way of life." He laughed at the idea. "I don't feel like a millionaire when I'm crawling around in sheep shit, looking for a lamb."

We climbed again, along the route that Alexander Ross and a bunch of Hudson's Bay trappers took in 1824, when they became the first white men to cast their eyes on Galena Summit. We descended into Sawtooth Valley, below headwaters of the Salmon River.

"As pretty country as I've seen," he said. "Dad used to go down this hill with a Doug fir tied on behind, for brakes."

We pulled off the road at Frenchman's Creek. In August, Faulkner would ship ten thousand lambs a day from just such a place to a packing plant in Dixon, California. The Faulkner camp would feed anybody who showed up, including tourists; one morning the year before, his wife and sister-in-law had cooked fifty-six breakfasts.

"We need the high country to make our lambs," he said, of all the FS land. He wanted to hold onto his piece of this remarkable place. It was easy to imagine that he might not, in an age when woollies were no longer an integral part of the Western viewshed, and natural beauty was too valuable to be leased out for twenty-three cents a month for each animal. But the sheep did far less damage here than in more arid country, which might not recover from their passing.

"There's a Basco up there," Faulkner said, nodding toward the mountain. "Name's Basilio. Look for a wagon and a band of sheep."

I came back the next morning. A dirt track followed the creek for a time and then plunged in; absolutely clear water rose to my axles, and tiny trout streaked away to hide under the grassy overhangs. Except for a trap in the form of a metal cage, baited for bear by Idaho Fish and Game with a hunk of salmon, there was no sign of civilization.

Willow bottoms and lush, watery meadows kept that way by tribes of beavers stretched between scree slopes interspersed with buckbrush and juniper. Big twisted ponderosas hung in the angles of rocky outcrops farther up. You could see a bear coming a mile away if it dropped over one of the ridges, but the trees in the vortex cast lovely deep shadows in sunlight bright enough to blind.

A weathered blue camp wagon stood in a grove of lodgepole pine a couple of miles up the creek. The curved roof, covered with tarpaulin to keep the rain out, was punctured by a crooked stovepipe. Detachable wooden steps hung from the front of the wagon; a wooden commissary wagon was tied on behind, and tied to it was a little saddle horse, a gelding, its ears pitched forward.

I got out of the van. Two white-faced Border collies appeared from nowhere and barked. The camp wagon's Dutch door hung half-open onto living quarters not much bigger than a closet. A wood-burning stove sat in a corner, next to a pail of water—the herder's kitchen. Cans of tomatoes and a ripped carton of Winstons rested on the shelf; a new pair of black shoes stood against the wall.

Someone inside said, "Oy?" and the dogs barked again. A man emerged from the shadows, where he had been napping. He had a marvelous red nose and white hair scissored close to the skin. He wore Levi's and the traditional black Basque sash tied in the back, and exploded shoes with red socks peering through. He stood for a moment in the doorway, looking down at me and scratching his stomach.

Finally he said, "You writer?"

"Yes. Yes, I am."

He scribbled on his callused palm with an imaginary pencil. The notion struck him as so absurd that he laughed out loud. Then he said, "Johnfaulkner say you want bullshit me," running his employer's first and last names together.

"That's right."

"Okay."

Already bored, he went back for a cigarette. He returned with a .30-30 Marlin lever action, which he left on the steps while he strolled out into the meadow to set up a target, an empty condensed milk can. The rifle had teeth marks on the stock where the gelding had gone after the salt from Basilio's hands.

"For *oso*"—bear. He smacked the gun, and added, "No worry."

Soon we were blasting away at the can. He used the Marlin as an icebreaker, a kind of prebrunch social activity smelling of burnt cordite instead of mimosas. It had quite a kick. He mostly shot coyotes with it, he said, with bullets provided by Johnfaulkner.

I could barely see the sheep up the canyon, drifting in and out of the lodgepole stands like bits of cumulus, but I could hear their bleating. Basilio went in to put on a clean white shirt, for it was Sunday. Ordinarily he ate lunch about ten in the morning, having been up since four, but the foreman was expected with a load of supplies and so he was waiting to cook for him as well.

The pickup appeared on cue, driven by Guillermo. He got out and shook hands, a bare-chested Basco with a red bandana tied jauntily around his neck, wearing cutoff Levi's. "Goddamn Jesus Christ son of a bitch," he said happily. He would have been there earlier but there was some problem with a Peruvian herder down the supply line. Guillermo had yet to deliver to the Mexican herder over on Smiley Creek. While he talked he unloaded the supplies: a sack of Gold Medal flour, cardboard cartons of groceries, some kerosene. He and Basilio shoved the wooden steps into the wagon. They dropped the old metal tongue over the hitch on the pickup and hauled the camp a mile up Frenchman's Creek.

They conferred about the proper aspect for the wagon in the stand of lodgepoles, speaking a strange singsong language. Basilio took a shovel and dug holes for two of the tires, leveling his house for the next week or so. Then he replaced the steps, climbed inside, and tossed a bota—a leather wineskin—out the door.

Guillermo caught it. He cocked his head back and directed a purple jet into his mouth, then passed the bota to me. I got the wine into my mouth all right, but left a trail down the front of my shirt. "Maybe you want a glass," Guillermo said, laughing. "Goddamn Jesus Christ son of a bitch."

He or Faulkner bought whatever supplies the herders requested. Basilio required no more than one pair of pants a year and considered even that an extravagance. He had yet to put on the new shoes.

Smoke emerged from the chimney: lunch was in progress. I had expected warmed-up corned beef hash or bologna sandwiches but realized that something else was in order when Basilio pulled a chicken out of a cardboard carton and began to chop it up with a huge butcher knife. He worked on a board with a single hinged leg that stayed folded against the wall when he wasn't cooking or eating off it.

He floured the chicken and dropped the pieces into an iron

skillet full of hot oil. A handful of peeled and sliced garlic followed. He flattened out handfuls of dough, using a gallon jug of Carlo Rossi as a rolling pin, and threw these big pancakes directly onto the hot stovetop. The smell of the bread and garlic and the taste of the wine in the hot, clear air lent my hunger a sudden, glorious edge.

Basilio had seen the little tape recorder in my van. Now he rummaged around in the back of the wagon and came out with a cassette of Basque fandangos. I put it on the machine, in the grass, and a thin, furious music rose beneath the trees, full of accordians and a plangent, repetitious melody that reminded me of Cajun songs. Guillermo tried to translate, but the lyrics seemed incomprehensible in any language.

We ate lunch from a board suspended between a fir log and a can of diesel fuel: soup with dumplings, coq au vin, and hot fresh bread washed down with wine from the bota, followed by salad and canned fruit cocktail, the most enduring of camp desserts. Talk was of sheep, and Peruvians. "I don't give them wine," Guillermo said of the Peruvian herders in his charge. "You give them a gallon, they drink a gallon. You give them two gallons, they drink two gallons. Goddamn Jesus Christ son of a bitch."

Basilio would not denounce the Peruvians; instead, he criticized their cooking. "I don't like."

They were pretty good herders, he added, but none too strong. "Little," he added, measuring.

The Peruvians, and some Chileans, were still working under three-year contracts, as these Bascos had done in the beginning. Guillermo had been in the United States for twenty-three years, Basilio for seventeen. Basilio had worked in California, with Mormons in Utah, and in Colorado, but he liked Idaho best. "Not too much people," he said.

I asked if he had a family in Spain. "No wife, no children," he said. "Just sheep." He laughed explosively.

We stretched out on a piece of canvas and had a smoke. The tobacco tasted fine after that meal. Guillermo had to go tend to his Mexican. He unloaded salt bags for Basilio's sheep, hay for the gelding, a fresh ham and a slab of bacon, which Basilio stashed in a cardboard box—his larder—insulated from the stove by a stack of fresh-split wood.

Guillermo said, "Goddamn son of a bitch Jesus Christ, it's a beautiful Sunday," and drove off.

Basilio had to turn the flock downstream, to be nearer camp. He explained that coyotes and bears were less likely to come so close to the smell of man—in this case, garlic. A good herder stayed close to his sheep, anyway. He didn't try to count the sheep every day but kept track of the thirty black ones as floating indicators; if a dark woolly was missing, he figured about sixty white ones were off in the woods with it, and went looking for them.

If I wanted to go fishing, Basilio said, he knew a beaver pond where trout congregated. Fish would be nice for supper, and he had no time to catch them himself. He saddled the horse, named, appropriately, Bolero, and I got my gear together. We set off across the wet meadows, the dogs excited by the prospect of an outing. Border collies have faces of unnerving intelligence. Probably the last breed on earth uncorrupted by show breeding, they are still linked directly to a profession going back to paleolithic times in Europe. These were named Mike and Bat—Basco for Number One.

"Look!"

Basilio had turned back in the direction of camp. He bent slightly at the waist, sash swinging, forefinger raised. I thought he had seen a bear. Then I saw a station wagon piled with folding chairs, bumping uncertainly up the road—an unusual sight in these remote parts. "Tooor-ists," he said, rolling the word around in disbelief and alarm. Not only did tourists bother the sheep and compete with herders for available space, but they also complained on occasion of domestic animals eating grass and browse, and cluttering up the view. Tourists were a clear and present danger to Basilio's way of life, whereas bears, coyotes, rabid foxes, rattlesnakes, and blizzards merely inconvenienced him.

The station wagon turned around and disappeared; Basilio sighed with relief. We skirted a beaver pond and came up from the south side, with a view of wild brookies and brown trout marshaled in the clear, shallow water. I assembled my fly rod while Basilio looked on skeptically: it had remained lashed to the roof of the van through some great trout country, and now the leader was corkscrewed and the reel covered with dust.

I tied on a fly; Basilio's skepticism hardened. "No worm?" he said.

Without waiting for an answer, he took the dogs to inspect the next pond. I worked the fly into the range of the trout, who fled.

Basilio returned five minutes later. "How many catch?"

"Basilio, I just got started."

"I go sheep."

I fished for three hours, floundering in the mud and tripping over submerged willow branches. In the distance I could see Basilio moving the sheep and hear their bleating. He sat with great patience on Bolero, doing what, I could not say, but the herd moved with a calm persistence in and out of the woods, pushed slowly but relentlessly by the dogs. There was something profoundly restful in the sight.

Basilio moved sheep until seven-thirty. By then I was back at camp, propped against a spruce, writing in my journal and watching the shadow of the opposing mountain climb the slope. Mountain sheep sometimes descended the scree and coupled with the ewes, Basilio said, but he had not seen one in two years.

I had caught two small fish. I told him, and he said, *"Dos?"* He repeated it. *"Dos,"* he said a third time, trying to come to terms with the idea of someone catching just two fish in Idaho—a perversity.

It was clear we would need more than that for dinner. He told me to save them and quickly peeled potatoes in the waning light, refusing to let me help, and then beat half a dozen eggs for a kind of potato omelet. He embodied a remarkable economy of motion, first flipping out the shelf on the Dutch door, unhooking the washpan from the outside wall of the wagon, soaping his hands, and tossing out the water in the same gesture with which he replaced the pan. He started the fire with diesel fuel and cooked a complete meal faster than any short-order specialist I had ever seen.

I brought out a bottle of Mendocino cabernet, which he sampled. "Hot," he said, detecting high alcohol; otherwise he liked it. He liked the wines of Rioja best, and Spanish food, but Spain wasn't what it had been, he added.

A curious thing had happened. Without a third party to witness our linguistic inadequacies we were talking quite easily in pidgin English and Spanish, the dogs cocking their heads and looking at us as if we were crazy.

Basilio came from the coastal province of Vizcaya. He had been back to Spain the year before, on holiday, but was unimpressed with everything but the food. The *curas*—priests—now wore clothes like everybody else. "Half Catolicos no go church." He remembered Franco, whom he disliked. "Franco kill lotsa Basco. But lotsa job with Franco. No much money, but jobs. Now no jobs in España. Bums," he added.

There were cars everywhere in his province, where before there had been almost none. "Idaho better," he said. The notion of public domain amazed him. He called it, simply, "the land," with a sweeping gesture implying vastness. Everybody in America could act like a king, he said, because of the hunting and the grazing. There was no BLM in Spain, no Foresta like the Sawtooth, and no twenty-five hundred head of sheep in a single herd. His brother ran a few sheep and cows on a farm in Vizcaya, as his father had, but the scope of herding in the West was considered a fantasy at home.

"United States good," he said, nodding. "Not all good, but Reagan good." He thought for a moment. "Dollar strong."

I asked what he did with his money.

"CD."

"Certificates of deposit?"

He nodded, and said, "Better interest."

He had almost eighty thousand dollars in the Gooding bank. With average annual expenditures limited to a pair of pants, it was easy enough to save. Faulkner had told me that one of his foremen had a quarter of a million dollars in CDs. Some Basques had ended up owning sheep outfits they herded for, because the accumulated debt to them was so great. Two years before, Basilio had bought the radio for $150, what he considered a great extravagance, although every day he listened to the

Spanish language broadcast, his only source of outside amusement; he seemed quite happy to miss it if there was something else to do.

Some years he attended the annual Basque picnic in Gooding, but usually he stayed by himself. Most herders worked in pairs, one to cook and one to herd, but not Basilio. The teams often had disputes, usually over women. If a woman showed up the odd man out had to sleep under the wagon while the lovers partied a few inches from his face. That led to arguments, and worse.

It didn't get dark until ten. We drank brewed coffee after supper, Basilio stirring sugar into his with a fork handle. I found out too late that the water had been dipped from the creek downstream of two thousand sheep. If I developed giardiasis, at least I got it in a beautiful setting, in good company. I could see the dogs' eyes shining outside. The bawling of distant sheep filled the night; the stars had a new intensity. We sat watching moths kamikaze against the wheezing, white-hot lantern. Basilio's freshly skinned head gleamed in its light. He had been up since four in the morning, had cooked two epicurean meals, moved his camp, tended his sheep, fed his horse and dogs, split wood, entertained a stranger, compared two California wines, and delivered a treatise on Spain and America. If a herder's life was easy and narrow, his was no good example.

He was up before dawn the next morning, making bread in the light of the Coleman. He mixed a big wad of dough in a metal bowl, wrapped the whole thing in an old shirt, and stuffed it into his still warm bedroll. We set out in the darkness to move sheep, he on Bolero, I on foot. In first light I could see Basilio across the meadows, still mounted, urging woollies off the scree slope with infinite patience. Sheepherding is not one of the world's great spectator sports. Basilio made an odd hissing noise from time to time when the animals browsed where he wanted them, and his voice rang out when he, Mike, and Bat had them on the prod, but mostly the mysteries of his profession remained intact.

When we returned to camp three hours later, the dough was pushing up the bedroll. He made a fire and took the dough out and kneaded it. He fondly sprinkled it with flour and eased it down into the greased Dutch oven. "Pretty soon," he said, which meant another hour to rise again and another to cook.

We dozed until it was time to eat. He made another fire outside, squirting a long column of diesel fuel onto wood piled between two rocks. He took a side of bacon from the ubiquitous cardboard box and hewed off a couple of slabs that were soon spitting in the hot skillet. I could smell the bread. Basilio took the lid off the Dutch oven, revealing the gorgeous crusty top of a round loaf the size of a hatbox. He removed the bread and set it aside to cool.

"Get fishes," he said.

I fetched the trout from my ice chest.

"Dos," said Basilio, looking at them one more time, and then slipped them into the hot grease. They were followed by half a dozen eggs. He slid them sunny side up onto cracked enamel plates warmed by proximity to the fire, and poured cupfuls of Cribari. He hugged the fresh loaf to his chest and cut swaths of steaming bread with the butcher knife, with great unbroken scythelike strokes. We finished up with a can of Budweiser from a six-pack left by a tourist from Phoenix as a peace offering—a digestif for the sort of meal outdoorsmen eat after a hard day in the bush, except that it was just ten o'clock in the morning.

The sky was hazy from blazing national forests. From Arizona to Washington State the West was on fire; I wanted to help fight one but couldn't tear myself away from Frenchman's Creek. If Basilio and I had nothing else in common, we had food, courtesy of Johnfaulkner, who knew that a well-fed herder was a happy one. I contributed what I had. Basilio was not shy about accepting, or rejecting. He disapproved of American bread, which he called "sack bread." Peanut butter was clearly an abomination in his eyes. He went through my store of fresh plums in ninety seconds, swallowing the best and ejecting the others like cannonballs. This was a man accustomed, after all, to good Navarran fruit. He wouldn't eat my carrots, so I fed them to Bolero.

One night he came in at dusk, tied Bolero to the commissary wagon, unsaddled and fed him, started a fire outside with the usual barrage of diesel fuel, washed his hands, carved two ham steaks, and began cooking them, all in about seven minutes. The usual fistful of garlic went into the skillet, followed by a can of tomatoes. He gave the dish a stir with the empty can and tossed it into the darkness with his usual economy of gesture. He always picked up before moving camp, but in the meantime Basilio wasn't going to bother with putting empty tomato cans in plastic bags. Some bread also went into the skillet. We were eating within fifteen minutes, a meal of such flavorful intensity that all I could do was gasp.

I had no way of determining Basilio's anxieties, if they existed, but he certainly seemed happy. I had never met anyone more at home in his life, good-natured, generous, devoid of pretension and apparently of material needs. I wanted to send him a present when I got home but couldn't imagine what. I asked if he wanted a cassette player like mine, and he said no. He didn't mind listening to fandangos occasionally when someone came around with a little machine, but basically he considered them unhealthy. He liked to eat fish but had no interest in catching them. Reading was a chore. "No want nothing," he shouted, laughing.

We did not shake hands before I left. Formal partings were not Basilio's style. He spent much time alone and had developed a humane means of dealing with the interruptions, with some protection built in for himself. He led a life that must have had its moments of intense loneliness. Since he didn't celebrate arrivals, he didn't celebrate the leavings either. It was all part of a larger process, one in which people showed up with food, or appetites, or both, and went away fuller than he imagined. He just stood there in the sunlight, ruddy nose pointed up-canyon, talking loudly about sheep.

Then he turned and strolled away.

4

THE RANGE as we know it wouldn't be complete without those famous itinerant workers who often own neither cows nor land—the cowboys. They originally came out of Texas, having been taught to ride by Mexicans, hardly an all-American experience; yet they evolved into an American myth of valor and individualism. In reality, they were closer to nineteenth-century hippies than to the image projected by John Wayne.

During the course of my trip I worked briefly with contemporary cowboys in New Mexico, Arizona, and Utah. Most of them did something else for a living and wrangled on the side for friends, relatives, and themselves. With the solitude and the sense of freedom their avocation entailed came some dirt and brutality. No one who has taken part in a spring roundup will soon forget the choking dust, the acrid smell of burning hair and hide, or the moans of a calf beneath the white-hot dehorner and the castrater's blade. That is not where the cowboy legend lies, however, but in the notion of movement, risk, and an endless succession of purple mountains and green valleys. These last ceased to be a reality in much of the West soon after cows and cowboys moved into them, but no matter.

Wild longhorn cattle originally made cowboying an extremely dangerous profession. Longhorns, too, are a thing of the past, but wild horses are not. They exist in great numbers in the West, and pose some danger to those responsible for rounding them up. I heard that the men who did it were considered mavericks by ranchers and government agents who dealt with them, just as their forerunners had been.

Southwest Idaho meets Nevada in alkali flats, dry lakes called playas, and stringy mountain ranges of deceptive height and distance, furred by blue bunchgrass growing on their flanks. The valleys stretch away under sage and greasewood—and squirrel tail and Indian rice grass, if the BLM brochures are to be believed. The BLM owns 86 percent of Nevada, and a lot of the country looks very lean.

On the edge of the Great Basin, roads far from the Interstate run for miles toward some immense stony wrinkle before making an abrupt turn and running for miles more. The lights of Winnemucca, Nevada, floated in a trough of evening shadow, as I came to the end of a long day of desert driving. The casinos on the main drag cast bright nets for passing motor homes. Winnemucca was no tourist attraction, but then gambling is a local pastime in Nevada, where townsfolk drop a five-dollar bill on the roulette table as casually as some people buy a newspaper.

I parked on a side street and ate tuna fish from a can for dinner, watching cowboys and girls in Levi's jackets tromp between the pools of glitter and Winnemucca's grainy darkness. I needed a place to park and sleep, and found my way to the BLM headquarters a couple of blocks from the last casino. I woke up the next morning to a full parking lot and the sight of people working in the offices.

They were expecting me. An hour later, I rode west across more desert with a soft-spoken, intense range con who for two years had been trying to get out of Winnemucca. "If you're a GS twelve, you have to move every four or five years," he said, "or you lose your effectiveness. People at the office get used to looking at the same face. The ranchers you've trespassed think you're an SOB."

A trespass was a citation for grazing more cows on government land than were allowed; judging by the view, any stock at all should have constituted trespass.

He said, "What can I tell you about Nevada? It has its share of unconventional people, is the main thing. We've got outlaws and renegades right here. They stab people, steal things, run mustangs."

Each of the six BLM management areas in Nevada is larger than Massachusetts, and each harbors wild horses that have to be rounded up. That requires a special sort of cowboy.

"This one's the best in the business," said the range con, indicating a collection of trucks isolated in big country at the foot of the Humboldt Range. A steel corral had been set up amidst the sage, and a few lone riders sat casually on their cow ponies, looking toward the mountains. We left the BLM Suburban near the road and hiked up. The contractor's name was Dave Cattoor; he was a small man with a horny hand and a slightly misaligned eye. The brim of his straw cowboy hat had been mended with epoxy, and his jacket bled goose feathers.

His lariat had a piece of chain attached to the end, for looping over the saddle horn after he roped a mustang. "It'll stay on the saddle that way," he said, to no one in particular. "Saddle might not stay on your horse, though."

He and his partner had earned half a million dollars in the last eight months. That seemed a lot of money, he said, until you realized that the weekly fuel bill for the helicopter alone was more than fifteen hundred dollars. Two had crashed since Thanksgiving. The previous year, a big semi belonging to the outfit had overturned in northern Nevada, and Cattoor and his men had set up a corral beside the highway and winched forty live mustangs out of the wreckage.

Cattoor and his partner, the helicopter pilot, paid all those expenses, plus wages and board for four men, and a bonus if things worked out well. They were paid sixty-nine dollars for each mustang they captured, and had to earn two thousand dollars a day to break even. However, they were making money.

The wranglers all bunked at the Two Stiffs Motel, in Lovelock, for weeks. So did the pilot. We could hear him working the canyons, the rhythm of the engine changing as he turned and began to push the sound toward us.

"Here he comes," said Cattoor. "Get behind the horse trailer and stay out of sight."

The chopper flew low to the ground, while half a dozen horses raced ahead of it. They passed a mile to the north, bound for another canyon, but the chopper flanked and gradually turned them. They came charging into full view, coats dark with sweat. Cattoor had tied his horse behind the trailer and led a pony down to the open end of the corral, camouflaged with hay bales and sage. He crouched, waiting for the herd.

"That's the Judas horse," the range con said. The Judas horse stood patiently while the wild ones—a bay stallion, three mares, and three ponies—charged past. They wheeled as the chopper cut them off and drove them back toward the trap.

Cattoor released the Judas and it trotted obediently between the fences, followed by all but the stallion. At the last moment it turned and reared, making for the narrow slot between iron bars and that clattering machine. I could see the pilot clearly now inside his glass bubble, in a Windbreaker over an old plaid shirt, faded Levi's, and boots, a technological cowboy unhappy with this recalcitrant stallion forty feet from his rotors. Even I could tell that the horse was not going into the trap.

Men rose up with a long tarpaulin and ran across the mouth of the trap, cutting the rest of the horses off from escape. The stallion charged the helicopter. The pilot performed a sleight of hand inspired by the vision of a severed equine head, buckets of gore, a broken rotor blade, and oily black flames. The chopper swung heavily to port—reeled, really—the pilot silently screaming at an animal that had not known of his existence half an hour before.

Out of my peripheral vision charged two riders, leaning forward in their saddles, at a clip not commonly seen outside racetracks and the speeded-up versions of old TV Westerns. Men and horses seemed to vibrate with the effort, over rough country full of prairie dog holes. The stallion disappeared in a draw, followed by the riders, then emerged, a little smaller, the men seemingly close enough to reach out and put a hand on that sweaty flank. One tossed his lariat and missed, then Cattoor tossed his and the stallion came up hard at the end of it, pawing the air.

The range con beside me said, "Goddamn, he got him."

The lariat cut off the mustang's breath, bringing it gradually to its knees. It rolled over, and Cattoor dismounted and cautiously approached. With a hank of rope he tied fore and hind hooves together before the horse revived, then left it to be picked up when the truck came around collecting hog-tied animals as if they were battle casualties.

"That Judas horse almost ironed me out," Cattoor said a few minutes later, seeking shelter in the horse trailer from some rare Nevada rain. The horse had kicked at him when he released it.

Another BLM agent had brought more observers to the roundup. One was a wild horse advocate from Austin, Texas, named Deedee. She stood for a while with her hands deep in the pockets of her jeans, watching Cattoor. Then she told him that she had a special interest in his profession, being a founder of the American Mustang and Burro Association, which was a relative newcomer to the extensive wild horse lobby.

"We have members in thirty-eight states," she said. "We're one of the fastest-growing wild horse interest groups."

Someone said, "It ain't supposed to rain in Nevada."

Deedee's organization had joined the much larger American Wild Equine Council, and had paid for her to fly to Nevada. In addition to exercising influence there, she was on the lookout for another mare for her Texas household. She planned to adopt one of the mustangs. "We like the idea of horses running free, their manes flying in the wind," she said.

The range con later told me he badly wanted out of wild horse work, one of the most time-consuming and frustrating tasks in the BLM. "You can't imagine how much coordination goes into it."

I asked how many roamed Nevada. He thought there might be as many as forty thousand.

"Forty thousand?"

Mustangs are destroying what's left of the range, but public interest groups prevent the government from dealing with them the way it deals with other, less harmful creatures. Coyotes are shot from helicopters or poisoned, but wild horses roam free, eating four and five times as much of the sparse ground cover as a cow. Some are trapped and shipped to feedlots, at ruinous expense, where they live until they drop of old age. Thousands of horses behind government fences eat their way through government forage because a few people consider them related to the old Spanish war mounts, and a symbol of wildness. So they cannot be sold as meat or turned into dog food, as an old steer might be.

The horses may be adopted, and for a year government agents have to visit these orphans to make sure they are being properly cared for. This part of the program, like the expense and the ban on productive use of wild horseflesh, arouses ridicule in the men who round up mustangs.

Mustangs aren't a good symbol of the wild, unspoiled West. They have nothing to do with the conquistadors but are the progeny of mares and studs turned out on public land during the Depression, when their owners couldn't afford to feed them. A few may be descended from draft horses let loose when the cavalry disbanded in the 1890s. Yet there are sixty-nine organizations fighting for their rights.

Behind Deedee, in the corral, tattered, bony, murderous animals with bloody legs, white scars on flanks and withers, and chunks missing from their own hides routinely sank their teeth in other horses. The fighting went on more or less continuously, and not just in captivity. Now the whinnying reverberated for a mile and more, hooves rattling against the metal bars and drumming on other equine rib cages.

A wrangler urged them into the collecting pen, careful to stay clear. Once the roundup was complete, the animals would be trucked to Palomino Ranch, a BLM feedlot north of Reno set up just for mustangs, where they would be processed, inoculated, and fed. Prospective adopters occasionally came by; most were discouraged by the sight of equine orphans kicking one another and demolishing the odd horse trailer.

A little mare lay in the weeds. A wild horse had stood on her neck until someone noticed and moved him. Now the mare's eyes assumed a terminal glassiness.

"Shock," the range con said.

"Our sign fell down," said one of the cowboys.

He dragged the dead horse away, tied to the pickup, and left her in a sage clump where predators would take over.

I later found out that in fiscal 1985 the BLM had spent $17 million on wild horses. Congress had passed the Wild Horse and Burro Act fifteen years before, at the urging of the wild horse lobby, stipulating that mustangs had a place on the range. The BLM operates its wild horse program under a continuing resolution; the program includes squiring around visiting journalists and horse lobbyists, holding public meetings, hiring permanent wild horse and burro specialists, conducting environmental studies and horse counts, and hiring cowboy entrepreneurs like Dave Cattoor. It also involves publishing expensive brochures that reflect the political reality of wild horse sentiment: "Like the relics left by ancient Indian tribes," says the BLM's Special Wild Horse Issue of *Our Public Lands,* "and the still visible ruts made by wagon trains, wild horses and burros are important links to our heritage." The wild horse program provides high visibility for the BLM's new role as preservationists at relatively little cost, while overgrazing, mining, and timbering continue.

Cattoor asked the BLM range con for a time extension. Ordinarily roundups stopped at one o'clock, to keep the wild horses from overheating, but it was damp and cold now, and Dave had not made his minimum. The range con radioed the BLM's wild horse specialist, who was sitting in his Suburban down on the highway, and got permission. Within half an hour the chopper was pushing forty more mustangs down out of the Humboldts.

A BLM investigator with a carbine under the seat of his Bronco would spend the night there, to guard the herd from renegades. The horses would be loaded and trucked the next day. Dave and the others drove back to Lovelock, and I followed them. They seemed close to the real notion of cowboys, in a state that in one way, at least, closely approximated the Old West: Nevada was still largely unfenced. I suspected that the men who went after mustangs were similarly unrestricted, but my questions about their occupation were met with disbelief, and amusement. Cowboys don't like talking about what they do when they are doing it, because the work is hard and exacting. They don't like talking to strangers about it when it's over, because those who have never done it can't imagine what it's like. Also, cowboys see almost everybody else as aliens, opposed to their way of life or, at best, unsympathetic.

We ate a quick meal full of cryptic references and plate-rattling silences in Lovelock, around the corner from Rose's Chapel of Love.

"Some guys say they dally-rope mustangs," said a wrangler.

"Sure, and watch their fingers fly off."

"I used a sloppy loop on that ole chicken-necked sorrel."

"You think that tarp'll hold 'em if they decide to turn around?"

"Sure it will."

"When they put the hammer back," said Cattoor, "you'll know it."

Talk turned to recreation. Someone said, "I hear they're having them camel races in Virginia City this weekend."

"I didn't see any camels last year, but I saw a lot of drunk people."

"They had some mighty friendly whiskey up there. Wasn't nobody on the fight, or nothing."

"I told myself then," said Cattoor, "that if I was ever in Nevada when the camel races were going on, I'd be there."

"Not many colts today," said Jim Hicks, the chopper pilot. His face and arms were covered with scar tissue left by burns, and the backs of his hands bore the permanent imprint of bandages. "Mountain lion's working the hills, or maybe a human type."

"You said you couldn't herd no more," said Dave. "Then you came down with a whole shitload of mustangs. That's attitude improvement."

They had been working together for eight years and had collected twenty-five thousand wild horses. Jim had flown in the Vietnam War, doing low-level reconnaissance over the Cambodian border in the late sixties. Back in this country, he flew predator control over public lands in the West. One night when driving a fuel truck outside Elko, Nevada, bound for his helicopter, he blew a front tire and the truck turned over. Gasoline covered the highway and ignited. He crawled out the window and through the flames in a T-shirt; the only part of him that wasn't burned was the palms of his hands.

When he got out of the hospital, he tried selling asphalt roofing but couldn't stand it, and was soon back in the wild horse business. "There's a challenge to this. These old horses are wild, and smart. You can't fly a helicopter like a cutting horse—it's too hard on the machine. And once those horses realize a helicopter can't hurt 'em, then you're in trouble. Then you need a roper."

"It's high risk," said Dave. "It's hard to work around wild horses day after day and not get hurt. You've got to go full speed over them dog holes. These old horses kick and bite. We've been lucky."

"Been a bad year for helicopters, though. In November I had engine failure at forty feet. Rotors cut off the tail boom when I hit. That's standard. We had it rebuilt, and the exact same thing happened two months later."

I asked how he had escaped unhurt.

"Oh, you just wait for things to stop flying around. Then you jump out."

"The insurance companies don't love us no more," Dave said. "The premiums are horrendous. Sometimes we don't collect from the government until we're sixty thousand dollars in debt. The credit card people get mighty nervous," he added, handing his American Express card to the waitress.

They were up before dawn, a Saturday, eating sticky buns out of cartons tossed onto pickup dashboards, and drinking coffee from Styrofoam cups, racing for the Humboldts. I rode with Cattoor. The horses would be shipped to Palomino Ranch that day, and the state brand inspector was already at the corral when we arrived, checking the few brands among the herd and squirting these horses with gentian violet paint, so they could be picked out later.

While setting up the loading chutes, Dave talked about mustangs. He had never seen one made into a decent mount. Mostly they were "chicken feed horses," best used in processed pellets, except that the mustang lobby had made it impossible to productively use the animals.

At one point the government had attempted its own roundup in Colorado, Dave said. "I told 'em I wanted the contract, and they said no, we want to learn how to run horses. I said your life's not long enough. But they did it anyway and spent about a million dollars to get seven hundred horses. The ones they couldn't catch they shot."

Dave's driver backed the semi across the desert and up to the chute, and the wranglers started prodding the horses into the trailer. Halfway into the first load a big mare reared, driving its head against the metal cover of the trailer, and collapsed.

"Horse down!"

"She'll get up again."

But the mare didn't. It lay amidst clambering hooves, its neck bent double, evidence of the delicacy of the equine spine. A short, sturdy, blond wrangler named Scott climbed in with a length of chain, drove the others back, and wrapped it around the rear hooves. It took three men to drag the mare through the straw and fresh manure. The animal's head dangled over the lip of the trailer like a fish, then its body sprawled onto the ground, awkward in death. Dave wrapped the chain around its neck and dragged it off behind a pickup, onto a sage flat, the mare's legs moving as if in a dream of trotting.

The truck rolled off toward Reno and another took its place. Horse hooves drummed on the metal floor of the trailer. Occasionally I could hear wind whistling in the hollow ends of the metal poles, and the sound of childish laughter. A rancher had brought his wife and kids up to watch, joining two BLM range cons, the wild horse specialist, the investigator, the brand inspector, a TV cameraman and reporter, and one print journalist. The wild horse advocate had gone back to Texas.

"It's a goddamn carnival," Dave said. "Some days you can walk among the horses and they'll never touch a gate. But, oh, they're skittish today."

The second semi was gone by one o'clock. The rest of the catch went into a spare corral on the neighboring ranch, where the trucks were kept. The rancher wanted the mustangs off his grazing allotments and his neighbors', and was very accommodating to the contract cowboys.

We gathered, during a sudden cloudburst, to water the mustangs and the working horses, and to scatter alfalfa over the ground. The cowboys' boots were caked with mud—gumbo, they called it. Then they stood around Dave's pickup, cutting slabs of Spam with folding knives and sorting out the rest of the day.

A young wrangler named Bob took off for Lovelock in another truck. Greg, the only one wearing specs, got a chance to fly with Jim, who had to deliver the chopper to town for a flywheel inspection. Greg seemed thrilled at the prospect of hopping over the Humboldts, although the sight of those dark canyons would have discouraged most prospective passengers.

"The wind up there almost ate my lunch today," Jim said.

Four of us piled into Dave's front seat, to go back to the horse trap, where the helicopter was parked. Dave offered to race Jim and Greg to town, they in the chopper, we in the truck. When Jim accepted the challenge, Dave let them out half a mile from the lonely glass bubble parked in the cheat grass, to give us a head start.

"You son of a bitch," said Jim.

Dave's pickup flew over the empty road. "They'll be sitting on the runway before we get out to the highway," he said, but I wondered. The fog and the rain higher up looked grim.

"Do you think of sixty-nine dollars every time you catch a mustang?" I asked.

"I usually don't even count 'em. I just do as good as I can, and at the end of the season we work it all out and see where we stand."

He lapsed into one of his characteristic ten-mile silences. We were on the Interstate before he spoke again. "I've been on the prod since June. I've been away from home so goddamn much. My kids are old now, they're doing their own thing." His daughter was married, his fourteen-year-old son helping look after 153 cows on the Cattoor place in Colorado. That sounded tame compared to life in Nevada, and a long way off. He wouldn't be back there before November, ten thousand mustangs to the good.

We could see the other side of the Humboldt Mountains now; it looked just as stormy. If Dave was worried about the helicopter he didn't show it. "It's hard catching horses in that rough old country," he said, with affection. "I like the helicopter, and I like working the horses. I'm doing what I want to do."

Outside Lovelock, the clouds broke up. We looked over to see Jim and Greg flying along beside us, grinning. The storm had tied the race, forcing them around the mountains, and they sailed off toward the airport.

The truck drivers had delivered their loads to Palomino Ranch. The one named Mike had spent the rest of the afternoon lying around the Two Stiffs, drinking wine coolers. He greeted us from the open motel door, his capped teeth shining in the setting sun. Some days he made two and even three round trips in the big semi, over alkali roads that in dry weather turned him white from head to toe.

Dave went to his room and stripped. There were clothes piled on the floor, empty potato chip packages, and no mementos. Dirt ringed Dave's neck, eyes, and wrists, and caked the backs of his hands. He stepped into the bathroom for a shower, and emerged with wet hair carefully combed. When Jim arrived Dave was sitting on the edge of the bed, wiping the brim of his good felt Stetson with the damp towel.

He said, "You better hurry up."

"Oh, shit," said Bob, who was standing in the door nursing a can of Michelob. "We're going to *Reno!*"

I got a head start in my van, but they passed me twenty miles west of Lovelock, doing ninety: two pickups with three men to a front seat. I saw Mike tip up another wine cooler. I lost them somewhere east of Fernley, in big sage country with perpendicular rocks looking black in the shadow of mountains—populated, I now knew, with a lot of wild horses.

I caught up with the cowboys in Reno, at the Western Village Casino, behind the 76 Truck Stop. Their pickups were parked randomly at the casino door, the beds full of lariats, baling cord, plastic buckets, and bits of chain, the cabs littered with cups, chewing tobacco pouches, and empty wine cooler bottles. Inside, Mike drifted among the two-dollar blackjack tables, cradling his wine cooler, beaming at all the action. The others sat in a tight group next to the slot machines, drinking beer.

Dave slapped two keys into Jim's palm. "Two double beds in each room," he said. "We going to Virginia City?"

They had driven two hundred miles that day already, to work and back, and another seventy miles to Reno. Mike had driven twice that, in the company of fifty mustangs. Now they got into the pickups and happily drove another twenty tortuous miles into the mountains.

I rode with Bob, Jim, and Greg; Bob steered with great authority although he had been drinking Michelob for five hours. "I'm definitely not getting drunk tonight," he said, and then amended that slightly. "I hope they don't have no Everclear where we're going. I love that stuff. A hundred and fifty percent grain alcohol—God, it's got a kick. You can pour some in a Styrofoam cup, and seven seconds later the bottom'll fall out."

It was dark when we arrived. Virginia City had spent itself that day on exotic animal races and booze. A few tourists and more drunks tarried on the plank sidewalks of what had been the gateway to the greatest gold bonanza in the West—the Comstock Lode. Virginia City in the 1860s had offered the finest collection of gartered women and rot-gut booze east of the Sierra Nevada, as well as a chance to get rich or at least, as Mike said, to get interesting.

Camels were bedded down next to the parking lot, looking like bizarre stuffed animals in Virginia City's fluorescent lighting.

"There's a bunch of sulkies." Jim pointed to the wheeled carts. "They must pull 'em with the camels."

"The sulkies are for the ostriches," said Greg.

We all gathered on the main street, in a cold wind, watched by a pair of skeptical deputies: five cowboy hats and one Cat hat, belonging to Mike, that said "Older Men Need Love, Too," and one bare head. Scott steered Mike up the street, toward a Chinese restaurant, the only one still open. Jim kidded Dave about the lack of action in Virginia City, but carefully; Dave's eyes narrowed to slits in the glare of the red-flocked dining room. Waitresses and a handful of patrons watched apprehensively as Scott and Greg maneuvered Mike among the tables and propped him in a chair.

"Can we get some groceries pretty quick?" Dave asked a waitress; he was ready to go back to Reno, but people had to eat. Dave was the titular head of the family, so ordered Chinese for everybody. "Where's that other guy?" he said, meaning me. I was not part of the outfit but had attached myself in such a way that he felt responsible. He had spent some time with me but didn't remember my name—not because of unfriendliness, but a simple matter of priorities. He knew the names of the men he worked with, and after that recognition of the rest of the world fell off rapidly.

Mike leaned toward me, displaying his dentures. "You gon wri a ni stor bou our lives," he said, nodding. "Tha gon be rea ni."

The vegetables Hunan, fried shrimp, and Mo-shu pork went around once and disappeared. Mike slept with his head near the stack of empty platters. Greg made the sole comment upon the food—"That's the hottest fucking mustard I ever tasted"—and then we were leaving, Scott steering Mike back toward the door and the waitress chasing Dave with his American Express card. They had to be back at the Humboldts the next day, and they weren't going to waste Saturday night savoring foreign food in a dead town.

Half an hour later we were in the Red Rose, in Reno, a cavernous dance hall where couples in Western gear two-stepped and Cotton-eyed Joed to music from a live band that included a fiddle. We had a round of drinks, but before they were finished Dave was leaving, bound for Whiskey River and more action. We piled back into the pickups. At Whiskey River Dave danced with a younger woman; he seemed competent but a bit stiff amidst the jostling bodies and was smiling tightly. His wranglers elbowed in at the bar. The other men already there wore yoked shirts and boots, and some sported cowboy hats with feathers in the bands and had snuff can imprints in their back pockets. But they were for the most part car and appliance salesmen, and they seemed profoundly uneasy in the presence of these hard little cowboys and their loud talk.

Dave had enough of Whiskey River after two songs, and so it was back to the Red Rose. Now most of the available women were gone, and the band was squeezing out fiddle music too fast to dance to, trying to end the night with a decent frenzy. A blonde in tight jeans approached our table, wearing Greg's cowboy hat; she had met him in the parking lot, and he had gone off with her girlfriend after asking the blonde to hold his hat.

She danced with all of us, including Jim, who said he did not dance, pressing herself confidently against men who had not seen much of women in the last few months.

Her friend showed up with Greg, and the girls escaped giggling through the emergency exit. "She gave me her phone number," Greg said, but he had forgotten it. "I've got to start packing a pencil."

It was late. No one had a girl to take back to one of those double beds, but no one seemed to care much. Mike was sleeping in one of the locked pickups. Tomorrow it was back to Lovelock and from there to the wild horse pens, to provide more water and alfalfa. Nowadays most wrangling involves mechanized chores on marginal or tax-deductible ranches, without much excitement. But these men bore some resemblance to the cowboys who had pushed herds north from Texas across the land that belonged to no one, just for the hell of it. The work was dangerous at times, difficult and unconventional, and they thrived on it; yet the institution of mustang management—the money spent, and the protection of wild horses—dismayed and disgusted them. The irony was that mustangs and cowboys were both remnants of an age perceived as glorious and reflected in the odd longings of people gathered in smoky dance halls, in the shadow of dry mountains.

5

THERE IS AN ASPECT of the range that still exercises extraordinary influence on the imagination—six-shooters and those
who wield them. Public lands have supported as much lawless-
ness as any domain in the West, but finding a contemporary
gunfighter seemed to me an unlikely prospect in an age of universal jurisprudence. However, midway through the trip, I
heard a story about a body found in the desert with its head
resting on a red rock. Actually it was more a rumor than a story
and involved several bodies instead of one, all rustlers caught
too far out in the wilds to be brought to justice. A rock under
the head had been the hallmark of a certain nineteenth-century
lawman, and supposedly was used by his reincarnation, Ed Cantrell.

I began to hear other rumors about Cantrell: he could ride for
days without eating and bring down a horse or a man at a
thousand yards with a rifle; some personal misfortune had
driven him to the brink of despair; he could quote long passages
from Hemingway; he was near-deaf from practicing every day
with a revolver; he had the eyes of a rattlesnake, and quicker
hands.

I didn't believe them, of course. Then I found Ed Cantrell in
Wyoming.

East of the Wind River Range the plains break against the mountains in big, rolling swells. To the south lies the Great Divide

Basin and a lot of BLM land with a sad, colorful history of creaking prairie schooners, dispersed tribes, and gaunt cowboys pushing famished animals toward what was left of the grasslands. Parts of the old Oregon Trail are still visible in ghostly meanderings across marginal grassland and broad drainages.

To the north of U.S. Highway 20/26 lie the Bighorn Mountains, a maverick thrust of the Rockies and one more techtonic wrinkle in mostly dry, difficult country. The road passes through Shoshoni and along Poison Creek above the Rattlesnake Hills, through Hell's Half Acre and the town of Powder River. From there, headwaters of the river of the same name flow north past the old Hole-in-the-Wall, once the roost of unrepentent badmen, and on up into Montana.

Powder River is little more than a Texaco station and a bunch of pronghorn antelope looking at it. The traveler can buy a few groceries there, as well as gas, and drink a cup of coffee at the table in the corner before continuing on to Casper. The table was occupied when I arrived by three men and two women in Levi's, who regarded me with more skepticism than my out-of-state license plates seemed to warrant. But then rustling is still a recognized vocation in this part of Wyoming, where lack of water means spreads of a hundred square miles and larger, from which livestock is often taken to slaughter in Colorado and Nebraska, against the owners' wishes.

When I mentioned the name Cantrell, the biggest of the men said, "What do you want with Ed?"

"I want to talk to him." I added that Cantrell's lawyer had given me a phone number but no one had answered there.

One of the women said, "Ed was drunk at the sheep fair. We didn't think we'd see him for a few days, but he came through this morning."

"They don't have that telephone no more," said the man. He got up and moved behind the cash register. "You have to use the radio phone."

He showed me how. The operator had to place the call and call us back; only one person can speak at a time on a radio phone, so conversations tend to be short and to the point. Mine was listened to with something akin to rapture by the coffee drinkers, while wind rattled the Texaco sign out front.

The voice at the other end was cautious, a bit hoarse, gentlemanly. "You've caught me unawares," it said, as if that was more than a little unwise. Then it said, "All right, come on out. What kind of vehicle are you driving, and how many are you?"

Not everything I knew about Ed Cantrell was rumor; there were some facts. He had shot a man to death in Rock Springs in 1978, during the wild days of the oil boom, when Cantrell ran that town's law enforcement agency, such as it was. The dead man was one of Cantrell's own officers. Cantrell was tried for murder and acquitted after a dramatic courtroom battle in which he demonstrated the speed of his draw. The publicity made Cantrell famous in the intermountain West, but afterward he could not get a job in official law enforcement. Since he had worked as a free-lance range detective before going to Rock Springs, he went back to the range, dropping out of sight with a rare collection of guns, telescopes, and experiences.

Finding him had not been easy. I had called a security agency in Rock Springs where Cantrell worked for a time after the trial. Ed was a good man, said the one who had hired him, but he liked to work alone. He gave me the name and number of a lawyer. The lawyer said he would check with Cantrell, but couldn't reach him. Finally a secretary came up with an old telephone number and mentioned the name of a ranch outside Powder River.

It belonged to a Casper banker—170,000 acres, about half BLM land, north of the highway. The dirt road split and after ten miles split again, without houses or trees or landmarks other than fence posts with an occasional sheep skull on top. There were thirty thousand sheep out there somewhere. If a person didn't pay attention to directions he might find himself out of gas and luck, stared at by antelope down from the Bighorn Mountains to look for water, and maybe by Ed Cantrell.

A sheep rancher had once told a newspaper reporter that he hired Cantrell to kill some sons of bitches and that Cantrell had stopped the rustling on his range. "Rustlers aren't afraid of the courts," the rancher said, "but they're afraid of Ed." What they were afraid of was his gun. Most everyone in the West had one, but Cantrell supposedly *used* his.

Handguns are emblematic of the intention to defend oneself,

not the active engines of destruction they once were, and have a symbolic power greater than their collective muzzle velocity. They arrived in the West from Connecticut by way of Texas. The revolver became what the historian Walter Prescott Webb called "the first radical adaptation made by the American people as they moved westward from the humid region into the Plains country."

War against the Plains Indians in the early nineteenth century was a hopeless proposition for Europeans armed with swords, single-shot pistols, and breech-loading rifles. The Indians were infinitely better horsemen and, as Webb pointed out, could loose a continuous fusillade of arrows from beneath the neck of a pony going at full tilt. Those short bows were potent enough to send an arrow through the body of a buffalo. The Indians also carried twelve-foot lances with which they regularly skewered fleeing white men, and those trying to pour gunpowder into their smoking barrels. Even cartridge rifles were of limited use on horseback against a daring, fleet foe with a reputation for the most artful forms of torture should he find occasion to employ them. Little wonder that early settlers looked around for an equalizer.

The Texas Rangers had Comanches and Mexicans to contend with. After Samuel Colt invented the six-shooter in 1836, it became known as the Texas because of its popularity there. With such an invention a ranger could get off five or six shots without having to dismount, and he could reload quickly. The effect was revolutionary. Literature of the period is full of the amazement of Indians up against the revolver for the first time. But the Texas Rangers were a small outfit and their enthusiasm wasn't shared by the rest of the country or by the U.S. government. Colt went into bankruptcy in 1842. It was Texans who got him out again. Rangers fighting with other Americans against the Mexicans as Texas sought statehood in 1845 used their own pistols—Colts—and General Zachary Taylor, impressed, ordered some for his troops. Like many an entrepreneur, Samuel Colt was finally made wealthy by government requisition.

Guns in the West amount to more than protection. They provide a sense of mission to some isolated lives. I knew a man who had come out from the East to work for the BLM. He knew nothing of guns when he arrived, and disliked them, but he turned to target shooting as he might have to squash or clamraking in another environment. The men in his district office were hunters, and "self-loaders"—they loaded their own shells. One had sixty guns that he kept in a dark room, like wine. The newcomer started shooting for relaxation and as an antidote to loneliness. First he bought a Marlin .30-30, a lightweight lever-action rifle. He traded it on the open market for a .41 magnum Ruger Blackhawk. He bought a Smith & Wesson nine-millimeter automatic. He traded the big Ruger magnum for a .22-225 Ruger rifle. He traded the nine-millimeter automatic for a stainless steel S&W .357 magnum on an L-frame with a six-inch barrel. He bought a Remington 12 gauge pump shotgun and a .30-40 Craig, an old-timey drop-bolt, center-fire military rifle, just for the romance of it. He started loading his own cartridges and derived pleasure from placing three bullets in a space the size of a quarter from 250 yards, knowing the bullet traveled at the right speed, with the proper impact, the proper trajectory.

This was an erudite man, with shelves of books that included a two-volume set of Kipling, Gray's *Anatomy,* a plethora of Western history. In the living room sat a workbench supporting trays of empty brass cartridges, a loading press, a delicate scale, quart containers of gunpowder of varying potency, and a stack of manuals. He carried a Ruger under his jacket; and under the seat of his pickup he kept a .45 Long Colt loaded with hollow-point slugs he had tamped down himself. He also owned a .22 Colt New Frontier in a camouflage nylon holster, modeled on the old six-shooter; a .45 Winchester Challenger in a velvet-lined holster, half as long as a rifle; and a couple of guns he was building from scratch.

From the top of a ridge in huge, empty country, I looked down on a lambing shed and a dozen old herders' wagons. The abandonment of the herding system in this part of Wyoming had meant greater loss of unsupervised sheep, which rustlers supposedly loaded onto trucks in remote canyons at night. In front of a little prefab house stood a pickup painted military green.

Even the cottonwoods out back had the harsh radiance of an overexposed photograph. I drove down and parked. The screen door opened and a wiry man with a full white mustache appeared on the porch, squinting in the sun. His denim shirt was gone at the elbows, and unbuttoned to reveal dog tags on a metal chain. "I'm Ed Cantrell," he said, shaking hands tentatively. It seemed as if he didn't want the right one tied up too long. "Come on in."

He sat on the couch and fished a Camel from his pocket, moving with the care of someone prodigiously hung over. Ed Cantrell had a recruit's buzz cut and a recruit's body, but his face looked every bit of its fifty-seven years. While we talked he never took his bloodshot, cornflower blue eyes off mine. The room was spare as a barracks, with a television set and copies of the Bible, *Bury My Heart at Wounded Knee, Gun Digest,* and *Guns and Ammunition* on a shelf. Eleven rifles and shotguns stood propped against the wall.

"I travel with them," he said. "They keep me from being so lonely. I touch then, and, well . . . they've been with me a long time. They give me a little stability."

There were two .30/06's, a legendary Weatherby, a Remington 12 gauge shotgun he had given to his father, now dead. The others had come to him gradually over thirty years of law enforcement, starting as an MP in Germany in 1948. He had few other mementos. The afghan on the couch had been knitted by his mother in Illinois. On the wall hung a framed Grandfather Achievement Award.

I asked if he had to shoot people in his present line of work.

"Why do you think I'm here? Not because I teach Sunday school. This man hired me because he wanted something done about sheep stealing. You have to make it in the world, and this is all I know how to do. The sheep that come out of this country go somewhere. They don't disappear. It's my job to find out what happens and stop it. The fact that you're talking to me north of Powder River doesn't mean I might not be sitting in Texas tomorrow. I follow a lead anywhere. There are some pretty hard people involved in this. If I stay more than two nights in a place, I get nervous."

He gestured toward the four walls. "This is a good place for me to rest. Some of these rustlers I know, but they *all* know me."

The question had not exactly been answered, but then Cantrell didn't care for direct inquiry. You had to work up to the point with him and then sit through some profound silences.

"I'm a renegade," he said. "You have to understand that. I'm more vulnerable working alone, but I'm also more effective."

"What would you say if someone asked you about bodies in the Red Desert?"

"I'd say I didn't know what the hell he was talking about."

His father was a preacher. Cantrell worked for the Indiana State Police after the war and came west in the early fifties, looking for space. He found it in Wyoming, where he assisted various county sheriffs and gradually learned the trade of range detective. The ranchers apparently liked his style. "I don't just work for rich people, but if you can't afford me, you can't afford me." That meant twenty thousand a year, plus expenses. "This rancher is a good Christian man. I told him I wouldn't sign a contract. If I didn't like the way things were going, I'd roll my bed and move. I don't have any strings on me."

One of his two sons was killed by a drunk driver, Cantrell said, about the time Rock Springs boomed. He was offered the job of police chief, and accepted, to get away from his own misery. "It was the biggest mistake of my life."

The town had tripled in size, with thirty bars and reportedly twice as many pimps. "It was a zoo. People were lined up outside the bars twenty-four hours a day. The police would go in and get beat up and thrown out onto the street. We got rid of the pimps first. You know what a pimp looks like? Big floppy hats, big cars. I'd go up to one, and say, 'You know me, don't you? You know what my job is, don't you? You're not going to be here after today. I'm going home to dinner, and if you're still here when I come back I'm going to start shooting at you.'"

He did not get along with his undercover narcotics agent, whom Cantrell suspected of pocketing the contraband. One night, sitting in a squad car outside the Silver Dollar saloon, the two men fell into an argument, in the presence of two other cops. Cantrell shot the narcotics agent. His name was Mike Rosa and his death galvanized a city already charged with corruption and unbridled, murderous behavior. Cantrell said he shot Rosa in self-defense when he saw him reach for his gun; the two cops remembered it differently. Cantrell was in jail for three weeks before the ranchers of eastern Wyoming came to his rescue. "I had no money. They flew over from Casper," and hired an attorney to defend him. "The bond was five hundred thousand and those fellows just happened to have it."

The prosecution claimed that Cantrell had threatened to kill Rosa before; the charge was murder, since Rosa had no gun in his hand when it finally happened. The defense claimed that Rosa had reached for his gun, after cussing Cantrell, and that Cantrell flat outdrew him. "I had to demonstrate three times in the courtroom," Cantrell said.

He showed me now, reaching for an imaginary pistol in an imaginary holster and aiming at my head. "Can you imagine the pressure? After the first draw, you could see the jury relax, because they saw I was fast enough. Then they understood what had happened that night, and they all sat back and crossed their arms."

Cantrell was acquitted, but as part of the bond deal he had to be out of Sweetwater County within four hours. "*Four hours!* Let that sink in. I had just bought a corner lot and house. I went back and threw my camping gear in the back of the Bronco and took off. I won't say my wife wasn't supportive—that would be cheap, and she's not here to defend herself"—but they had lived separately ever since. "I've paid a terrible price for what I am," he said. "I don't run with anyone, I don't trust anyone. It goes with the territory."

There was something appealing about Cantrell that went beyond the hangover and the pain in the eyes and the anachronism—a vulnerability associated with age, and isolation. Like so many Westerners he grew up in Webb's "humid regions," shooting squirrels out of leafy green trees and imagining an open, arid frontier. He had become the dream of every ten-year-old boy who went into a Saturday matinee between 1920 and the time television killed the Western.

* * *

"I want to tell you something about what my life is like."

Cantrell was driving his pickup toward a sheep camp, up a narrow winding road. He sat forward, hugging the steering wheel, watching the ridgelines, looking more like a Prussian artillery officer than a detective, with his mustache and gray crew cut. The immense landscape, undifferentiated to the urban eye, took on subtle variations in color: pinks and pale lavenders, and dark shadows on the edge of sunlight.

An unlit Camel dangled from Cantrell's lip. He wore no gun, but several were packed in the truck, which growled unnaturally, trailing water from a leaky radiator. He preferred a horse to pickups or all-terrain vehicles because a horse was quiet and did not raise a cloud of dust.

"From time to time I like to drink a few beers," he said. "I get a little unconscious. There's a bar in Shoshoni I go to. The owner's a friend of mine. I know the people there, they know me; I feel comfortable. I can sit and listen to the juke box and ogle them ole dried-up gals, like I like to do.

"One night this guy comes in and sits up at the bar. He's a cowboy-looking guy. He stares, which starts to bother me. Then he comes over and says, 'I know who you are, and I know you're after me.' Well, he's drunk, and I'm not. I say, 'I never saw you in my life.' He keeps on pushing. It gets heavy. I say, 'I don't want to hurt your feelings, but I never heard of you, and I'm not after you.'

"He goes out into the parking lot and comes back with a pistol under his jacket. I can see it. He sits up at the bar and keeps turning around and looking at me. Finally I tell the waitress to call the sheriff and get him out there before I blow this son of a bitch off his stool. It turns out—now get this—that he's the former son-in-law of an old friend of mine. He beat up my friend's daughter, and my friend told him he was going to take out a contract on him with Ed Cantrell. Only trouble was, he never told me about it."

He laughed at the irony. "No matter what I do, I'm in a bad position." He added, almost wistfully, "People use my name." I had the impression that a multitude of arguments hung out there in the middle distance, waiting to be resolved.

"I'll tell you a story. I was riding down the road and saw this fella pushing some cows. I stopped to watch. He rode up and said, 'I know who you are, you son of a bitch! Don't screw with me,' and rode off again. His daughter was roping, so I drove over and asked her what was wrong with her daddy. She said, 'Who are you?' I said, 'I'm Ed Cantrell.' And she said, 'You're what's wrong with him.'

"I went to my boss and told him about it. 'I want you to know the situation,' I said, 'because if that son of a bitch talks to me that way again, I'm gonna blow him out of the saddle.' "

The road looped and rose some more; evergreen appeared—a sign of moisture. "You never know when somebody's watching you in this country," he said. "That's why I thought you might want to drive your own vehicle." He carried two sets of binoculars, one of them for night work, and a telescope on a gun stock. "Every time I look through it, I wonder if somebody's looking at *me*. Don't worry, this isn't the right time of year to get shot."

The right time was autumn—slaughter season for lambs, and maybe a human or two.

"Why hasn't some rustler already shot you?"

"I've often wondered that myself."

After reflection, he said, "It's dirty, boring, tedious work, but I keep coming back to it. I've laid up on these ole ridges many a cold night. I like to ease into a place, and stay a few days, watching. You get where you know who the people are, or you have strong suspicions. It's a close-knit bunch here, old-timers. They learned rustling from their dads. It's so isolated they get a bunch of sheep out there and shear 'em so there's no paint brand. All that's left is the earmark. They take 'em to another state and change that. It's easy."

The sheep camp consisted of a knockdown corral, a beat-up trailer, two saddled horses, and two Mexicans standing warily by, waiting to see if I worked for Immigration before they bolted. The ranch foreman came out and shook Cantrell's hand. He was Chris, a born-again Christian who worked as lay pastor of the Home of Our Shepherd nondenominational church in Powder River as well as ranch foreman. He invited me into the trailer to have coffee with an Anglo herder while Cantrell dipped water from the spring for his radiator.

"Ed's made a difference," Chris said. "Last year we lost three hundred sheep, down from a thousand. This year we haven't lost a one."

A thousand sheep were worth sixty thousand dollars, not counting wool and lambs. The economics of rustling made sense, when several hundred sheep could be packed into one cattle truck.

"Just having somebody on the place helps. That, and Ed's name. The price of lamb has turned some honest ranchers into thieves. It's a hard old way. Now Ed makes 'em think. If he catches you, will he arrest you or will he shoot you? I wouldn't want him to catch *me* rustling sheep."

"He's pretty quick," said the herder, watching Ed through the window. The herder wore a leather holster for his Skoal tin, above greasy chaps. "He can stand up and spin around like that." He snapped his fingers. "He can look right through you and make you feel like you've done something wrong." He sucked coffee through his mustache. "You'll be out working in the middle of nowhere, thinking you're all alone, and you'll turn around and there'll be ole Ed."

The murder trial in Rock Springs had raised both men's estimation of Cantrell. "After his arrest," said Chris, "he never tried to hide his face or anything. And it was hard on ole Ed."

On the way back down the mountain, Cantrell told me he had created his own job security. "I'll run the rustlers off this place, and they'll go next door. Then that rancher'll hire me. The winters are tough, though. You really feel 'em when you get older."

He planned to retire in three years, he said. He wanted to buy a little house on a quiet street in Casper and maybe help raise his daughter's son. He hoped people would let him be.

He stopped on the hill above the house, then rolled the pickup slowly down. He took a worn black holster from beneath the seat, and strapped it on after he had gotten out of the truck. He unloaded the revolver, a .38 with custom grips made of mesquite. "People are too rigid with handguns," he said. "You have to be fluid, and use the same motion every time you reach for it."

He moved his hand in circles, like a conjurer, starting at the bottom of the holster and coming up with the pistol. "It's a muscle-mind thing." He repeated the process twice, pulling the trigger each time. *Snick . . . snick . . .* "If you do something once, it's one thing. If you do it ten thousand times, it's something else. You don't stab. Just reaching for the pistol can get you into trouble—you break the motion and have to start again. This way I can begin to pull the trigger as I come up to here."

Snick . . .

"We're talking milliseconds. You drop your shoulder a little and shoot from the hip. It's the opposite of the FBI crouch, which is supposed to help your balance but really's bullshit because it takes too much time. My way, you don't have to absorb any lead. Don't shoot for the body, it's a waste of time. If you have to shoot him, shoot him in the face."

He turned to me, five feet between us. "This is knife range. Now the natural tendency is to shoot low. I have special grips, to level the gun when my finger's on the trigger. Automatics are especially bad because you have to bring them up. I can shoot with just the feel of this gun. That's why I like a heavy six-inch barrel. I shot Rosa with a six-inch barrel."

"Where?"

"Right between the eyes."

He reloaded and holstered the pistol, and turned as if to go into the house. Suddenly the gun was in his hand again, cocked, his wrist pressed against his hip. I looked at this slight, wiry man with his very blue eyes, and saw in them a natural, utterly impersonal force that made the hair stand up on the back of my neck.

The gun went off with a terrific roar, throwing up dirt a dozen feet away. The bullet had nicked the upper edge of a red rock the size of a half dollar.

"Shooting high today," said Cantrell.

· II ·

HARVEST

The West has always meant opportunity. It fueled the fantasies and fortunes of millions, from the days when Kentucky was considered the West and the transmississippi wilderness had all the allure of a galactic outpost. Some saw opportunity in the grandeur of the West—an opportunity for the expansion of the American consciousness that Frederick Jackson Turner talked about. Others ignored natural beauty and spiritual growth or, more accurately, found beauty in the kingdom's ability to provide material value.

That version of the West is a larder where successive generations of the hungry and avaricious have rampaged, usually in collusion with government. And the West is still an awesome generator of product. The BLM's income from grazing and other fees in fiscal 1985 was only $227 million. But oil, gas, coal, and mineral leasing earned the agency an additional $1.2 billion. The Forest Service's total receipts for fiscal 1985 also amounted to more than $1 billion, including everything from timber production to royalties paid for Smokey Bear stuffed dolls. That kind of cash flow puts both agencies on a par with the biggest multinationals, in fact with whole nations. If the BLM and Forest Service charged a competitive rate for grazing and lumber, and received royalties from mining operations, the figure would be much higher.

I wanted to understand the specifics behind this bonanza. Choosing among a multitude of money-making schemes was not easy. A uranium mine or a clear-cut slope, drilling rigs, a ski resort, or some master plan for a similar project hangs in every view of public lands, literal or figurative. The most remote, self-sufficient, innocent life can't escape the scars and enticements of development.

· · · · ·

1

GOLD MINING is the most enduring symbol of opportunity in the West. Curiously, gold is also the most illusive. It riveted attention on the West in 1848 like nothing else had, not the expedition of Lewis and Clark, or the war with Mexico. The discovery of gold in California provided the factory-weary and the farm-bound the first glimpse of fast wealth. The speculative impulse so prevalent in development of the West might well have started at Sutter's Mill, on the American River. It flooded the Mormon and Gila trails, and the steamers taking prospectors south around the Horn or across the isthmus of Central America and up the coast—a hundred thousand, more or less. Newspaper editorialists inveighed against the abandonment of traditional values, and Thoreau declared the Gold Rush "the greatest disgrace on mankind."

Those who came west looking for gold weren't impressed with such moralizing. "The California they knew," wrote J. S. Holliday in *The World Rushed In,* "gave new meaning, even reality, to the most American of myths—the pursuit of happiness."

Happiness ended up in a relatively small number of hands. Then the rush moved to Nevada, to the Colorado Rockies, the banks of the Gila River, to southwest Canada, to Montana and Wyoming. Stories of great wealth carried weight, like that of Henry "Old Pancake" Comstock, who sold out for a mere eleven thousand dollars and didn't seem to care that his mine was worth a third of a billion. The big mining companies made most of the money, over the long haul, but it was the unlikely stories of gold that had the tightest grip on popular imagination: the sourdough miner washing several dollars' worth of gold from his beard; nuggets found lying in the dust in front of brothels.

The government owned the land by right of conquest, but miners didn't pay for what they jumped and rummaged through and left. Gold not only inspired some of the great excesses in the West, it also gave rise to laws that had the effect of depriving the rest of the citizens of the United States of payment for their treasure, and allowing miners and miners manqué—of which there were and are still thousands—to live on public land so long as they kept it in a state of perpetual disruption.

An early effort to sell public mineral lands to pay off Civil War debts was subverted by a senator from Nevada named William Stewart. He had made a fortune in Virginia City gold and silver, and he later piggybacked his mining bill onto another that had passed the House, assuring that minerals found on the public domain were free. So was the use of the land. That and the subsequent Mining Law of 1872, which included hardrock mining, amounted to a radical departure from the usual disposal of the public lands, whereby some of the wealth is shared by the populace. That law is still with us.

My pursuit not of gold but of gold miners brought me to Arizona in the spring; I left the desert and the environs of Phoenix and crossed the marvelous high saddle of the Mazatzal Mountains, heading toward the Tonto National Forest. The conquistadors might have built their own Cíbola in the Tonto Basin, or along the Mogollon Rim, a natural fortress and the bottom wrinkle in the belly of the Colorado Plateau. But first they would have had to beat off the Indians and master the techniques of hardrock mining. Placer gold, the sort that shows up in pans full of silt, was rare here. But below the rivers and streams lay deep seams of quartz and precious metals. The Coconino, Tonto, Gila, and Apache-Sitgreaves national forests all entertain latter-day prospectors after gold and silver. Part-time miners from the Rockies to the Pacific use the antiquated mining laws just to set up houses or hunting camps on government land.

In the town of Payson I found a Forest Service engineer responsible for inspecting claims on the Tonto. Gold miners were something of a problem, he said. "They take shots at one another on occasion. A few hardheads think we're violating their constitutional rights."

Few claims become patented mines. "Ninety percent of these guys *think* they have something, but they don't have the capability or the intent of developing it themselves. They just want to be bought out. Some sell a hole in the ground—an out-and-out scam."

All a miner has to do to stay on public land is conduct a hundred dollars' worth of "assessment" work. That usually means pushing some dirt around with a bulldozer. Twenty acres goes with a patented claim, and many such "mining" camps are sold on the open market, in direct violation of the law.

The mining operation I visited lay close to town, where FS land abutted the highway. A Lincoln Continental sat with the hood up, cables attached to the battery leading to a mobile home. At the edge of the clearing was an elaborate contraption where ore was pulverized; the tailings trailed down into a basin of caked yellow mud. Bits of machinery with no evident purpose lay in the shadow of a bulldozer of great vintage.

A piece of plywood next to the rutted entrance said "Shumway," not a mining procedure, but the name of the owner. He stood in the shade of a mesquite with another man, next to a pile of old electric motors. I heard Shumway tell his neighbor, as I approached, "If this one don't work, bring it back and take another one."

The neighbor went off with his purchase, grunting under its weight. Shumway tipped his cowboy hat low over his eyes and watched him go. "He's got a leaching mill," he said, as if we were old friends. "He's trying to get gold out of cinders. Volcanic rock. What'd you say your name was?"

Like so many users of public lands, Ray Shumway was perfectly willing to discuss his life with a stranger. He was a miner, he said, and the other man was a promoter. The mining fraternity was pretty evenly divided between the two, but interaction was constant and often critical. One man's mine could be part of another man's scheme.

Before I could digest that bit of lore, Shumway asked, "Want to see some gold?"

Out of the pocket of his jeans, which were burned full of holes, he took what looked like two golden Hershey Kisses and dropped them into my hand. They weighed about three ounces each and were worth about two thousand dollars. One had a reddish cast; the other shone with the brilliance of a new wedding band.

"People love to see gold," he said, taking his back. "You hand it to them, and they don't want to let go of it. I've seen people's hands start to shake, holding gold."

He was sixty but didn't look it, a big man with dark lashes covering blue eyes that could have come out of some cinematic version of the quest for El Dorado. He drew the toe of one boot through the dust, completing the image. He had dropped out of school when he was nine, he told me, up in Utah, and started digging uranium when he was thirteen, learning enough geology along the way to make it as a miner. "Vanadium and uranium travel together," he said, "generally in a sandstone formation."

That's where he had dug, earning enough money to buy a motorcycle and, later, several Piper 210's, in which he had buzzed his claims from Colorado to Nevada.

He showed me around. A retort oven, used to melt down concentrate from the mill, sat in the dust outside his cinderblock office. Inside, we stepped carefully among the electroplater for separating gold and silver from baser elements, containers for sulfuric acid (that explained the holes in his jeans), a machine for making distilled water, a scale in a glass case accurate to half a milligram, more cowboy boots, gruesome oil paintings of Apaches, and a girlie calendar. He did his own assaying amidst an almost incredible clutter of dust, rock, and containers of strange substances. If this is modern alchemy, I thought, no wonder gold is so expensive.

The falling price of gold to about $350 an ounce had taken

some of the gleam out of his operation. The mill was worth half a million dollars, he said, and that didn't include the earth movers, the dump trucks, the machinery, or the mine itself, located a few miles north on FS land. Shumway lived in the mobile home, where two cushionless aluminum chairs sat on boards in the blinding sun, with one of a succession of wives. Her name was Randy. I had seen the rustle of a curtain when I drove up, but that was all I would see.

"She's a city girl," he said. "She don't like the country, and she don't like mines. I think them holes scare her."

The mill was idle, he explained, because he needed at least thirty days' worth of ore guaranteed before he could crank up and hire a crew. So he and Randy spent a fair amount of time shopping down in Phoenix, waiting for the price of gold to go up. They ate out on Saturdays in Payson, and danced at a club with a big floor and a good Western swing band. Shumway liked dancing. He wanted to go public with his gold company and had filled out all the papers and hired a lawyer. Once it was done, he and Randy could move to Colorado.

We walked out to the mill. Here ore was pulverized in a drum and passed through a bowl with a centrifuge that separated the "heavies"—precious metals—from the "lights," the dross. The former went into a chemical froth called a float, which bonded air bubbles with bits of gold and silver and brought these heavies to the surface. The product was high-grade "con"—concentrate of sufficient density to justify feeding it into a smelter from which emerged the gold Hershey Kisses, or bars stamped .999 ad infinitum, the official designation of ultimate value.

"Gold ain't worth anything," Shumway said. "Just what value people put on it. Gold brings out the greed."

His life seemed crowded with enemies. While he and Randy were in Phoenix, a friend stole thirty-five ounces of heavies out of the bowl and Shumway's front-end loader. The thief took his haul clear to Kansas before the police stopped him. That was inconsequential compared to Shumway's problems with other miners. Some neighbors tried to jump his claims, he said, and to shut him down. He found his bulldozer tipped over one morning, and dirt in every gas tank on the place. There had been confrontations at the mine shaft, and two lawsuits.

"That's greed," Shumway said.

He figured he had spent twenty-seven thousand dollars on this particular feud, and that didn't include equipment and attorneys. "I was new to Arizona, I wanted to get along with everybody. I told the lawyer it would be cheaper for me to run these fellas off with a gun. He said I'd better not do that, then charged me a hundred dollars for the advice."

I asked why he had given up uranium for the chancier prospect of gold.

"I came down to drill for uranium, and some boys here showed me the gold. These little mines have a fine grade, too fine for the tables"—vibrating slabs that had been used for years to separate lights and heavies. Also, he liked the climate.

That was seven years ago. He had filed a claim and a mining plan with the FS. The site containing Shumway's mill, mobile home, office, and menagerie of machinery did not belong to him, but to the federal government. He had to pay a five-dollar filing fee and put up a bond assuring that he would restore the land if he pulled out, and that was it. He paid no taxes on the thirty acres he occupied, and no royalties on what he mined. Such were the anomalies that kept small miners afloat, and had made big ones wealthy on public resources. Once the site was patented and its commercial viability proved, then Shumway could buy the land at a nominal fee.

"The Forest Service might try to keep me from patenting," he said. "Depends on the man handling the application," another potential enemy. "The Forest thinks the land belongs to it, but it don't. It belongs to everybody."

He invited me into the trailer. The bleak exterior had not prepared me for the clean carpets, upholstered chairs, a coffee table supporting a book of Andrew Wyeth's paintings, a neat kitchenette with wine glasses lined up on the pass-through, a collection of butterflies in a glass case. Shumway was clearly a man of two parts, and he kept one of them carefully hidden in Payson.

He took off his hat and ran a hand through gray hair. "I'll probably get back into uranium, after we go public. I'll build a fence here, and hire somebody to run the place."

"What'll you do if the public offering doesn't work out?"

"A miner can always make money." He nudged a coffee table leg with a toe. "You can always dig some ore and sort the big chunks, mash it, and pan a line. You have to know what you're doing, but you can make a living."

I could hear Randy moving around at the far end of the trailer. The telephone rang. Shumway was expecting a call from his lawyer—another hundred dollars.

"Mining's fun," he was saying. "You never know what's behind the next rock outcrop. One day you're poor, and the next day you're rich. That's the thing about mining."

I drove down the highway. The mill owned by the competition made Shumway's operation look like a paragon of order and environmental concern. I stopped the van in a cloud of dust, which drifted across a few scoured federal acres and the apotheosis of Rube Goldbergism: long strings of white plastic pipe held aloft by poles and baling wire; green plastic bins that once contained apple juice and were now full of chemicals for floating the heavies; random piles of dirt and ore; patched hoses snaking from hut to hut; staved-in metal drums full of con; derelict machinery providing shade for sleeping mongrels; an old sedan without wheels or a windshield; skeletal metal frames out of the deep industrial past; flapping sheets of corrugated steel; rusted high-pressure tanks; wooden carts with wheels splayed under impossible loads of junk; sagging conveyer belts; dozens of empty Dove detergent bottles for more chemicals; and an abandoned pit full of something toxic.

The dogs began to howl. Two young men came out of a trailer to stare. One wore a Cat hat that said "Payson General Store—Gateway to the Mogollon Rim." The other wore BMW sunglasses and a Beatles' haircut. I introduced myself. They were Marshall and Michael, brothers, age twenty-eight and thirty, foremen of the mine, as well as shareholders. They told me immediately that it would make them millionaires.

"We're still putting this thing together," said Marshall. "We had to spend some time in court, and get some new investors."

I asked about their dispute with Ray Shumway.

"He tried to jump our claims. He put an armed guard on

the mine. I wanted to shoot him, but you can't do that. And Ray's too old to beat on. I just get up in his face and yell at him."

We strolled about, trailed by the dogs. Marshall turned on the crusher, a demonstration; the structure shook so, I thought the coyote skulls would fall off the shelf.

"It's backbreaking work," Marshall said, "but I get off on it."

Their mine was located a few miles north, on FS land. They called it the Golden Wonder. A hundred years before, they said, the owner walked into the tunnel with his small daughter and emerged with two chunks of gold as big as his fists. With them he bought a fine cattle spread up by Twin Peaks. Indians had mined the Golden Wonder before that, according to the brothers. They had been following the same seam for seven years.

"We need five one-hundredths of an ounce to break even," Marshall said. That meant twenty tons of pulverized rubble for an ounce of gold. "We usually haul a quarter-ounce or better. We run the assays down to Phoenix. It's a real good mine. We might have ten million dollars waiting in there, we might have two hundred million."

Marshall had a little mustache and big knuckly hands. "His daddy told me he's pretty rough," Shumway had said, without rancor. Michael had been a commercial artist outside Phoenix before he responded to the call of El Dorado in this rural slum. "A lot of my friends in the valley would like to live up here," he said proudly. He and his brother watched plenty of television, he added, and shot deer and javelina anytime they felt like it.

Marshall shut off the crusher. The heat, the dogs lolling in the dust, the glare of sun off metal, and the sight of bulging plastic containers full of witch's brew did not seem worth the discovery of a one-ounce ton, or even a five-ounce ton.

"We might be willing to sell," Marshall said, "if someone offered us an outrageous price."

"What would you consider outrageous?"

"We might take four million," Michael said.

"Hell, no!" said Marshall, and his brother backed up a step. "At least ten million!"

One of the dogs chewed on a rotten two-by-four supporting a rickety sluiceway. He must have been doing hundreds of thousands of dollars' worth of damage.

Michael shoved the dog aside with a boot. "We're either going to make it big," he said, "or we're not going to make it at all. This is my only chance to make a million dollars."

"You gotta be positive," said Marshall. He slipped his right hand into the remaining pocket on his Levi's and arched his back. "There's a main of minerals that runs from here to Globe. We figure we found the pot. Two hundred more feet down and we'll be picking up chunks of gold you can break apart with your fingers."

Meanwhile, they were going fishing on Roosevelt Lake.

"This is our year," Michael said.

As I was leaving I asked about the dark pond.

"Oh, that's just a cyanide pit."

The next morning I went back to Shumway's. The Continental was gone—he and Randy were shopping in Phoenix, according to the neighbor who had bought the used electric motor. He owned the leaching mill across the highway—big plastic tanks where acid was poured over volcanic cinders that supposedly contained precious metal. Now he was inspecting an old vibrating table once used to separate heavies, now discarded in the weeds.

I told him I wanted to write about gold mining. He stood up and looked me over speculatively. He wore sunglasses of impenetrable density and shifted a toothpick from one side of his mouth to the other, trying to decide if I was worth a pitch. Finally he said, "I want to show you something."

We went over to his pickup. He lifted a black rock from the bed and held it up in the sunlight. "A cinder cone. It's full of little silicate crystals. See how they shine? Lots of platinates, too. Go on, feel how heavy it is."

I hefted the rock; it was indeed heavy.

"We've found free gold in these the size of this toothpick," he said. " 'Course, it's hard to assay because it's got so many chemicals in it. Right now my ore's being assayed in Frankfurt, Germany, in Zurich, Switzerland, in Tucson and Houston. The big boys are interested in my platinates." He went through a list of exotic metals, counting on his fingers. "I'll just sell them the cones, and let them extract it. Nobody's ever tried to get precious metals out of cinder cones before."

For twenty years he had worked as an equipment foreman for the global construction firm Morrison-Knudson, in Vietnam, Indonesia, Iran. He retired and was driving around Arizona with a friend, he said, when they saw a mountain of hardened lava. "I said, 'Look at that mountain. It don't look like the others.' It was *shiny* black. We went up and took some samples. Those old volcanoes vaporized the precious metals as the magma rose, then dissolved and trapped them in what they call gas bombs. Big boulders, like. Trapped in there was gold and silver and, of course, platinates. We own the rights to eighty-five million tons of the stuff."

He wouldn't try to develop the cinder cones himself. Too expensive. Besides, he said, one of the majors would do a better job, after they bought him out. Some large-scale gold mining had been revived in the West, and if the price rose, there would be more.

Patriotism was his primary concern, he added. "This will help revive mining. Mining's in a real mess in this country. We're getting our platinates from Russia! Pretty soon the dollar's gonna crash and America'll be scrambling for its own mineral resources. We'll be in the right spot."

He replaced the toothpick with a thin cigar. "Ray here's no poor boy," he said, looking around. "He's got a Hatfield-McCoy thing with those boys, but he knows what he's doing. This is a real nice mill. It'll get the gold and silver out of my cones, but it's not sophisticated to get the rest. I run thirty-seven tons through it, and my platinates ended up in the tailing pond."

"Why don't you try to recover them?"

"I own eighty-five million tons of the stuff. Why do I want to fool around with Ray Shumway's tailings?"

Meanwhile he was negotiating with Shumway over used electric motors and an antiquated vibrating table. He could make some money shaking con for other small miners in the area, until the majors came to their senses and bought 85 million tons of lava.

2

I HAD SEEN mining on a small scale in Arizona, but I waited until I reached eastern Montana before I took a look at the other sort. The BLM has a million acres under coal lease in the West. That is not much out of the BLM's nearly 180 million acres in the lower forty-eight states. But it is still a lot of country—almost sixteen hundred square miles of potential desolation.

I had visited the plains of eastern Montana fourteen years before. There Meriwether Lewis had recorded in his diary that coal he found "burnt tolerably well [and] afforded but little flame or smoke, but produced a hot & lasting fire." In the early 1970s that coal had set off a small war pitting miners and their allies against those convinced that the country roundabout would be devastated. The *Atlantic* had sent me out to investigate, and the piece I wrote predicted developmental nightmares and a wrecked landscape.

Northeast of the Custer Battlefield National Monument, a narrow state road crosses rolling, arid country where winter wind blowing down from the Arctic Circle picks at sandstone tors and pushes the shallow topsoil around in little clefts and valleys. The valleys shelter some cattle and a dozen native grasses, greasewood, and sagebrush, as well as sharp-tailed grouse, deer, and antelope. Ponderosa pines stand on the ridges above pinkish "burns," where coal smoldering for thousands of years left clinker too hard to erode, part of a huge coal deposit—34 billion tons, more or less—that slops over into the Dakotas and Wyoming. Most of the coal belongs to the BLM, the railroad, and the Crow and Northern Cheyenne; it represents about a third of America's reserves.

The landscape changes abruptly just south of Colstrip, a town created by the Northern Pacific Railroad in the 1920s to fuel its engines. Big serrated loaves of spoil are left from the old strip-mining operations. A dragline, a huge machine for stripping coal, still flays the putty-gray earth, and smokestacks stand like exclamation points on the horizon, their coordinated strobes flashing to ward off aircraft. When I first visited Colstrip, the tallest structure was the dragline's boom.

The town's history says a lot about railroads and mining in the West. In an exchange typical of the nineteenth century, the federal government had long ago given the railroad land along its proposed route to offset the cost of building in vast, dangerous country. Sections bequeathed to the railroad alternated with those remaining in government hands, creating the so-called checkerboard pattern still found throughout the West, a constant reminder of the unprecedented bonanza in land enjoyed by the likes of Collis Huntington and Leland Stanford.

Northern Pacific's Colstrip operation remained small potatoes until the appearance of something called the North Central Power Study in 1971. Produced by the Bureau of Reclamation, the study asserted the need for forty-two huge coal-burning power plants in the West, half of them located in eastern Montana. By then Northern Pacific had become Burlington Northern, with more than 2 million acres of its land underlaid with coal and rights to another 6 million acres of coal under private land. The BLM also owned huge coal deposits in the area.

Colstrip had been a podunk highway stop in those days. I remembered a little sundries store, a gas station, and a handful of dilapidated houses. In the intervening years it had become a dryland Levittown, with trailered outboards in the driveways, a Taco Shack, and an eight-lane bowling alley. Fourteen years before, there were posters in the roadhouse window announcing that Montana Jack and Tonto—jackasses—were available for stud. Men fought with their fists as often for recreation as from anger, and judges looked more kindly upon homicide than cattle rustling. Now there were no stud ads in the window of the bowling alley. It was owned by Minnesotans, offered Bowlarama Sweepstakes on weekends, and had an air of prefab gentility. You could drink mushy margaritas out of goldfish bowls if you behaved yourself, and sprinkle your own bacon bits at a vest-pocket salad bar.

The Montanans I had met in 1971 preferred Ditch—bourbon and water—or VO and Squirt. They danced to bands like the Cridland Trio, and some got their horns scraped, as the euphemism had it, in a Sheridan cathouse. The more responsible ones did not like the idea of boom times from mining coal in Rosebud, Powder River, and Big Horn counties. Some had taken uncomfortable positions in the community, opposing what they foresaw as bad air, bad neighbors, severed aquifers, and destruction of their landscape and way of life—all for the sake of quick profits from the megawatts to be fed into air conditioners in God-knew-what distant cities.

Wally MacRae, a cowboy who had done difficult service for an environmental group called the Northern Plains Resources Council, had testified in the 1970s before congressional committees and had traveled the state questioning the methodology of the Bureau of Reclamation, Burlington Northern, and Montana Power and its mining subsidiary, Western Energy. Now I called him and was surprised when he offered to meet me in town. Formerly he had been reluctant to come to Colstrip and risk getting into a brawl with company employees.

We met in the Miner's House, an equally laminated alternative to the Colbowl, with paper doilies on the tables and framed photographs of old stripping operations on the walls. MacRae was more than welcome there. The double-jointed brim of his beat-up cowboy hat hung down in front of a face ravaged by the Montana winters. His eyes were turquoise studs driven into an old stump, and conversation with him was one long dalliance with a Pall Mall.

MacRae owned a big ranch south of Colstrip which had been in his family for 104 years. "All my fears have been realized," he said. "A lot of things happened here I didn't want to see happen. A lot of people left, or cut themselves off. The big issue was construction of the plants, not the mining. Any rational person will recognize that you have to mine some coal in the United States. This is a pretty good place for that, but a horrible place to convert it into something else. I and other people in the Northern Plains Resources Council said the power plants were not needed, they were too big, and not in the right place. Montana Power went ahead and built the stupid things and then couldn't get a rate increase."

The power plants had risen, but the demand for electricity forecast by the Bureau of Reclamation had not. Therefore, two of the plants sat in a squalor of nonproductiveness while their owner, Montana Power, tried to refinance, and a third ran at a fraction of capacity. Still, mining kept things prosperous, and tax revenues from the area around Colstrip, MacRae said, made Rosebud the Cinderella of Montana's counties.

"We have a stainless steel Olympic-size swimming pool at the high school. We need that like three holes in the head. Do you know how much it costs to clean a stainless steel Olympic-size swimming pool? And how many BTUs it takes to heat it? They say, 'It's a mere pittance,' and then they fire tenured teachers. So a good education boils down to a stainless steel Olympic-size swimming pool."

He had burned out on the environmental circuit, he said. "I was a hired gun for a while, consulting, traveling around helping citizen groups. I got interviewed so many times that I'd wait for that little red light on top of the TV camera to go on, then I'd push my hat back"—he demonstrated, and accentuated his twang—"and say, 'This land as far as you can see is mine, and them sons of bitches ain't gittin' any of it. Okay, cut and print.' "

Now he was a cowboy poet. "I've got a book of poetry out, I'm working on another. I write plays, too."

He had formed a local theater group called the Coal and Cattle Country Players. "We've done dinner theaters at the Moose Club—*The Fantastiks* and *Prisoner of Second Avenue.* Sold out. We got our best response to my melodrama, *Maids A-woo and Derring-do upon the Sparklin' Sea.* That last part's in parentheses. I directed it at the high school, where I graduated. We had great props—an old saloon and a mine shaft and a Victorian parlor. Played to a full house three nights, and turned people away."

MacRae lit up a Pall Mall.

"There was a time when I wouldn't come in here because it wasn't physically safe. Now I'm a goddamn hero. We at the NPRC got laws passed for reclamation, and well-scrubbed power plants. Even the company people nowadays will come up and tell you they're environmentalists."

I spent the night on a ridge above Western Energy's mining site, under a waxy three-quarter moon that popped up over North Dakota. I cooked a steak on my gas stove and looked out over the twenty-four-hour operation; it reminded me of the view of Queens from the Fifty-ninth Street Bridge at 2:00 A.M. Webs of lights surrounded the four power units, only one of which was humming in the darkness, and the lighted coal conveyer hung like another bridge between mine and town. Two monumental draglines grunted and snorted, miles apart, in the ever-widening sumps of their own industry, red lights flashing to keep airplanes out of the rigging. Murky pools of dust roiled the night air about them as they swiveled back and forth, back and forth, the incoming roads threaded by the tiny beams of what were really huge coal haulers and trucks loaded with tons of water to spread over the roads.

A snake of natural electricity struck off to the southwest, followed by heat lightning and the rumble of localized rain. The clamor of the draglines competed with the thunder, and for a time it was hard to distinguish one from the other.

"These guys in scrapers are just working the overburden," said Cathy Doran. "They strip another area and hand the topsoil over to us. It's known as a direct laydown; it keeps the grass seed from going sterile."

She was a mining engineer for Western Energy, involved in reclamation—returning the land to some semblance of its former state. Slightly built, with wisps of blond hair ringing her hard hat, she drove the company pickup with precise motions along a dirt track between manmade mountains. Aflutter with red and yellow ribbons, they were really enormous rock piles waiting to be given a gentling layer of topsoil. Eventually they would support stands of native wheat like those on neighboring slopes, an impressive bit of reclamation that a decade ago seemed impossible. The land did not look the same, but neither was it wrecked.

What lies between the miner and the coal is the overburden—a graphic mining conceit. "You blast the overburden," Cathy said, "set up a dragline, and remove it. You clean the top of the seam with front-end loaders. You drill it and blast it, then bring in a piston shovel with a twenty-five-yard bucket and load it into the one-twenty-ton haulers. It's pretty simple, really."

She had once worked as a secretary for the BLM, typing up coal leases. The process described in the leases interested her considerably more than typing, and she became one of three women in an engineering class at Montana Tech. Her father had been a miner in Butte, her brother was one still. Now she was in charge of grading roads where they appeared and disappeared overnight. The roads, and blasting overburden, were two formerly masculine endeavors she had taken over for Western Energy. Her husband also worked for the company, as an accountant. Their children attended school in Colstrip and swam in the Olympic-size stainless steel pool. "My daughter wants to be a mining engineer," she said, "and my son wants to be a dragline operator. I guess I'm a pretty good role model."

We approached the dragline, known as a Marion 8200. It cost $22 million to assemble and supposedly weighed 9 million pounds, although it would be difficult to get an eight-story iron box on the scales. The Marion 8200 looked like something out of Hieronymus Bosch, with cunning passageways and strange declivities. Occasionally I could see a tiny face, or faces, in a remote window. The body of the machine sat on a vast drum with great club feet that could walk the monster backward, away from the precipice created by its own snorting, clanking endeavor. The boom, longer than a football field, dangled a cleated steel bucket the size of a room, polished to mirrored brightness by 75 cubic yards of shattered rock picked up in each scoop—3,000 cubic yards an hour, 16 million cubic yards a year.

Cathy radioed the operator of the Marion 8200 for permission to board. I felt like a passenger in a dinghy between two cresting waves. The machine ceased its swiveling while I grappled up a steel ladder, then commenced again, groaning and shrieking now. The young man in plastic glasses at the top of the catwalk handed me plastic earplugs and led me inside, past howling exhaust fans and generators with liquid diodes flashing and big flywheels reeling four-inch steel cables. Somewhere out in the dust storm a minor disaster occurred every time the bucket struck earth.

The power control room, PC-One, insulated from the noise, reminded me of the bridge of a large ship. The operator, dressed in cowboy boots and a snap-cuff shirt, was seated in a glorified barber's chair, hauling on levers and pumping pedals, chewing on a wad of gum, looking out into the canyon of his own making. To the younger man, the oiler, fell the duties of maintenance and the computer watch—checking the power surges, the cable feed, and the temperature of components that could bring a Marion 8200 to a costly shutdown.

Western Energy's mine in eastern Montana had a bright future. The oiler made forty thousand dollars a year, he said. He was a Montanan and a former farm boy named Dennis Maag. Operators and oilers here originally came from the East, brought by the coal companies from other mines. Now they came from ranches and farms in the West. Dennis had decided to become an equipment operator after one too many winter mornings when he got up before dawn and knocked icicles off the noses of his father's cows. Now when it was forty below he worked in relative comfort.

In winter, he said, steam rose from water seeping from exposed aquifers, and the mine shut down during blizzards because the bucket hung too far out in the storms to be seen. In summer, the temperature inside the engine room reached 120 degrees. Outside, the handrails got too hot to touch.

The operator took a break, and Dennis sat down in the barber's chair. "This thing's like driving a car to me now," he said, resuming operation. "Basically there are three motions—swing, drag, and hoist. Eighty percent of the operation is in the swing."

He dumped several tons of overburden in an explosion of blue-gray dust, and swung back to the trough, providing a hair-raising account of what could go wrong: a severed boom, and crumbling earth that theoretically could dump 800 million pounds of steel into the trough. Yet Dennis was afraid to drive in Billings traffic.

The Rosebud seam lay about eighty feet below the drum, and the McKay seam below that, all property of the BLM, which had leased mining rights to Western Energy. "It's pretty good-looking coal," Dennis said. "This is a fifty-year mine, and most of it's already sold. I'm not sure I want to mine it all my life. I'd like to get into computers."

I told him I was getting seasick.

"I know," he said. "I threw up two or three times when I first started."

Sarpy Creek, a few miles to the west of Colstrip, was unspoiled range when the land scouts and energy companies arrived twenty years before. One family, the Reddings, had held out for years against development. Bud Redding's father had brought his family from Indian Territory in 1916 to homestead in Sarpy—rolling, isolated country between the Little Wolf Mountains and the Crow reservation. The day they stepped onto their half-section it was thirty degrees below zero, with three feet of snow on the ground. For a year they lived in a tent. Bud Redding and his brothers grew up in the log cabin that was eventually built; when Bud was twenty-one he married a girl named Vella and moved her in with them.

Bud and Vella eventually bought their own half-section from the government for a dollar an acre and raised corn, wheat, hogs, and cattle. They survived the Depression, bought land from discouraged homesteaders, and raised their children in the same log cabin. Their daughters married and moved away, but their son, John, built his own house just down the road. Bud Redding finally adorned the cabin with asbestos siding, and electricity, and from the front steps he could often see his grandson, John Rial, playing in the coulee where his father first arrived by wagon.

In 1970 the Crow Indians, encouraged by the Bureau of Indian Affairs, sold the coal under thousands of acres of private land to Westmoreland Resources. Some of that coal lay under the Redding place. Anyone homesteading after 1914 had received only surface ownership, and a law dating from the time when Anaconda Copper and the Montana legislature were synonymous gave mining companies the right of eminent domain. They used the threat of condemnation to force ranchers to sell and to keep prices down.

Bud Redding refused to sign a contract because he didn't want his land destroyed and a strip mine yawning in the distance. He resisted the efforts of lease gatherers, who came in shifts and kept the Reddings up all night.

"They'd tell us that all our neighbors had signed away their land," Bud had told me when I came to Rosebud County in the seventies, "and that if we didn't sign, we'd get nothing. We wouldn't sign, and they'd go to our neighbors and tell them we had signed. They offered royalties on the coal under our land to anyone who could get us to sign—even our relatives. Some things went on around here you wouldn't believe."

The Reddings hired several lawyers, only to see them fall under the influence of the energy companies. Bud's son, John, had fired a rifle between the feet of a surveyor who insisted he was entitled to work on Redding land, and forced a helicopter full of executives to land after it violated Redding air space.

Bud Redding had died in the years since my first visit. I wanted to see how his wife, son, and grandson had fared, and approached Sarpy Creek in the early evening. The dirt road I had once taken was now blocked by a yawning strip mine. A new road led me around the mine and dropped me into the valley I remembered, except that it was now devoid of stock, crops, and, as far as I could tell, people. It had the feel of abandonment, and I had only to look back toward the ridge to see why. The boom of the dragline punctured the horizon, out of scale with the surrounding country, ominous and undeniably depressing.

The Redding place stood surrounded by little cottonwoods and parched sunflowers. The garden out back had gone to August weeds, under gray skies that would not release their moisture. Drought had brought a plague of grasshoppers that summer, and they moved ceaselessly in the dry grass.

I could see someone in the shadowy kitchen. I opened the gate and rapped on the side of the house. An old woman came tentatively out onto the screen porch, wearing an apron. It was Vella Redding. I reintroduced myself through the screen and reminded her that I had been to Sarpy Creek before.

"There's no one left," she said. "John Rial's living up in Livingston with his mother, the hired man's in Johnny's house."

Before I could ask why, she said, "My husband had a heart attack, you know. He was too nervous to withstand the pressure. People who haven't been through it don't know what it's like. They come at you this way and that. They found out we were in debt, they came by and talked so rough."

I asked about her son.

"Johnny's dead, too. He was the picture of health, and then he started having these chest pains. He went up to Billings. The doctor said his heart was all torn up, that he had never seen anything so bad. The aorta was worn paper-thin. I wanted to get him the best help, but the doctor said there wasn't time. He had to operate right away."

We stood on either side of the screen, listening to grasshoppers tick against the asbestos siding.

"After Bud's death, me and the girls all turned to Johnny. It was real bad, losing him.

"If the neighbors had all stuck together," she went on, "I think we could have beat them. But they go after you one by one, they make you feel you're going to end up with nothing."

She had settled for a hundred acres, the house, and some money—a small life estate in arid, now neighborless country, with a view of the dragline boom, explosions that rattled the windows, and the spectacle of the mine stretching toward the house.

"The company lawyer told me, 'You're a rich woman.' I said I didn't want to be a rich woman, all I wanted was my home and my family. I guess I shouldn't have said that. We agreed not to fight the development. I just wonder if all this would have happened without it, if Johnny wouldn't still be here, and John Rial living down the road. I know I shouldn't say that, but I can't help wondering."

She asked if I believed in prophecy. I didn't know what to say.

She asked, "Do you believe in the power of dreams?"

"Yes."

Sixty years before, her nephew had died suddenly, and the family had buried him up by the schoolhouse, a mile away. Later her father said they must move the body, that he had dreamed of the destruction of Sarpy Creek.

"We asked him, 'What was it, a tornado?' He said, 'No, not an earthquake, either. I don't know what it was.' We moved my nephew to Hardin, where he's buried today."

Heat lightning flashed on the western horizon. Dry wind rattled dry sunflowers.

"I've been here seventy years," she said. "I think I'll stay here until . . . My daughters want me to come live with them, but I don't want to leave. It's nice up there, but it's sure not Sarpy Creek. I don't believe there's anyplace like Sarpy."

▪ 3 ▪

THE TREE had been a seedling about the time bigger ones were being cut in Europe to build the *Niña,* the *Pinta,* and the *Santa Maria.* It had risen steadily through the Oregon mists for half a millennium, triumphing over weeds, competing with alders and pines for sunlight, then breaking free. Lately its growth had become so slow that it would be almost indiscernible in the tight grain just inside the bark, known as clear in the trade. This top-grade product makes old growth—virgin timber—famous, and is the unblemished best that can be bought.

It was still dark when I arrived with a lumber contractor named Dale Bonnell at the "side"—a place where timber is cut—in Oregon's Umpqua National Forest. The two cutters were already there, lacing up their calk boots, the tightly cinched leather giving their legs a spindly, delicate look. Brass buttons on their overalls gleamed in the headlights of the pickup. One cutter was white-haired and had a tape measure on his belt. His Swedish chain saw sat on the side of the road, next to plastic fuel cans. A felt patch strapped to one shoulder padded the saw blade when he had to pack it.

Ordinarily, cutters work alone, but these two would cut as a team this morning because they were going after massive old-growth Douglas fir. They worked ahead of the main operation, like scouts, felling trees weeks before the siding crew came in with portable steel towers and long skylines—cables—to haul the logs up and deck them and load them onto trucks bound for the mills on the west slope of the Cascades.

The white-haired cutter had worked for Bonnell for fifteen years; he was nimble, and easy to get along with—a refutation of the notion of logger as burly tobacco-hawkers with five days' growth of beard. His name was Vic, and when he came up to Dale Bonnell's open window to tell us he was ready, he brought with him the faint redolence of after-shave.

Cutters aren't the first people into the woods; those are the "cruisers," like Dale Bonnell, who check out the timber for the bidding. But cutters are the next step in the process. Vic assembled his saw, attaching the forty-two-inch bar and threading the chain through; then he bent the bar slightly and snapped the chain into place, like an Indian stringing his bow. The saw cost seven hundred dollars and carried a Scandinavian name that the cutters shortened to Husky.

Vic and his partner would be working in the canyon that day, a two-thousand-foot hike down, but first they had to cut this Doug fir beside the road, the one tree left from an earlier operation. It stood surrounded by slash and piles of YUM—bureaucratese for Yarding of Unutilized Material.

There was a blue light in the sky as we got out of the pickup. The assembling view off to the south included Mount McLoughlin and the Rogue River National Forest. It was a typical Oregon morning, enough mist on the windshield to require wipers, and heavy clouds that would burn off by noon. Dale and Vic stood with hands on hips, looking up at the tree, which measured close to five feet in diameter at the base. This part of the Northwest is the only place that old growth is consistently logged. It takes place on public land, and the economies of whole communities are dependent upon the cutting, moving, and processing of trees.

Dale was thick as a stump, and his black hair was neatly roached; he wore the same kind of wide-bottomed trousers the cutters wore. He had thirty years' experience cruising and was known to be tough and at times abrasive.

Vic said, "I guess she's about a hundred and thirty feet. No more than a hundred and forty, that's for sure."

"And there's no quality past the first thirty feet."

It was light enough to see the branches toward the top—the "grouse ladder." They seemed incongruous on such a massive trunk.

Dale said the tree was "ripe. A little cankery maybe, but solid."

They talked about where to lay it. There was YUM to be avoided. The land fell away steeply on the other side, toward big boulders that would damage the tree if it went that way. They decided to fell it across the decked trees, and from there they could buck it and roll the logs downhill to a level spot where the loading shovel could hoist them onto a truck.

"Climb that little tree," Vic said jokingly, pointing to a dead pine, "and put your hat on top of it, and I'll hit the hat with the tree."

Dale was not amused and did not offer his hat as a sacrifice. If the big tree wavered as much as ten feet it could fall on the loading shovel, an expensive piece of equipment and a considerable percentage of the company's assets. The tree weighed upward of fifty thousand pounds.

It stood very straight. Vic's incision could not vary more than two inches from absolute square, in order to minimize waste and allow the mills to process the log more easily. He got his ax out of the pickup and walked around the tree, hitting it with the flat of the blade, almost affectionately. He found a soft spot. When he got the undercut in, he would know if the rot was extensive enough to affect his strategy. Then he might get Dale to move the shovel.

Vic jerked once on the Husky cord. The saw rattled to life. In the moment it took him to adjust the idle, the tree's immortality ended. In the cool morning air I thought I detected a sentient something in those high, wispy branches. Vic applied the chain just above the roots for the undercut, and bark flew. He started upward at a forty-five-degree angle to meet the later horizontal cut, so that when he was finished and the V-shaped plug was removed, the tree would have a perfectly flat bottom. This left the waste on the stump, as loggers liked to say—a money-saving device.

The tree was too thick to cut all the way through. Vic withdrew the saw and walked around and began cutting into the far side. The snarl of the Husky and the smell of gasoline filled the air. Water ran down from inside the tree, collected there for years from some opening high up—a hole in the arboreal roof. A logging truck trundled past, the first of that working day, raising a cloud of dust. It was loaded with carcasses that bore little resemblance to this still standing, living thing, the pesky activity at its base not remotely equal to its height, girth, and grandeur.

The piece from the completed cut was too big to handle, so Vic sawed it in half. He knocked out his half with the ax, and his partner knocked out the other. The wood showed a clear grain indicating top-grade lumber, and profits, with a single dark spot where the water had stood. If all old growth had been so close to the road, so easily cut and transported, many more fortunes would have been made in the logging industry.

Vic stepped around behind the tree and began the back cut. His partner took a yellow plastic wedge out of his back pocket, inserted it in the crack behind the saw and gave it a lick with the ax blade. He moved over eight inches and inserted another wedge.

"That's enough," Vic said.

He continued to cut. The tree trembled, the stress of gravity perceptible in the branches. If Vic encountered enough rot to influence the fall path, he gave no indication of it. The saw went deeper. The tree was in serious trouble, as was the loading shovel, it seemed to me, with nothing to guide that monolith but two little plastic wedges and the "pinch," the hinge of uncut wood running through the approximate center, no more than two inches wide.

Slowly, almost whimsically, the Doug fir began to lean. As it did so, the saw stopped and Vic unhurriedly withdrew the blade. He turned and strolled up the bank, not even looking back at the fifty thousand pounds of "grade" that gathered sudden, terrible speed. It fell directly over the decked timber and onto the dead pine, as Vic said it would, raising dust and a very solid sound that faded away to leave birdsong and a large piece of sky.

The whole process had taken twelve minutes.

* * *

Trees drifting on ocean currents were an early indication to European voyagers of the near-impenetrable forests lurking beyond their western horizon. Trees were carried by storms to distant beaches, and added to the early daunting view of America. The forest, and with it the absence of light on arable soil, was probably the greatest difficulty first overcome by settlers, as well as their great good fortune: trees provided an endless source of building material and their first export.

Forest preserves had once been the province of kings. Henry David Thoreau, watching the trees fall around Concord, Massachusetts, mused on the possibility of a forest province "in which the bear and panther, and even some of the hunter race, may still exist. . . ."

Formal recognition of the value of timber to watershed came in 1878, with the Free Timber and the Timber and Stone acts, but these did little more than legitimize the burgeoning cut on public lands. They were the woody equivalent of the mining acts, protecting the cutters rather than the trees. The Forest Reserve Act three years later empowered the president of the United States to create forest preserves, and the Organic Administration Act of 1897—a prescient name for a piece of nineteenth-century legislation—actually charged the government with the responsibility for their health and well-being.

President Benjamin Harrison proclaimed the first forest preserve, Yellowstone Forest Reservation, adjacent to what became in 1872 the country's first national park. President Grover Cleveland set aside 21 million acres in thirteen forest reserves, but some of that land was later returned to private ownership. Teddy Roosevelt, the outdoorsman whose physical well-being and reputation rested upon his Western experience, amassed forests in the name of old-fashioned decency—150 million acres during the time he was president.

Gifford Pinchot, an Eastern patrician, had studied forestry in Germany before becoming the pivotal figure in U.S. Forest Service history. There is an evocative photograph in the FS archives of Roosevelt and Pinchot, dressed in formal clothes, standing on the deck of a boat headed down the Mississippi River in 1907. The president wears a top hat and rears back with a thumb hooked in his vest pocket, looking up at his lean, bareheaded forestry director, who has a military mustache and an air of easeful command.

Pinchot urged Roosevelt to add an unprecedented amount of acreage to the federal forest. The same year that photograph was taken, Congress amended the Forest Reserve Act to end the presidential prerogative to set aside lands and attached the amendment to Agriculture's appropriation bill to assure that it would pass. Before signing it, Roosevelt sat up most of the night with Pinchot and added another 16 million acres to the national forests. Western politicians denounced the action but could do nothing about it.

Pinchot wrote in *Breaking New Ground,* "Forestry is Tree Farming . . . to make the forest produce the largest possible amount of whatever crop or service will be most useful, and keep on producing it for generation after generation of men and trees."

Today the national forest system in the Forest Service's six Western regions produces 8.5 billion board feet of timber a year—about 25 percent of U.S. commercial production. Half of that comes from FS land in Oregon and Washington.

The Cascades under low clouds, with lichen-covered rocks and twisted madroña trees overhung by the bigger timber, suggest a Japanese print. Dale Bonnell had been working this country since he was fourteen years old. He peeled piling (stripped bark) in those days, using a spud (an ax), and cut three-foot-square shake bolts for roofing. He sawed logs by hand well into the fifties, using the old misery whips that now hung, painted with forest scenes, on the walls of his home in Glide, Oregon, a community where the satellite dishes are painted with pictures of logging trucks. He had seen the logs grow smaller, with less grade in them; he had watched the standards go down as well. "It used to be easy to get vertical grade, without knots"—big, fine boards that went into bleacher seats and other places where resistance to weather was important.

Old growth is the only source of such grade. Although he steadily cut it, the fact that old growth was dwindling seemed to make him angry. So did the fact that the feds had some say about the speed of the cut. The tension between dwindling natural resources and government control was as old as the West, irking Dale and others like him who felt the resources belonged to them because they got there first, or at least ahead of most of the competition and before all of the environmentalists. Statutory limitations, however modest, reminded him that the resource was finite; he focused his anger on government agents, and backpackers, and occasionally on a fellow logger.

Dale had been a high climber for twenty years, before the industry went to metal spar poles and towers with skylines to hoist trees out of the woods. He put up $160, as did two other men, and one who put up $500, to buy out the assets of a gypo outfit, as small logging companies are called. Over sixteen years it came to be valued at $1.5 million, and Dale ran it as a minority stockholder. It had sixty-five employees operating out of a pre-fab warehouse on the outskirts of Roseburg. Dale did all the cruising and all the bidding on government timber sales, competing against half a dozen other gypo outfits. They all wanted contracts to cut BLM and FS trees. "It's a tough, dirty, competitive business," he said, driving toward the next logging site.

He wanted to take over the company but hadn't figured out exactly how. "When my partner dies or retires or whatever he does, I'll be the major stockholder." But Dale worried, anyway. "He could go senile on me."

The Umpqua National Forest contained 10 billion board feet of old growth, part of the national treasure in the keeping of the Forest Service—more than enough to last through his retirement and that of his two sons and son-in-law, who also worked for the company.

I asked Dale what he saw when he went for a walk in the woods. He braked, and we got out of the truck. Dale led me across the road and into a stand of larch, with Doug fir and a few ponderosa pine. "What I see is peeler number one . . . peeler number two . . . peeler number three. Grade quality. I look for knotholes, conky material. When I'm cruising I try to come up with the log that's gonna represent the whole sale. If I've got a thousand logs laying here, they're gonna be a two-hundred-board-foot average. Some might be sixteen feet ten inches with a five-inch diameter, another might be five feet long with a thirty-six-inch diameter.

"I look for the distance we've got to log. If you can get thirty logs an hour, that's one log every two minutes. Or three logs every six minutes in a turn—a round-trip cycle. If those logs are two hundred board feet, that will give you six thousand feet an hour. Okay. As the distance gets shorter, you can get more logs per hour. Then as the logs get bigger, you can't get so many logs, but you get more scale. Five hundred board feet a log means you only have to get twenty of them an hour to get ten thousand feet per hour. You work ten hours, you got a hundred thousand board feet. See?"

He looked for landing sites, guyline stumps, adequate tail-holds for rigging spar poles, tailholds for the skyline on the perimeter, and lead trees to get the rigging in the air.

On this particular day Dale had three logging sides to check on, and a drum of gasoline to deliver. A side was usually just a level spot on the mountainside where they could set up the yarder—a tower with a cable and a motorized lift that skidded logs up out of the canyons and across thousands of feet of forest. A side included decked timber, a shovel with pincers for lifting and swinging logs onto the trucks, and Caterpillars and other mechanized land turtles for heavy work. A side was built on public land, in this case the Umpqua, a million acres running up the spine of the Cascades, and on the BLM's O&C tracts— among the last and most extensive stands of old-growth Douglas fir.

O&C referred to the Oregon and California Revested Lands, formerly the property of the Oregon and California Railroad, acquired from the federal government in the same checkerboard pattern that prevailed in eastern Montana. The other squares in the checkerboard remained in government hands. The O&C lands were later absorbed by the Southern Pacific Company, which attempted to sell them for more money than the charter allowed, and in larger parcels. Consequently, in 1916 three million acres reverted to the old General Land Office. They ended up in the BLM and became the economic salvation of southwest

Oregon, where today local communities receive a prescribed percentage of the revenue from the trees cut in their area. According to the BLM district manager in Roseburg, his agency was in "the timber growing and harvesting business." That meant half a million acres that produced about 250 million board feet of lumber annually.

The year before my visit, the BLM's O&C lands produced $128 million worth of lumber. At the current rate of cutting, the BLM estimated, all the old growth would be harvested within sixty years. Local people still objected to any government regulation that took some of the forest out of production.

Dale drove his new cinnamon Chevy pickup with the speed and confidence of a man who had built some of the roads himself, going into the ditch to let a logging truck pass. The worth of the lumber he was now logging meant nothing to him. He had contracted to cut and move it for a mill in Roseburg and was concerned with volume, getting out his six thousand board feet a day with minimum down time.

He left the truck at the first siding. He moved among the fallen timber with agility, despite his girth. This was a Cat job, using the machine instead of a skyline to haul the logs up to where a shovel snorted and wheezed, the big clamps gripping a log and dropping it neatly into place on the truck bed.

Smoke puffs rose from the Cat on the far side of the hill. "What's taking that Caterpillar so damn long?" Dale asked. "It should have been up by now."

We could see the Cat and a smaller vehicle called an FMC, quicker but not as powerful. The metal tread had come off the FMC, and the driver sat with his feet up on the controls, talking to the choke-setters—young men in hard hats, calk boots, and suspenders, who put the metal noose around the logs, or "turns," so the Cat could drag them up the hill.

Dale said, "It's easy to come on a job like this early in the morning and find something to criticize," trying to control himself. He turned toward the Caterpillar. "That Cat driver's wife died last week from cancer. It's better for him to be out here working than at home, going out of his mind."

Dale shouted, "What are you guys hanging around for?"

The FMC driver's boots came off the control panel as if it were hot. "Track's off," he said lamely.

"Well, why don't you get that other Cat down here with the winch on it and pull this thing up the hill?"

"Winch's busted."

The Cat driver had never stopped working. He backed over a mound of dirt and YUM, and I thought he would tumble a thousand feet, but he didn't. He came up behind the FMC and began to push and snort.

"You're a Cat-skinner," Dale shouted at the FMC driver. "You ought to come up with a plan to get out of here."

We got back into his pickup and headed for the next siding. "You've got to stay on 'em to keep 'em sharp. People have to think for themselves to be valuable to me. But if you chew on 'em too much, they'll be afraid to make a decision and just sit there."

He turned his attention now to the logging trucks, which were going too slow to suit him. The drivers had hauled on the incentive basis, but Dale had changed that, giving them an hour for the trip from the logging side to the mill and an hour back. "They bitch about it, say they don't have enough time. Then they poke along like that dumb ass."

He turned and spread a large hand across the western horizon, driving fast with the other. "Look at that. They can't cut any trees in there because it's spotted owl habitat. They're talking about having two thousand acres for a pair of spotted owls. At forty thousand board feet per acre, that's eighty million board feet worth a total of one point six million dollars, for two goddamn owls!"

He grabbed the radio microphone and called his head mechanic for a shop update. The mechanic's exposition was a bit too leisurely for Dale. "I want to know instantly how long it will take to get the motor out of that Cat."

He found out instantly. When his senior partner came on the radio, Dale didn't get exactly deferential, but he did get cautious. They talked around each other for a while, and Dale hung up the mike. "I don't know why he thinks he needs any more money," he said.

Dale asked if I had ever eaten steelhead trout. I hadn't. He picked up the microphone again, and when the dispatcher came on, Dale said, "Telephone my wife and tell her I'm bringing one person home to supper. Tell her to thaw out some steelhead. Repeat—we will have steelhead tonight."

Clouds had settled into the valley, and blue-green timber rose steeply to meet them. Massive Doug fir overgrown with hoary, almost phosphorescent green moss on the north sides of the trunks resembled long-backed sloths in some superthyroid stage of evolution. There were still thousand-year-old trees out there, but they were hard to find.

I asked Dale what grade lumber meant to him, hoping for some flight of imagination.

Dale said, "It means larger logs."

"Well, what do you think of when you see a bucked log with a lot of grade?" A bucked log was one ready for transporting.

"A big log. I like the big logs, but it doesn't make any difference, really. It takes fifty little logs to make a load, and only six or eight big logs. If you get forty dollars a thousand for a big log and you can yard ten thousand feet an hour, that's four hundred dollars an hour. In order to get that same amount of money logging little logs, where you get five thousand feet an hour, you have to get eighty dollars. Tough to do. But little logs are easier to handle than big logs. Big logs take bigger machinery. Big logs in a tough show are really tough. Little logs in a tough show you can carry."

A tough show lay before us—a tower and a three-thousand-foot cable with a motorized lift running up and down it, attached to the cable. "Now this is gonna get tough," he said, "when they have to reach way out there over that rock. They get fourteen loads a day, but before they're done they're gonna be down to six."

We heard the snort of the engine at the base of the tower. Far below, men like insects, their hard hats just silver dots, labored in a green, unfathomable trough. "My prediction is about eight loads a day for this sale—forty, maybe forty-five thousand a day."

The site had to be cleaned up after the show was over. It cost three hundred dollars an acre to pile YUM. "I refuse to pay less than five bucks an hour," Dale said. "Even I couldn't sleep nights if I did."

The next day I followed bits of bark west along Oregon Highway 138. They led into the scaling station and out the other side, and on through the town of Roseburg, to a lumberyard and mill occupying a mile on both sides of the road, known as Roseburg Lumber Products. I had an appointment with Allyn Ford, son of the founder, who wiped his boots on his own doormat when he came in.

Ford said, "I can give you a quick and dirty tour."

His family's plant ran off hogged fuel—bark and other leftovers from the vast timber harvesting process—that produced excess electricity sold to the local utility. Huge saurian tractors picked up whole truckloads of Doug fir and ponderosa in a single pinch and stacked it amidst continents of ready timber. Roseburg Lumber had been in operation since the thirties, when the first plywood plant went up. Since then it had chuffed out high-grade particle board. The company had also added a sawmill with an electronic scanner to determine timber quality and computer-driven machines to twirl, trim, and dismantle whole trees that a few days before had stood in dark, silent, lichenous forests.

I followed the trail of Doug fir logs from the time they left the piles to their emergence as planks, studs, or thin sheets sandwiched together with glue, steam, and tremendous force to make plywood. The plant used all the residuals, from bark to heartwood, but the best was grade.

"We're always going for grade," Ford shouted, above the shriek of huge circular saws, mounted on rockers, cutting the logs to appropriate length.

They trundled on down the line to meet their angular fates in the teeth of fifty-five-foot band saws strung on drums and regulated by computer. They cut through the wood like so much tofu. "Basically, we're making a square product out of a round product," he said. Since grade lumber lay in the outermost sphere of each log, the results of each cut had to be judged and sorted, either by man or machine, and sent on to some further refinement. The residuals were collected along the way—about fifty thousand tons' worth every month—some going on into particle board and some into the furnaces.

We passed a bearded figure in a glass box, playing the "piano"—an automatic sorting machine for the planks that flowed past like salmon. I asked how much of the product came from FS and BLM land.

"I'd say eighty-five percent comes from the feds."

The good smell of wood rose from the planing plant and the kiln, where the logs were steamed to make the bark slough off more easily: "Like a cooked apple," Ford said. "Easier to peel."

He nudged a ribbon of chewed-up metal with the toe of his boot. "That's a piece of a band saw that hit something. If a rotary saw finds a metal spike, you'd better not be standing there. The teeth come off like bullets out of a machine gun."

In the machine shop we found fifty-five-foot metal loops with new teeth cut in them, looking like props for a bigger and better remake of *Jaws*. "The filers are the best-paid people here," he said. If a spike took a dozen teeth out of one of these monsters, the entire band had to be cut down and new teeth filed.

In the plywood plant, the logs were sorted according to the size of the desired plywood sheets, and pushed along by a man with a pickeroon—a spiked version of an ax. Metal claws on opposing rotors hoisted a massive trunk from the waiting pile and began to spin it. I remembered a Doug fir with a grouse ladder standing beside a road at dawn fifty miles to the east, and the sound of it falling. Now the spinning log was shuttled on pulleys toward the lathe, which bit angrily into the white wood. The tree began to shrink.

"You're watching history," shouted Ford.

A charred spot appeared on the body of the tree. It could have been a pitch ring, he said, left by Umpqua Indians setting a fire two centuries ago, to clear the ground under the big trees. Before Ford's explanation was done, the pitch ring had disappeared, part of an unending ribbon of wood bound on rollers for the enormous wheezing press and, eventually, the sides of a house on a distant lot somewhere in America.

4

THERE IS A HARVEST taking place on public lands that is illegal and disruptive to the environment, human and natural—marijuana. That grown in northern California, known as Humboldt lightning, is seedless and reputed to have a particularly boltish effect on human ganglia. It has brought as much as two thousand dollars a pound on the streets of Washington and New York.

In California, marijuana is reportedly the largest cash crop, worth $2 billion a year. Marijuana growers have been known to rig booby traps in the woods with shotgun shells or with fishhooks strung on monofilament, to discourage interference with this lucrative trade. The assault by government agents on the marijuana crop fills the pages of West Coast newspapers every fall.

South of Eureka, the road abandons the coast and climbs gradually along the Eel River, passing beneath cathedral redwoods scarred by fire and through high, open meadows. To the west lies the only stretch of California beach lacking a ribbon of concrete, the mountains being too steep and rain-drenched for a highway. There the King Range National Conservation Area, sixty thousand acres of choice BLM land, rises from black sands littered with the severed trunks of *Sequoia sempervirens* and Douglas fir, to the aeries of golden eagles. This part of the kingdom is used by mountain lions, black-tailed deer, and occasionally by people carrying automatic weapons.

The Eel looked flat and docile as I drove along it at summer's end. A sign at the edge of the highway commemorated the flood that scoured the valley in 1964, when the heavily logged slopes of the Coast Ranges were unable to absorb the rain for which Humboldt County is famous, and natural dams of felled trees and old slash in the canyons gave way, transforming the narrowly contained Eel into something approximating the Nile. It washed a lot of cattle out into the Pacific. Timber as an industry was already dying in southern Humboldt County and since then has virtually disappeared.

In Garberville, women in serapes and tassled boots sold pipes and other drug-related curios from the pavement, and bearded men in backpacks lofted thumbs at passing pickups. I checked into the Great Western at the north end of town. In the last few weeks there had been gun battles among local sinsemilla growers in Humboldt, and at least one death associated with marijuana.

Federal, state, and local agencies had formed something called CAMP—Campaign Against Marijuana Planting. The weekly *Redwood Record* condemned the CAMP raids on grounds that children of marijuana growers developed an antipathy to police by seeing their parents being arrested. Garberville seemed a prosperous one-drag town blessed with clear skies and the clatter of old Volkswagens. The sight of drivers in bandanas and steel-rimmed spectacles touched a strong chord of memory. School buses parked in the street had been converted into movable homesteads, with crooked stovepipes protruding from the roofs and tattered blankets over the windows. Long tepee poles were tied on top, amidst the household clutter of discretionary gypsies. The sides of the buses bore the happy painted faces and hieroglyphics of the ongoing Aquarian dream of the sixties.

To pay for their fries at the Great American Hamburger Company, two young men had to shove aside .45's in holsters to get to their wallets. The window of Brown's Sporting Goods was full of guns, including an A-14, of Vietnam notoriety, but the local favorite was the Uzi.

"There's no doubt people are growing pot around here," the local real estate agent told me, between telephone calls in a narrow office next to the Eel River Café. "That doesn't mean they're bad people. There's a point where the money's just irresistible."

Customers paid cash for a few acres with south-facing slopes; the most prized nuzzled up to Forest Service and BLM land, including the King Range. The price of real estate around Garberville had doubled every three years for the last fifteen, when the marijuana boom began.

The closest thing to a mayor in town was the president of the chamber of commerce, a motel owner and real estate investor who had a philosophic view of Garberville's main industry. "This is a market area that supplies a product," he said, drinking coffee in his combined living room and reception area, watching the traffic. "The old formula of supply and demand has driven up the price of marijuana, and that has attracted the big entrepreneurs. The mom-and-pop operators have been here for years. They wanted to live in the wilderness. They're talented, hardworking, naive. I'd love to see them turn their talents to pinot noir grapes or kiwis."

The CAMP team was staying in a motel at the far end of the strip, he said. They went out only in large groups, for protection. Old tires piled in the truck parked outside their doors were used to kindle confiscated marijuana at the helicopter landing zone. Black plumes of smoke against the Humboldt County sky bespoke millions of dollars' worth of sinsemilla offered up every evening as an object lesson.

There were stories of civil rights violations by CAMP, of helicopter harassment and scattered livestock. Other stories told of tons of growers' fertilizer leaching into the ecosystem, thriving garden supply stores all over southern Humboldt, miles of black plastic pipe snaking over the county floor like varicose veins. A poison known as d-Con was scattered by growers for the wood rats and deer, also fond of marijuana, causing them to die of internal hemorrhage. The poison worked its way up the food chain to raptors and other predators. Salmon and steelhead trout in the Eel and Mattole rivers were not immune.

The Environmental Protection Information Center occupied a storefront on a side street. An Invasion Response bulletin

board hung on the wall; paper cups had been set out for contri-
butions to the Sinkyone Wilderness and other funds. A middle-
aged man in a long pigtail sat at the table, his bulky cardigan
held together with a Mick Jagger button. He said, "The fertilizer
thing has been sensationalized. This is a media-created industry."

NBC had come to Garberville to film a report. The town had
been discussed on the "Phil Donahue Show." In the beginning
people had grown a little pot to support themselves. Then it was
no big deal, he said. "It gets people back to the land, but I can't
stand the yearly paranoia anymore."

A woman came into the office and stood listening to our
conversation. She wore new thermal boots against the an-
ticipated rains, and a wool cap pulled down to her eyebrows.
Her Japanese version of a Land Rover sat outside with two
wheels up on the curb.

"It's a cultural thing," she said, trembling. "Because we don't
pay war taxes they chase our children in helicopters, to practice
chasing children in other countries, where they kill them."

The next morning fog hung in elbows of the Eel valley. It had
burned away by ten o'clock. I drove out toward the King Range,
under cobalt skies seen through madroña and tan oak trees
lining the winding road. Before the advent of synthetics for
preserving leather, the bark was stripped from tan oaks and
delivered to distilleries that pumped wood smoke into the nineteenth-century air. Thousands of people lived directly or in-
directly off the tanbark boom, from shippers at Shelter Cove to
prostitutes. For centuries before that, the Sinkyone Indians had
collected tan oak acorns for winter food, burning brush beneath
the big hardwoods and leaving healthy, clean-swept bits of forest floor that must have been something to behold.

The big holes I saw in the road signs had not been blasted out
with conventional weapons. Most gates were locked, and most
dirt tracks posted. I turned into an unmarked lane that dipped
toward the Mattole River and the eastern slopes of the King
Range. I got out of the car in front of a cottage with a tin roof
and a droopy wooden gate. A white-haired woman holding a
paperback in one hand opened the door and waved me in. Her

husband, although house-bound, with two canes, wore coveralls. The house smelled of wood smoke jammed up the chimney for half a century.

They were Hilma and Fred Wolf. He had been born down the coast in 1901 and had belonged to the original survey team that crossed the King Range in the early 1920s. "It was all new country then," he said, easing himself down into a cracked leather chair. "All we had were blanket rolls and a change of clothes. There were eight of us—the chief, two chainmen, four brush-cutters, and the cook. I made sixty dollars a month, and board. By God, did we eat! The cook was German. He made Parker House rolls, ham and eggs, everything. But you had to keep the whiskey away from him."

Kings Peak was visible from the window. Wolf had spent weeks up there with a friend fifty years before, looking for gold, living off the land. "I've seen the boom in Shelter Cove, five hundred fishing boats, and a plant for processing salmon. Then the catch went right down to nothing. The marijuana's the biggest change. There are five patches within a mile of where we're sitting."

That night a vast, bruised, lightning-threaded front moved down the coast. In the gloom of the Branding Iron, I met a grower who was drinking bourbon before driving back to his house in the hills where two German shepherds stood guard over his harvest, which was locked up with the wood stove to dry. Thieves had taken the last 10 percent of the crop, he said, before he could get it picked. "They violated my space," he said, with a kind of wonder. "I followed their trail, they knew all the secret ways. I fired off a clip from my Uzi to warn them, but they'll be back next year."

I'll call him Terry. He was in his midthirties, a Vietnam veteran, with a beard, a new Pendleton shirt, and a straw cowboy hat with a pinched crown that gave him the look of a friendly back-up guitarist in a C&W band. He had started smoking marijuana as a teenager in southern California and continued in Vietnam, a practice that did not interfere, he said, with his soldiering or his patriotism. After eighteen months in the infantry he was threatened with being sent to Fort Benning, and so he re-upped. He traveled all over Southeast Asia, but he liked coming back to the United States. "It was like *This is where I want to be*. . . . There are a lot of 'Nam vets in these woods. It feels like home here—the rain forests, the remoteness, the dope."

He married a neighbor's relative. She was a big, good-looking woman—a Sagittarius, he added. She had been married before. They moved to Idaho with her son and changed their name, to keep the boy from his real father. They had two daughters of their own. Terry worked as a high steel painter there, and took his stepson hunting and fishing in the parts of Idaho famous for it. Then the Carter recession smote the construction industry in the Northwest, and he accepted an offer to sharecrop sinsemilla in southern Humboldt with his brother-in-law. "He said I could make a hundred thousand dollars a year."

Actually he made half that, hard at work for a brief period each year. "During harvest you get filthy. The stuff gets in your hair, your clothes, your food." The skunky smell of THC—tetrahydrocannabinol—in the resin was inescapable, but the profits were nothing short of amazing. He bought his own place next to a plot of BLM land a few miles from the King Range, and grew his own crops. It was a family enterprise. The children weren't interested in smoking the marijuana, but they helped out with the drying and with fighting mold. "They trimmed, and got a hundred dollars a pound, like any other trimmer. They had their own bank accounts. I was proud of that. Any time I can farm and put clean clothes on my kids and food in their stomachs, I'm proud."

For a time CAMP used the BLM plot next door as a staging area for its helicopter raids, and Terry and his family would sit on the hill and watch the lawmen below practice maneuvers. "They'd put on bulletproof vests and charge up and down. Then they'd get into the choppers and fly off somewhere." They would return with a net full of marijuana. Once two big marijuana buds fell into the road and the girls picked them up on their way home from school. "They said, 'Hey, Mommy, Daddy, look what we found!'" That added several hundred dollars to the family income.

"I'm security minded, always have been. I don't want to blow it on coke, or some new machine. I put it away." In Ziploc bags, buried under madroña leaves. "It was a good family life. Then my wife got strung out on coke. She started buying things," but mostly she bought more dope. "It happens all the time here. People can't handle all the discretionary income. I'm a Taurus— easily manipulated. She started abusing me, then shooting at me. The last time she had a forty-five, leaning out the upstairs window, naked, her tits flopping, pumping slugs into the pickup while I was driving off with her son."

Terry and his stepson smoked their first joint together, to ease the tension. The boy had since gone back to live with his real father, and Terry's wife was in southern California with the girls. "I did everything with that boy. Now he's gone. My wife's suing for child support. She's got a photograph of me standing next to an eighteen-foot marijuana plant she's using to prove I can afford big alimony payments."

He sipped his bourbon and said, "I want my daughters back. I feel like I'm an adolescent again. I'm elated at all the freedom, but I'm also scared. What am I going to do?"

He gave me his telephone number.

"Maybe you can come out to the place," Terry said. "We could cook some ribs."

"Look at this," said Dave Howard, BLM's special agent, opening a glossy leather briefcase on my motel bed and revealing a pair of cuffs and a nickel-plated .38 Police Special. He took out a photograph of a homemade device for firing a shotgun shell, with a spring-driven hammer and a trip wire attached to the trigger. It was, he said, an indiscriminate killer; he had tripped it accidentally, on a drug raid near the Klamath River, and remembered the heavy metallic sound of the falling hammer. "I thought it was a grenade. I hit the ground."

Nothing happened because the firing pin had jammed. The incident didn't bother him at the time, but he later dreamed that the device went off, and woke up yelling.

Howard had chestnut sideburns and wore wheat jeans. The hair on his wrists curled over the cuffs of a well-washed flannel shirt. We sat in the Great Western, watching the rain come down. Howard had worked for the FBI before coming to the BLM as a special agent, and before that was a military policeman in Vietnam and Korea. As an FBI agent in Montana, he arrested more draft evaders than anybody else in the state, going to their families' homes at holiday time and hauling them away from Thanksgiving and Christmas dinner tables. "Five of my best friends were killed in Vietnam," he said. "I had a special interest in the subject."

Now he was in charge of law enforcement on 18 million acres of BLM land in California. Howard had his problems with the bureaucracy in Washington, and what he saw as its Western extension. He had difficulty getting shotguns for his special agents. His insistence that the law be enforced on BLM land didn't earn him friends in the agency. It was common knowledge within the BLM and Forest Service that trespass often went unreported. There was still no regulation specifically outlawing the growing of marijuana on BLM property. The CAMP haul that season was five hundred tons, worth maybe $350 million. They had also confiscated more than two hundred guns and a lot of vehicles, including three-wheel all-terrain vehicles. Much of the haul came from public lands, yet marijuana fell in the same category as corn or tobacco—all illegal on public lands.

"Campers and other Americans are afraid to go on federal land," he said. "Federal *employees* are afraid to go on federal land." Cadastral survey teams assigned to the King Range first put up notices of their intentions so they wouldn't be mistaken for pot thieves.

Howard and the director of California's Bureau of Narcotics Enforcement came up with the notion of CAMP. The idea was to pool resources of federal, state, and local agencies. Some agencies devoted men, others gave vehicles, radios, bulletproof vests, fireproof shirts, diesel fuel, helicopters. Howard went to Washington and briefed BLM chief Robert Burford, who fell asleep. Howard held deer repellent used by the growers under Burford's nose, and the director clawed his way back to consciousness.

"He'll never forget me," Howard said.

He proposed "pre-eradication" on the King Range, which meant cutting down the plants before maturity. Fixed-wing aircraft pilots spotted the crops and punched the coordinates into a Loran system like the ones used on sailboats. The BLM put out a map with latitude and longitude tics on a plastic overlay, pinpointing the best locations for growing. One was less than half a mile from a public camping area.

One year CAMP destroyed five thousand plants on the King. "One grower was flying up from Santa Monica in a private plane every weekend. He had battery-operated drip valves on miles of plastic pipe, pulling off three Doughboy swimming pools"—the collapsible kind, filled with water and Sup'r Grow chicken manure. Howard took part in the raids, slashing and burning. The total cost to the BLM was only forty thousand dollars. "That year they spent three million dollars just chasing wild horses."

The motel maid came in. Howard asked her about marijuana, a friendly question. "They bring it in plastic garbage bags," she said, leaning against the wall, arms folded. "They manicure in the rooms," using Wiss sewing scissors from the Kash Saver grocery, where they were sold by the bucket. "Now that the rainy season's started, this place will be packed. They spread our sheets on the floor and trim the buds over them. They turn up the heat and leave for a couple of days, to let the stuff dry out."

She had found sinsemilla buds under chairs, and stranger things. "Would you believe rose petals? Piled up to the level of the bed?"

Howard and I walked out of the room. Two doors down, a battered silver pickup was backed up to the motel; a young man and woman in Levi's were tossing black plastic garbage bags onto the pavement. He glanced at us, and said, "Is that them?"

She said, "Yeah."

They kept tossing.

Howard had no arrest power off public land. He walked into the motel office and told the owner that one of his rooms was filling up with cannabis.

The owner said, "We don't ask questions. We can't let a million-dollar motel go down the drain." He needed the business, and apparently we weren't good for it. "Everybody knows you CAMP people are staying here."

"I'm not with CAMP," I said.

Howard and I drove slowly up the main street in his rented car. Needles of moisture assaulted the windshield, rain that would continue on and off until April.

"Did you see the way that maid was hugging herself?" Howard asked, unconcerned by the discovery of his sudden notoriety. "She's scared of those people. I don't think Americans should have to be scared."

A sheriff's deputy stood in the street, marking a car tire with a piece of chalk. Howard stopped to tell him about the couple at the motel. He gave him the room number and wrote the number of their pickup's license plate on a piece of my notebook paper, handing it to the deputy.

"We'll take care of it," the officer said, stuffing the paper into his pocket.

Howard and I ate soup and sandwiches in the Water Wheel. He was clearly bothered by Garberville's laissez-faire economics. "It's against the *law.*"

The Humboldt County sheriff's substation sat directly behind the Great Western, less than a hundred yards from the silver pickup. I dropped by to ask if they had received the report about the couple off-loading pot into their motel room. The sergeant in charge said, "We get them all the time," and tipped his metal chair against the cinderblock wall. "We're a poor sheriff's office, we don't have the manpower to follow them up. I would have to stake the place out and drive to Eureka for a warrant. That's five, six hours."

Marijuana had worked its way into the political system, he said. The elected sheriff had recently proposed that CAMP warn suspected growers twenty-four hours before dropping in on them. "The DA's not interested in drug-related arrests. I had a guy run a woman and her kids off the road, part of an old drug-related feud. He bumped her twice, her car rolled over five or six times. I charged him with assault with a deadly weapon and the DA reduced it to hit and run. Because the guy stopped and told another driver that the car had gone over, the DA dismissed the hit and run.

"Ninety-eight percent of what we get is drug-related. We were chasing a burglary suspect over in Redway. We searched three garages. Two had marijuana drying in them. One was owned by a sixty-seven-year-old man. He just laughed at us. He said, 'I've got three gardens. You and CAMP might get two, but I'll get one.' "

He opened a plastic evidence bag and dumped torn bits of photographs onto his already cluttered desk. "I want to show you something." He picked out a piece showing a young girl's face and a hand holding a pointed green leaf. "The guy who took this has just been charged with molesting his two stepchildren, ages ten and twelve. What's that he's holding in front of her face?"

It was marijuana.

That night Dave Howard and I drove to the motel at the other end of town to meet the CAMP team. I was to go out with them on a raid the next day, and I was uneasy with the knowledge that some people in town thought I was an active participant. Those on the street seemed to look at me with new interest; in their minds I had crossed from observer to antagonist, or so I imagined.

Six men wearing flannel shirts and jeans sat around a curtained room, watching television and drinking Olympia beer. They were all on loan from police departments around the state. Two girls waited outside, wanting dinner at the Brass Rail over in Redway, but the men had stories to swap about the day's raid and wouldn't be rushed.

Arrests, I learned, were not part of the package, for the same reason the Humboldt County sheriff's substation declined to crack down on the silver pickup: it was too expensive.

The team leader, Jerry, a BLM agent working out of Eureka, projected a kind of redheaded wholesomeness. He asked me if I wanted a Sanvik, a Swedish machete effective in attacking sinsemilla stems. I did not.

"Well," he said, "dress warm. And it'll be muddy as hell."

I changed rooms at the Great Western. The last thing I heard before going to sleep in my new bed was the whisper of garbage bags being dragged into the room next to mine.

"We're going in."

The pilot deftly turned the helicopter on its side. The verdant earth, including the eastern slopes of the King Range, rolled upward. Five men wearing sidearms, knives, webbed vests, canteens, and Sanviks found themselves jammed together, looking down at a house in a narrow valley on a tributary of the Mattole, planted round with corn, sunflowers, pumpkins, and the tall, unmistakable green stalks of sinsemilla.

A yellow Volkswagen bus tore up the hill, escaping, skidding in the mud. The helicopter set down in its wake and we all piled out. Wind from the rotors lashed the roadside ferns as the pilot took off to fetch the rest of the team. A crouching deputy with an AR-180—another Vietnam variation on the automatic rifle— secured the area, the brim of his hat pinned up like an Aussie commando's; he was on loan to CAMP from the Los Angeles Police Department.

Jerry, in webbed vest and California Department of Justice Cat hat, stopped a woman walking along the road with a baby in a backpack. Her handknit wool cap was covered with bits of manicured marijuana. "I have to make my town trip," she said, and he let her pass.

In the sudden stillness I could hear the Volkswagen in the next valley. A dog barked at the house, still hidden by trees. We started down the hill and immediately were into marijuana— modest eight-foot plants in mulch and Sup'r Grow. "Purple kush," said the AR-180 man.

The plants were reddish and sticky with resin. I waited for the report of a rifle, a shot from the steep, scrubby slope beyond the house. It would have been easy enough to plug a machete-wielder, and shooting down the helicopter with a deer rifle would have been just as easy.

The chopper returned, its throb filling the narrow valley and scattering horses in a distant field. The rest of the team came down the hill, digging in their heels. Now the woods were crowded with people in fatigues and boots, some with automatic pistols in their free hands—all CAMP members. The Humboldt deputy stopped a woman coming through the gate from the house. Listlessly, she pulled away from him. She wore a long skirt and corduroy bedroom slippers, and had an odd, waxy complexion. She ignored his questions, staring at the marijuana plants being dragged into the clearing. "Look," she told him, "you're doing your thing, I'm going to do my thing."

He took her arm and led her back toward a house with a shake roof, a breezeway, and a trellis for the morning glory. Peacocks strutted in the yard, next to the solar-powered water heater. Pot plants grew along the stream a few yards from the front door; some men laid into them with machetes while others searched behind the house. The owner had left the back door open, and there was a plastic garbage bag full of buds and "shake"—marijuana leaves—in the streambed.

The deputy asked the woman's name. She said, "You're ruining my day."

"If you don't give me your name I'm going to have to arrest you."

"Everybody knows you haven't arrested anybody this year."

Three raiders stood on the drying shed porch, peering in the window at wire racks suspended above a wood stove. On the racks were piles of plants, some of them tagged with the names of buyers of sinsemilla futures. An agent broke the lock with the grower's crowbar and opened the door, releasing the smoky, feral smell of drying marijuana.

"Nice stuff," said the only woman on the team. She was wearing a bulletproof vest, and she hefted a sinsemilla bud a foot long, heavy as an eggplant.

She and her colleagues dumped the contents of the trays into the grower's garbage bags and dragged them out onto the porch. They weighed 125 pounds, worth about a quarter of a million dollars at the other end of the marketing chain. The woman in the bedroom slippers watched the bags go past on their way to the pile of fresh-cut plants. "This has been a very stressful day," she said, adding, "totally."

The deputy read her rights aloud from a printed copy of the Miranda decision; this time CAMP was making an arrest.

Another deputy came out of the house carrying a .30/06 and

a shotgun. I followed Jerry inside. Marijuana pipes lay scattered over the coffee table, and sticky Wiss clippers. We looked in the bedroom. A small pair of blue sneakers had been left under the bunk beds; on a child's desk, next to a plastic horse and an empty Barbie doll box, sat a paper plate. On the plate was a six-inch pile of trimmed marijuana.

The helicopter throbbed overhead. The pilot's static-ridden voice came over the short-wave receivers: he had spotted black plastic pipe on the other slope, the universal tentacles of the hidden pot garden. We crossed the stream. A light rain began to fall and some raiders pulled out ponchos. As soon as they got them on, the rain stopped. A slash of blue appeared on the eastern horizon, backed by more clouds. A concrete tank full of water and fertilizer fed a system of plastic pipe fitted with drip valves; the plants had been concealed in a laurel grove. Some of the stalks were tagged with genetic coding. Sinsemilla came from the female plant, the male plants having been chopped down just before germination to stimulate eternal flowering.

The team waded in. "Smite the heathen," said the AR-180 man.

"Pipe bomb!"

We dropped like stones into the leaf-molt. Later, creeping forward, I saw a device that looked suspiciously like a home-made water sprinkler. The BLM agent gingerly tied a cord to it and backed off behind a tree; the rest of us groveled in the Sup'r Grow while he jerked it, but nothing happened.

The plants had to be dragged back down the mountain and across the stream. There two men crawled over the pile of stalks, stuffing them into a heavy plastic net. They were grimy, hands and fatigues covered with skunky-smelling THC. The rain began again, then let up. The sun broke through a smudge of south-drifting cloud, but no one cared. Every shirt was soaked with sweat and rain.

The chopper came in low, a hundred-foot cable dangling from its belly, and the air filled with a storm of dope. Cable and net were joined, and half a ton of sinsemilla rose, bound for a dousing of diesel fuel and the final burning.

*   *   *

CAMP was being honored that night at a dinner in a trailer park down the highway from Garberville. Some local businessmen were paying for beer and porterhouse steaks. Wives of local law enforcement officers had provided the hors d'oeuvres, including a centerpiece reflecting the CAMP theme: helicopters made out of ripe olives, with Velveeta slices cut into chopper blades, and bundles of oregano.

"I lost my Little League team to pot trimming," a highway patrolman told me, over Budweiser. He wanted to be reassigned.

There were speeches, including one by the sheriff. Wearing a cowboy hat and a new leather vest, he offered a toast to "the real Humboldt County." I had to marvel at his political acumen. Other than lawmen, the hall contained businessmen and a few old-time ranchers. The CAMP team, scrubbed and beaming in T-shirts emblazoned with sinsemilla leaves, stood in a tight circle and knocked back jiggers of tequila.

The BLM regional director in Eureka had agreed by telephone to drive me into the King Range, although he didn't sound happy about the prospect. I met him the next day at the BLM station near Whitethorn, where the BLM Jeep was kept; someone had let the air out of a knobby tire, an act of sabotage that the regional director accepted with equanimity. He stood bareheaded in the drizzle, down vest pulled up to his ears, watching a young ranger change the tire. Somewhere in the hills above lived Terry, the bearded grower with the unhappy marriage; I wondered if he was watching.

The regional director had studied English and business at a Midwestern university, unusual background for a BLM man. "We don't want a lot of publicity," he said, "about marijuana growing on public land."

He didn't care for arresting people, or the CAMP program. "It interferes with what we have to do—range inspection, road maintenance, issuing permits. The pot problem is more theoretical than real."

We drove for miles through the rain. Near Honeydew we turned west and passed a farmhouse. A board had been nailed to the fence, with the words "King Range" painted in black, and an arrow. The road, used by deer hunters in season and venturesome tourists wanting to view the wildest beach on the West Coast, rose through meadows long since grazed to the point of extinction. We dropped through second-growth timber. There were no pot growers here, although in the past a few had loaded seedlings and fertilizer onto three-wheeled ATVs and brought it miles up the beach from Shelter Cove. Driving on the beach was illegal but easy to get away with since the BLM did not patrol it or the back slopes of the King.

The regional director wanted the land used. "Our biggest problem is distance. Remoteness is what attracts the dope growers. The King Range is underutilized compared to other areas on the coast. If there were more people, it would discourage the dope growing."

The road descended through a wooded canyon, with views of steep, lost valleys in the back range, and the distant marine terrace at Big Flat. Douglas fir along the mountains' spine reached westward, the branches bent by prevailing easterly winds riding down toward the ocean. More than a hundred inches of rain could fall in a year. Before the big timber was cut, the ground retained much of the water and the streams ran full year-round; now they raged after storms, and salmon and steelhead waiting in the surf to spawn rushed inland on the flood.

We had lunch in an abandoned ranch house on the beach. The house had a battered screen door and a view of forty miles of sand littered with the whitened trunks of Doug fir, redwood, and sugar pine. It must once have been the most spectacular sheep ranch in the kingdom. A seal sat placidly on the beach; up behind us, a pair of golden eagles, large and dark against the racing clouds, worked the grassy terraces. Tracks of a dirt bike led toward the crest; within a few years, if the tracks went unfilled, the hillside would erode.

The BLM put up barriers at both ends of the beach to keep the motorcycles and ATVs away, but every year someone came with a bulldozer and pushed them down. I asked what the agency did about that. "We bring out our bulldozer," he said, "and put them up again."

It was the voice of the old General Land Office: let people do what they want on the land, since it belongs to them, i.e., to no one. We'll comply with the law, after a fashion, and not worry ourselves too much about the intent, or the particulars, or the inevitable decline of it all. A remnant view of remnant lands sounded strange in John Muir's state, at a time when the BLM was under attack for the paucity of its proposals for wilderness everywhere.

We drove back over Spanish Ridge and said goodbye without ceremony. Leaving the BLM station, I turned on impulse into the dirt road bordering the property. Terry lived back there somewhere. I passed a trailer set on cinder blocks, two wrecked cars and a pile of trash in the yard, by now a common sight. Up the holler in this county meant human detritus dumped into the watershed. I couldn't help admiring the entrepreneurial spirit of some of the growers, but the sight of their rain-streaked shacks and the inevitable mess they left was depressing.

The road led to a one-lane steel bridge without railings, with a twenty-foot plunge to the rocks below. The slick surface was glazed with rain. I drove slowly across and up the hill. The road forked, one side blocked by a chained gate, the other mounting steeply through mud and stone. I probably could have made it, but decided not to try.

I turned around with difficulty and found a car waiting on the far side of the bridge, a new but dilapidated Pacer with a smashed headlight. Two men sat watching me through rivulets of rain, making no move to cross.

Finally I drove onto the bridge. The Pacer held its place in the road and I had to pass it narrowly. I saw two beards, two Cat hats, two unyielding sets of eyes. If news of my association with CAMP had reached this far into the woods, I thought—my mouth full of cotton—I would know soon enough.

I drove straight to Garberville. From there I telephoned Terry before getting out of town for good.

"Hey, man," he said, "I'm sorry I can't invite you out, but I talked to some friends and they didn't like the idea. They said, 'You're leaving, don't step on any toes.' I'm selling out. I want the second half of my life to be better than the first half. I have to get someplace and get settled. It's over here, pot growing's finished. It's like the gold rush. I wish I had gotten in at the beginning, but I didn't. I'd like to get in at the beginning of the next rush, whatever that is."

He thought for a moment, and added, "Maybe it'll be coca leaves."

5

WINDMILLS WERE ONCE the salvation of the West and a sign of civilization, such as it was. Windmills drew water from shallow wells that meant the difference between survival and extinction in arid country. They stood like reminders of man's delicate supremacy from the Great Plains to the Pacific. Their contemporary counterparts still harvest from the wind—not water, but electric power.

East of Los Angeles and west of the Colorado Desert lies San Gorgonio Pass. The highway's approach is deceptively gentle, lifting between the San Bernardino Mountains and the San Jacintos, the same route followed by moist ocean air sucked into the breach by the force of sun on America's Saharan interior. John C. Van Dyke, an art historian from the East who wandered here at the turn of the century, wrote a book about it. *The Desert* has become an enduring, aesthetic comment on what was commonly considered unaesthetic country.

Van Dyke remarked on the force of air caught in a strange, cyclical dance: "The rush of it through that pass is quite violent at times. For wind is very much like water and seeks the least obstructed way. Its goal is usually the hottest and the lowest place on the desert."

On the slopes above San Gorgonio today stand armies of silver fins that baffle most travelers and dismay more than a few. The windmills in the pass bear little resemblance to their predecessors in the West. They are grouped in tens and twenties and even hundreds, aerodynamic in design, daunting in their numbers.

I saw them in the company of the person considered responsible for putting them there, Leslie Cone. She was a BLM area manager and the second woman in the agency's history to hold sway over such a large piece of real estate, extending from the eastern edge of Los Angeles to the middle of the desert. When I asked why she had chosen the BLM over private industry, she said, "Who else do you know who's thirty-three years old and manages two million acres?"

She had luminous red hair and a stellar smile—genetic imperatives among southern California women, it seemed. Leslie had studied forestry at Colorado State, and earned a graduate degree in public administration. The Forest Service had originally attracted her. "I objected to the regimentation," she said, "the uniforms, the rule book you have to check for every decision. The fact that you have to wear Smokey Bear earrings or no earrings at all."

Beyond the Little San Bernardino Mountains lies Joshua Tree National Monument, and all around it lies BLM land. "People have used the desert so long as a dumping ground," she said, as we came within view of the distant glass and reflecting steel that were Palm Springs, "for cars, garbage, bodies. Now it's a national conservation area, a BLM description that came in with the Federal Land Policy and Management Act, and people can't understand why they can't do whatever they want out there."

Theft of rock and cactus was rampant, she said, and a threat to the continued existence of some species. Even creosote bush, once considered worthless, was in demand for interior decoration. Collectors of creosote bush were required to pay three cents a stem, and some actually did. Landscaping in Palm Springs often involved government succulents and other desert bounty. But the citizens were outraged by the myriad shapes on the city's outskirts—big propellers, small propellers, weird elliptical contraptions like giant mobiles designed by Miró.

The valley floor lay breathless, but props high on the north slope spun merrily. Leslie turned off the Interstate in the direction of the windmills and took a winding dirt road that for a while carried us out of sight of civilization but not of the up-thrust San Jacinto Mountains, which belonged to the Forest Service and ran down to the Palm Springs city limits.

"It's frustrating," she said, "that Palm Springs, with all its air conditioning, won't stand for the sight of windmills. They've been cussing the wind in this pass for a hundred years, and now that we're making electricity with it, they don't like it."

She often received hostile queries from congressmen about windmills, and from friends of Ronald Reagan. "His kitchen cabinet winters here. William Clark is an old riding buddy of the mayor's. They all bypass me and go straight to the top with their complaints."

Three thousand wind machines stood in the pass, with as many more scheduled for erection. People accused them of pulling smog up from Los Angeles, and blamed them for dust storms going in the other direction. They complained of visual pollution, when there were already bundles of pipelines and transmission wires funneled through San Gorgonio Pass. In that route between desert and sea stood a power substation taking electricity from the Four Corners coal-burning complex and shoving it into the southern Californian urban maw.

"Nobody wants anything in their own back yard," Leslie said. "Dumps, prisons—it's a territorial imperative."

She had been called a communist at public meetings, and had her parentage called into question. "I've been cussed out over the phone. We shouldn't have to put up with that, but we do."

Palm Springs had sued the BLM. "They thought we'd change our position. 'Oh, my God, a suit!' Well, we get sued every day. We have lawyers who, if they weren't working on this suit, would be working on another one. They tried to get a restraining order and discovered that a fifty-million-dollar bond was required. Even *they* didn't have that much money."

We got out of the Suburban in the shadow of half a dozen turbines mounted on sixty-foot aluminum monoliths. An eerie metallic moan filled the air as the rotors turned. Computers located in locked boxes at the bases regulated the pitch of the blades and swiveled the machines to face the wind.

"This is fantastic country," she said, facing east and south. "We've got desert bighorn to worry about, and the infamous fringe-toed lizard—and seventy-seven golf courses."

At eight the next morning the desert was already heating up, but the big feet of the San Jacintos were still full of shadow, looking like burnt, crinkled tinfoil. A few vertical windmills on the valley floor, different from the ordinary wind machines, performed avian arabesques around their towers, and a thousand propeller blades moved in lazy expectation.

I drove through the clean, empty streets, in the shadow of transplanted palms and an exemplary low skyline, past the Harlow Haven, a hotel, the Alan Ladd Hardware Store, and Gilligan's Island Liquor Deli. Sinatra and President Ford both had streets named after them, as did John Wayne, Rock Hudson, and Jane Wyman.

Palm Springs' mayor agreed to see me. His name was Frank Bogert and he had played a bit part in *Beau Geste,* filmed many years before in sand dunes to the southeast. An engaging old pol, he wore a huge silver buckle, a scarlet bandana, and calfskin cowboy boots, and reared back in his chair when he talked. "We've had every president here since Roosevelt, except Carter. That sumbitch never came, but I didn't care—I didn't like him anyway. Kennedy came a lot, used to shack up with girls. Reagan comes every year and stays with the Annenbergs."

He referred to Reagan's friends as "the Boys." The previous year he had taken Secretary of Defense Caspar Weinberger and Interior Secretary Clark riding up in the canyons. "Clark rides like an old Spanish cowboy. Weinberger, that little shit, kept leaning over to one side. I had to stop all the time and pull up his cinch. Nice guy, though."

The mayor was a member of Rancheros Visitadores, who took moonlight rides with the president. "We pride ourselves on our desert view and clean air," said Bogert, "and now we have those damn things. Nobody knows if they'll make any money."

Palm Springs wouldn't tolerate windmills within three-quarters of a mile of scenic routes, even if they were on BLM land. The city didn't want them painted white because then they stood out. The medley of styles was a further annoyance. His main worry was the possibility that the whole enterprise would go bust after the tax credits were gone, and developers would leave the citizens of Palm Springs with several thousand Ozymandian reminders of bureaucratic hubris.

Oliver Treibick's stomach—an outgrowth of what he considered professional frustrations and the anxieties of entrepreneurial pioneering—peeked out from under a golf shirt with a hole in one sleeve. The stomach would disappear once his wind machines were fully operative, he said.

He had a cigar in his mouth—a Hoya de Monterey corona corona. His company, Energy Development and Construction Corporation, was owned by New Yorkers who had put up $6 million. Oliver ran it out of a prefab complex north of the Interstate, full of maps and blueprints and the smell of dark tobacco.

He led me out to the wind farm, riding a bright red Harley. His windmills were the vertical ones, known as eggbeaters, with a turning radius of thirty feet. They were set on a big tract of BLM land. The sun glinted off elliptical silver blades a hundred feet high.

"We took a shot here," Oliver said. "We're doing outrageously."

I asked why the blades weren't turning.

"They're in park. I'm testing stress for retrofits."

That meant strapping electrodes to each blade, to find out which components might need replacing before the wind farm came into full production. All twenty-six machines were expected to put out five megawatts in optimum conditions. The blades were troposkein, he said, a shape invented by a Frenchman in 1925 to turn regardless of wind direction. "It works on the basis of lift. Each side has both a leading and a trailing edge, developing an airfoil that turns the torque tube."

He stepped around a barrel cactus and unlocked a cabinet at the base of a machine, revealing computer chips and liquid diodes. He flipped a switch and the torque tube groaned into action, the huge beaters passing overhead. The vacuum created downstream at higher speeds made the eerie, high-pitched sound that had driven one desert recluse to shoot up a computer case.

"The motor takes it up to fifty rpm," Oliver said. "If the wind's not strong enough to keep it above that, the whole thing shuts down again. Same thing if the wind's too strong. Hold your ears—when the brake comes on it sounds like the New York subway."

The machines were spaced a hundred feet apart to avoid something called array loss—a downwind wash akin to the wake of a boat. To develop a placement prototype Oliver had mounted flour sifters on stands and set them in a wind tunnel, in a zigzag pattern. He did "worst-case scenarios" based on historical data and some limited site-specific investigations. "Based on some assumptions, like the hardware holding together, we think we can do no worse than break even. The upside potential's great, if you're willing to live in the desert."

During a ten-week test period, with twenty wind machines, Oliver produced, he said, 1.5 million kilowatt hours. He expected 360,000 kilowatt hours per turbine annually, and clear profits after six years.

"A million dollars a year is a lot to recover," I said.

"Look, we're in business. We're big boys—we took a shot."

He had gone to the California Energy Commission and found volumes about wind in the pass, including a draft environmental impact statement.

"What does Oliver do? He reads through it and has the boys in New York do the same thing. Turns out we're in an excellent potential area for wind."

Southern California Edison was eager to buy electricity from windmills.

"Part of our shot was an investment in meteorological equipment. We compared our findings with other data, then did energy production projections. We developed a graph with a power curve for our machines, according to wind speed. In a thirty-mile-an-hour wind environment we can do a hundred and sixty kilowatts. It peaks out at about thirty-seven miles per hour with a hundred and eighty-five kilowatts. Once we had that historical production data, it was like having money in the bank."

He walked up and down, raising dust. The motors were easy enough to replace, he said, and competitively priced since the Japanese were in the market. The extruded aluminum blades were Alcoa's. Metal fatigue was an unknown science in wind machines; the Energy Development and Construction Corporation was on the cutting edge.

"There's nothing sophisticated, if you listen to what I say. I'm just a Joe getting into this. My bottom line is, I have to answer to those guys in New York."

Oliver had been in Palm Springs for almost two years, on the edge of obsession. He said, "Living here, I get the feeling the boys on the hill—Mister Ford and Mister Hope and Mister Sinatra—have a hand in the difficulties of getting wind permits, and the strict specs."

He had attended public hearings on wind power in Palm Springs. "I'm out of the sixties, I don't want to give anybody any trouble. But I used to come out of those council meetings screaming."

He was forty-two. He had dropped out of college to join the merchant marine. The marine reserves saved him from Vietnam, he said. He went into real estate development in New York with his brother and made a lot of money "in the go-go years." Then he sold his house in Greenwich, hitched his Land Cruiser to his motor home, and headed west. He got a job as a sous-chef in one of Aspen's better restaurants, then became egg chef in another. "I was the best egg chef in town."

I asked how one went about investing in his company.

"One turbine in place today costs three hundred and fifty thousand. Cash, it's two hundred thousand. We've sold two machines, with seven partners in each. They put up fifty-six thousand, plus a fifty-thousand-dollar note. That's paid by the generation of electricity." The tax advantages were still good.

"What can I say?" he added, dragging on his corona corona. "I'm taking a shot."

People have made fortunes in the West with wilder schemes, and by doing a lot more damage to the land. I can't say the windmills are unobtrusive, but if they don't work they can be taken down and the view restored. That can't be said of the mined and road-riven BLM and Forest Service tracts from the Sierra to the Rockies. The people of Palm Springs didn't protest the flooding of Glen Canyon by the Colorado River, because that and projects like it provide water and electricity for distant places, and fit conveniently into the notion of "progress" upon which many a fortune depends.

THE KEEPERS

The BLM administers 178 million acres in the Lower Forty-eight and about 100 million acres in Alaska. It employs about ten thousand people and maintains fifty offices in the American West. Twenty-seven thousand work for the Forest Service, which is less endowed with land. The FS oversees a mere 23 million acres in Alaska and 146 million acres in the West, as well as a much smaller domain east of the Rockies.

Every day both agencies try to manage natural calamities the size of small wars, involving a thousand years of history. One of the things I wanted to see while traveling through our public lands was how government agents fit into a landscape rife with tradition, management objectives, and the contending needs and fantasies of users. I imagined myself for a time in the green trousers and khaki shirt symbolizing the FS, or assigned to a beige-colored BLM pickup with a decal on the door and a view of limitless country, and limitless regulations.

The BLM's land in the West includes 25 million acres of sufficient beauty and remoteness to be officially designated wilderness. In addition, there are 70 million acres of wetlands. About 20 percent of America's big game animals roam BLM land. Visitor days, the measurement of use of BLM land by recreationists, exceed 200 million a year. It is as if every American spent a day in one of the remote parts of the continent.

The National Register of Historic Places contains ninety archaeological and paleontological sites on BLM land. Before 1976, when Congress passed the Federal Land Policy and Management Act, the BLM had only to dispose of public lands; now it really has to manage and care for them under the rubric of "multiple use." That means a backpacker, an amateur geologist, or a fossil collector has as valid a claim on the land as a lumberman or a uranium miner. What had for decades been known jocularly as the Bureau of Livestock and Mining was forced to hire biologists, archaeologists, and other professionals to comply with the demand for broad and exacting inventories.

· · · · ·

1

ANASAZI is a Navajo word meaning the "ancient ones" or "ancient enemies" who lived in the Southwest before the Navajo. They were hunter-gatherers whose culture went back ten thousand or eleven thousand years. The Anasazi farmed in the shadow of red cliffs and created a dense social fabric over much of the Colorado Plateau. They dropped out of sight sometime in the fifteenth century, the victims of war or drought or some unaccounted-for demographic upheaval, and left behind a wealth of artifacts.

The early Anasazi were known as Basketmakers, an apparently random term bestowed by Richard Wetherill, a pot hunter of renown, who in the 1890s amassed a collection of Anasazi artifacts and sent them to the American Museum of Natural History in New York. I had gone to see them one bleak January afternoon, before coming out West. The collection had not been displayed in years and was locked away beneath the streets of Manhattan. A young archaeologist took me down into the basement and struck a match in a cavernous room to find the light switch. Tall metal cabinets leaped out of the shadows, full of bowls in smooth reds and grays, carved wooden spoons, and bundled mats too splendid to be buried. There were dried seeds of rice grass, pumpkin, squash, and piñon nuts; dice made from reeds; bone scrapers; clubs; chert bird points; a clay effigy of a dove. The tiny corncobs were Mesoamerican precursors of hybrids on Iowa farms. There were trays of gourd vessels, hafted ax blades, turquoise and shells strung on cords, evidence that these ancients traded with others who had reached the sea.

All these things came from what is now public lands. The West brims with Anasazi sites; locating and protecting them is an important part of the mandate of the Bureau of Land Management and the Forest Service, and not always a safe one. An Anasazi bowl in good condition fetches five thousand dollars, a basket, ten thousand. The goods move through the same marketing chain as other contraband, notably drugs, and share some of the same clientele. I read a story in a Western magazine about pot hunters in San Juan County, Utah, who reportedly laid down a line of cocaine on the 'dozer blade and inhaled it before falling on an Anasazi burial site in a collecting frenzy. There are stories of thieves cutting pictographs out of rock with chain saws and loading them into choppers for collectors as far away as Germany and Japan.

I decided to start my investigation on the Arizona Strip, the northwest part of Arizona between the Utah border and the Colorado River—a high, lost piece of the West cut off from southern access by the millennial crack of the Grand Canyon. The closest Interstate arches up from Las Vegas toward Salt Lake City, brushing the western corner and avoiding the canyons and other natural disasters as rich in history as in geology. Plateaus named for Indian tribes—Shivwits, Uinkaret, Kanab, Kaibab, and Paria—march off to the east, principal players in the grander production of the Colorado Plateau itself, eroded out of a continent's worth of rock. The broad valleys are silver-green with sagebrush, beneath high forested tablelands of confusing, often frightening aspect.

There are no cities and only two blacktop roads on the Strip, a few satellite Mormon communities, and 3 million acres belonging to the BLM and the Forest Service. Some of the country is so arid that 100 acres is needed to feed one cow for six months. It also supports black-tailed jack rabbits, desert bighorns, mountain lions, the Great Basin spadefoot toad, assorted lizards and rats, gila monsters, the desert tortoise, and an unusually large version of the mule deer.

The Strip is administered from St. George, just over the Utah line. There I went looking among the partitions of the BLM office for the chief archaeologist. Like most of his colleagues, he wore cowboy boots, a yoked shirt, and turquoise bracelets. His name was Rick Malcomson, and he wasn't a typical scholar, having spent twenty-three years in military intelligence. After retirement from the military he had stuffed himself with anthropological coursework and landed a job with the BLM.

Malcomson sounded more like a cop than a dryland Indiana Jones. Most of his friends worked in the sheriff's department, he said. All were members of the Elks, as was Malcomson. Mormons didn't officially recognize the presence of humans on the North American continent prior to about 400 B.C., so being an archaeologist was a bit awkward socially.

He exchanged ordinary spectacles for tinted ones, retrieved his Thermos of coffee, and led me out to the BLM Suburban that was to take us down along the Virgin River. On the way we passed a deputy sheriff in a big white sedan, and Malcomson waved. "There goes the Superior Past Exalted Ruler of the Elks," he said.

I wanted to talk about the Anasazi, but Malcomson talked about the Church of Jesus Christ of Latter-Day Saints—the Mormons. He divided them into two groups: those who tolerated his smoking, drinking, and opinions, and "the bigots." The latter sent their faithful around to his house, to try to convert him; they had turned his only friend in the neighborhood against him.

"He hasn't spoken to me in four years," Malcomson said, taking a cigarette from a metal case. "He used to come over on Saturday mornings for coffee. He'd smoke his pipe, and I'd smoke my cigar, and we'd talk. Then his wife turned Mormon. Well, the coffee went first. Then the pipe, then the conversation. . . . The Mormons have something for you to do twenty-four hours a day. I've taught Soviet intelligence for the Defense Department, and if I didn't know better I'd say Joseph Smith got the LDS system from them. Or maybe the Soviets got theirs from the Mormons."

We passed through the Virgin gorge, high rocky terraces where bighorns sometimes show themselves. Tamarisk bloomed along the river. The country around us was all owned by the BLM, as was most of the broad benchland where the Colorado Plateau swept down to the desert. We took an abandoned road off the Interstate and stopped in the glaring dust close to the Nevada state line.

"Watch out," he said, "for buzztail"—rattlesnakes.

We trudged out onto a point a hundred feet above the river. Potsherds and bits of flaked stone, some transparent, littered the sand. They reminded me of dirty snow piled in Central Park.

"Vandals," Malcomson said, puffing away at his Lark in the heat. "It makes me so damn mad." A cottontail cowered in a pot hunter's fresh spade mark, then bolted. "People carry shovels around in their pickups, and wire for sifting what they dig."

Malcomson wasn't interested in acquiring evidence here. The site had already been officially excavated and catalogued and the information entombed in some university. These pot hunters were just recreationists on a Sunday outing.

Malcomson saw himself beleaguered by artifact enthusiasts. "Formerly the BLM district managers in St. George have been either latent pot hunters or treasure hunters. One called me into his office and said he had just bought a metal detector. 'Can I take it on public land?' he asked. 'If I get a buzz, can I go for it?' I said, 'You can get a buzz, but you can't go for it.' He said I'd have to take him to court to enforce that one."

Sticking a shovel into a recorded archaeological site on public land, said Malcomson, violated the law under the Archaeological Resources Protection Act (ARPA). Probably 90 percent of Anasazi artifacts displayed in museums and private exhibits came from public land—mostly BLM. A few piddling arrests had been made. On the Arizona Strip, a BLM enforcement ranger working out of Vegas had arrested a man for pot-hunting, and found that the man's house was full of dynamite. "Posse Comitatus," Malcomson said. "If that agent had moved wrong when he was examining that stuff, he wouldn't be around today."

The BLM considered ARPA to be a prime headache. "I'm always being asked to violate professional standards. Somebody in the agency will come to me and say they want to dig a water catchment system for one of the fair-haired permittees. I tell them it'll take about a month and a half to excavate the site properly, and about nine thousand dollars for carbon dating, ceramic analysis, and publication. They say, 'Oh, no, just do the digging. We'll get the money later for the rest.' "

On the way back to St. George he showed me a golf course built on Anasazi grave sites. When the builders had excavated for the foundation for the clubhouse, they had uncovered pots and other artifacts. "The discovery was announced over the radio," Malcomson said, "and half the town came out to collect pots."

Petroglyphs had been chipped into the rock faces above the fairways; they were too big to steal and too difficult to climb up and deface. Passers-by had a view of strange, serpentine squiggles that have yet to be deciphered. The golfers I saw didn't seem interested in this Anasazi conundrum.

We parked and walked up a little draw where the development ended and public land began. Here the rocks bearing petroglyphs were more accessible; a truck had backed in recently to cart off a few for patio embellishment. Neighborhood children had turned a shallow cave into a clubhouse. The eye of a petroglyph gazed down from one wall, at a copy of *Penthouse* on an overturned fruit crate.

Malcomson flipped through the magazine, clucking at faded color photographs of naked girls. "Good Mormon kids," he said.

Malcomson introduced me to his assistant, Jennifer Jack, who did most of the field work. She had originally been hired to log the amazing proliferation of archaeological discovery into the computer.

As soon as Malcomson was out of earshot, she said, "I've been waiting for someone like you to come along. People think we spend our time finding out what's out there, looking for another Mesa Verde. But the government doesn't care. What we do is pure clearance for development. We don't do research. We run out in front of bulldozers and string up pink tape to keep them out of the archaeology."

She invited me to accompany her on an expedition the next

day, and I accepted. We met in the BLM parking lot. Jennifer wore a camouflage bush hat with a side of the brim snapped to the crown, and a breezy cotton blouse she had made on a treadle sewing machine inherited from her mother. The day was bright and already hot, and the traffic had agglutinated on the far side of the metal fence. The mechanics issued us a gas can, a spare fan belt, and rolls of colored plastic tape. Together we hoisted two big plastic water jugs onto the tailgate, requisite equipment for expeditions into the Shivwits and Vermilion resource areas. Resource specialists hereabouts often found themselves sleeping in the wild, Jennifer said, when there was more work to be done the next day, because it would take too long to return to civilization.

She had duties on the Paria Plateau, and a vandalized Anasazi site to visit on the way. "I like to check them out," she said, "just to encourage the range cons to keep reporting the violations. They get the impression nobody cares if people are stealing pots."

A random survey of the Paria Plateau, covering only 20 percent of that landmass, had turned up 539 sites of cultural significance. The Paria represents just a fraction of the Arizona Strip, some of it so remote that pots, baskets, and lithic points have sat undisturbed in the sun for hundreds of years. According to ARPA, all construction sites—whether for Interstate highways or cattle ponds—have to be certified free of artifacts before work can commence.

The vast matrix for cultural artifacts in the West has given rise to something called predictive modeling—a synthesis of the bureaucratic and the academic. Jennifer explained how it worked. "You go out and do a survey of maybe one-half of one percent of the land to be developed. You use different variables for what you find there—distance from water, slope direction, aspect, vegetative community. You feed it all into a computer and come up with a sixty percent probability, say, that each forty-acre quadrant with those variables has a high or a low site density. You draw zones on a map and give the maps to the developers, who are looking for low site density. Talk about a controversial subject. If you want to get into a fight, walk into a meeting of academic archaeologists and yell, 'Predictive modeling!' "

She earned fourteen thousand dollars a year. She and her husband, a contract worker for the postal service, rented a small house in the suburbs and carried a mortgage on forty acres of wilderness in central Utah. Her interest in archaeology went back to articles written by Louis Leakey that she read in *National Geographic*. She had collected fossils in east Texas, where her views on evolution got her booted out of Presbyterian Sunday school at age twelve. She had married young—she was the only pregnant valedictorian in the history of her high school—and moved to Reno, where formal studies began. She got divorced and married again, this time to a member of an LDS family who had rejected the faith. "He won't talk about his childhood. We live behind the Zion Curtain here," she added. "You've got to understand Mormonism if you're going to understand public lands in the West. It's a thoroughly nineteenth-century American religion—part Christianity, part Masonic Order. Since these are the latter days, and we don't know exactly when the end is coming, we're supposed to use the resources God put here while there's still time. That's why all these Mormon states are so prodevelopment."

The Vermilion Cliffs rose on the north, half a dozen shades of red that extended all the way to Marble Arch. They overlooked Antelope Valley in the foreground, too broad to fathom, dappled with cloud shadows the size of cities and scarred by washes that, had they occurred anywhere except in the neighborhood of the Grand Canyon, would have been counted among the earth's foremost accomplishments. Waves of green—sage, juniper, rabbitweed—rolled toward the distant upthrust of the Kaibab, and miles of blooming globe mallow—bright oranges and reds—seemed to reflect the color of the cliffs. I looked back to them, trying to understand this strange antiphon between botany and geology, and when I turned again the landscape had changed once more, with another set of colors and perceptual problems. No wonder John Wesley Powell, first man to run the Colorado River and surveyor of the Colorado Plateau, had navigational problems in this country, and great wonder that he and his crew survived at all.

Jennifer turned toward the cliffs, on a track through red dust. One arrest made under ARPA on the Strip had occurred close by: four adults with two babies and a sackful of broken pottery, caught by a Mohave County deputy sheriff. Rick Malcomson had the bag of artifacts under his desk at that moment, waiting for the hearing.

Jennifer suspected the same group had visited the horseshoe-shaped Shinarump Cliffs just ahead, and in fact someone had flattened the BLM's fence. We left the truck and climbed the sandy slope. "The Anasazi loved sand," she said. She used the word *Anasazi* guardedly. "It's one of those categories we archaeologists make up to describe something we're not sure about," she explained.

The Anasazi had dug pit houses here, with shallow walls that sometime in the last few hundred years had succumbed to gravity. Bits of corrugated pottery lay scattered about, what was left of cooking pots, and smooth gray and ocher shards. Some had elaborately molded lips, denoting a more advanced stage. All had eroded out of the red dunes, an indication that there were more to come. The middens—refuse heaps downslope—had also served as burial grounds. There, gaping holes had been recently dug; some had Tab and Carling Black Label cans at the bottom.

"These are the same kind of cans they found at the other vandalized site," Jennifer said. "If I can find a Pamper, I'll know it's the same bunch."

She took a bottle of Avon bath oil out of her pack and anointed bare arms, ears, face. She said, "This is the very best thing for keeping away gnats." Then she climbed down into one of the recent pits with a trowel that had her initials burned into the handle. "They dug all the way down into sterile." "Sterile" sand lay below the floor of the original pit. "These idiots don't know what they're doing. They destroy the strata so we have no idea where the artifacts come from, even if we find a few left."

The Anasazi had scratched beans and maize into the wash bottom. The mystery of their disappearance, like most things on the Strip, involved water. Rainfall and "moisture patterns" began to change somewhere around A.D. 1200. Not only was there less rain, but it tended to fall in the summer rather than winter and spring, when it did the most good. The Anasazi built check dams of flat stones to slow down the spring floods and spread the water over the bottomland, so it could soak into the earth. Then the bottoms could be planted. With drier springs, all horticulture suffered. But what precisely caused the Anasazi to pick up and leave, and where they went, has yet to be proved.

Unlike their neighbors in Mexico, the Anasazi had no highly developed writing and no monolithic political state.

"We don't try to clump traits together and say they belong to one cultural group," Jennifer said, holding an ocher shard up in the sun. "That's the old paradigm—the stuff that Dutton and John Wesley Powell were into. We're not as interested nowadays in a culture's history as we are in what made it tick. The big questions. Like what are the factors leading up to the adoption of agriculture in a semiarid environment? Why in 400 A.D. did they start to grow corn, beans, and squash? They had been grown in Mexico for thousands of years, so why not here? All sorts of questions spin off that, questions about environment, warfare, lack of water."

Overcrowding could have moved them out—a population explosion that put too much pressure on fields of maize and beans, and populations of deer and jack rabbits. The Anasazi's forebears, known as the Archaic people, hunted and gathered in constant migrations. Population control was probably built in, for there were no pack animals, and babies had to be carried. Some religious inhibition probably emerged to discourage producing too many children. The act of farming became the watershed between the Archaic people and Anasazi, who planted seeds and thereafter led a more settled existence.

When the rains failed, catastrophe followed.

"It could have been drought alone," she said, climbing out of the hole. She settled under a juniper, next to a flowering prickly pear, to take notes. "There could also have been some sociopolitical upheaval. The Toltec empire in Mexico fell about that time. We know there was a lot of trade between Mexico and

Chaco Canyon, and between the Virgin Anasazi and the Chaco Outliers. That's one working hypothesis, anyway."

I asked if she thought of public lands as a receptacle for Indian and prehistoric artifacts.

"Archaeologists dig for knowledge," she said, "not for things. Pots are receptacles of knowledge as well. We take pollen samples from what's in them. The floors of these pit houses could have told us a lot about the environment—what they ate, if more than one culture lived in them. Our kind of research can be useful—to policymakers working on the desertification of Africa, for instance. You have to understand the past to understand the present, and the archaeological past for most of the world's people is not in books. The big question is, How do people respond to environmental change?"

We raised the fence on our way out and hung a sign from it advising pot hunters that they were disturbing their own cultural heritage. "They'll just take it as a souvenir," Jennifer said. "The rest of the country would probably like to know what's going on out here. I've never been to the East Coast, but I don't think people there realize that the West is being ripped to pieces. There's no protection at all." The BLM agent in charge of the Strip worked in Phoenix, she said, and rarely came north. "They won't even let us monitor these sites on the weekends, on our own time."

We followed a dirt switchback up onto the Kaibab—de facto wilderness—and descended into a sea of globe mallow that was Houserock Valley. Jacob Hamblin's name was carved in rock somewhere out there. Hamblin had served as mediator between Powell and the Paiutes—the subject of Jennifer's master's thesis. One of Hamblin's wives was a Paiute. The Paiutes had embraced the Mormons as possible allies against the Utes and Navajos, who sold them into Spanish slavery and against whom the Mormons conducted their own vendettas. Powell found the Indians on the Strip the most primitive of all tribes left in North America; they were an ethnological treasure trove before gunpowder and disease brought them into the mainstream.

From Houserock we climbed up onto the Paria Plateau. There was to be a chaining in the Buckskin Mountains, she said. That sounded ominous. I knew that the BLM had a long tradition of helping ranchers develop the range, but I was unprepared for the extent of that help. Here twelve hundred acres of BLM land had been designated for clearing by dragging a huge ship's anchor chain, each link weighing eighty pounds, between two D-9 Caterpillars. The chain uprooted juniper and piñon, sage and scrub oak, and rent the ground so it could be seeded by airplane to produce new pasture. The slash would be stacked and burned. The cost of it all was thirty thousand dollars, none of it borne by the rancher who leased the land. The BLM spent millions of dollars every year for chainings and the construction of water catchment systems for ranchers.

"I wouldn't get pissed off if so much tax money wasn't involved," Jennifer said. "It's not just the cost of the chaining, it's also our salaries, the per diems and gas, all of it spent so this rancher can run a few more cows on land that isn't suitable for grazing in the first place. And it'll have to be rechained in fifteen or twenty years."

She had been working in the Buckskins for weeks, looking for cultural sites, colored tape at the ready. So far she had found only lithic scatters—places where Anasazi hunting parties from settlements like that beneath the Shinarump Cliffs had paused to fashion arrowheads and knife blades.

The tape created islands of cultural significance spared by the bulldozers. "Every pot hunter on the Strip knows those islands are full of artifacts." They escaped the 'dozer blade but were picked over by pot hunters.

It was late afternoon when we reached the BLM trailer sequestered between two twisted junipers. It offered the rudiments of civilization to range cons, wildlife specialists, and archaeologists with a lot of rough miles between their work and St. George: a disfunctional air conditioner, a propane stove, a scarred Formica table, and narrow wooden bunks. There was no reading material other than a copy of *Hustler* I found in a storage bin, and no food or water other than what we had brought. The trailer radiated dusty heat. I thought of all the people I had heard complain of bureaucrats in cushy jobs, and wondered how many of them would willingly pursue their professions here, as

Jennifer Jack had so often, with no more company than a wood rat gamboling on the roof.

The only food I had brought was corned beef hash with reconstituted potatoes; to open the can was to experience instant depression. Jennifer brought in her cooler and set it on the Formica. I watched jealously as she took out fresh strawberries, Brie, and a six-pack of Bud. Those provisions carried the weight of divine revelation. She had spent enough time on the Paria to know it, and to include greenhorns in her calculations.

"Have one," she said, tossing me a beer.

"We're a little slice of a very little pie," she said later, her papers spread on the table, where she worked on the endless reports. "Archaeologists don't produce timber or cattle, like other resource people. We don't have a lobby. What we are is a pain in the ass for everybody else, just another piece of paper that has to be signed off on."

I wanted to find a pot hunter. The Archaeological Resources Protection Act had made them publicity-shy and potentially dangerous. The arrest on the Strip for pot-hunting had been made by the deputy sheriff in Colorado City, Arizona, a polygamous LDS settlement hard up against the Utah border, isolated and schismatic. Pot-hunting was popular around there, but then so it was throughout Deseret, a Mormon word for honeybee, and an old LDS designation for the church's part of the Southwest. The patriarch of Colorado City reputedly had twelve wives and more than seventy children, and a power struggle was in progress to determine his successor. Outsiders were not welcome.

I had passed Colorado City the day before, on the way back from the Buckskins. It lay a mile or so off the two-lane highway, at the end of a rutted dirt road that would discourage the odd tourist from seeking a cold Coke and directions to the North Rim. Rough-hewn houses put up by their inhabitants remained in what appeared to be a long-lived state of incompletion, and were surrounded by public lands. Boys in crossed suspenders and bowl cuts, girls in long dresses with white smocks over the top, their hair in single braids, stood among the garden plots and watched my approach as I pulled in after the drive from St. George. I felt oddly exposed as I got out of the van.

The deputy sat with his elbows propped on a bare desk, a bright Mohave County patch on one arm. He was friendly enough, though guarded. Catching pot thieves on public land was not high on his list, he said, since he was one of only two deputies in a vast jurisdiction cut off from the rest of Arizona by the Grand Canyon. People had been collecting pots there for years; he was more concerned with car theft.

I told him I wanted to meet a pot hunter, expecting him to laugh. He said, "You ought to talk to Vernal."

Vernal was a woodcutter working on the Kaibab; when he got home the deputy's brother would drive me over to meet him. Meanwhile, I crossed the road to the communal cafeteria, where a school board meeting was in progress. The men wore shiny black suits and black ties, the women, black dresses and white smocks, fashions from another age. The proceedings seemed subdued for a town supposedly in the middle of social upheaval.

The sign on the coffee machine read, "The management appreciates people who clean up after themselves. Do it here and be a wife-saver." There wasn't much to eat: some well-cooked green beans, and oatmeal. The old woman at the cash register watched me with what I thought was distrust, then gave me a slice of fresh-baked bread with my decaf.

Later I strolled up to the co-op store. Big sacks of flour, hardware, and a few sundries changed hands, but I never saw any money. The salesgirls tittered at the presence of a stranger. I went back into the sunlight. A hammer rang in the late afternoon, a preindustrial sound. Children in their old-fashioned clothes ran in circles outside the adobe schoolhouse, clapping their hands and singing.

The deputy's brother was also a deputy, and a Mormon. He had a glass eye and the jaunty assurance of someone just graduated from law enforcement school. We drove around looking for Vernal, and I asked him about dissention in Colorado City. "Some of these people think they've been hard done by," he said, sitting low in the seat of his black sedan, a local boy made good. "This is all community property. If they decide to leave, they give up the improvements, which means the house."

The houses were incomplete, he said, because you didn't have to pay county tax on unfinished dwellings. "We've had a surge of problems lately—people apostatized for smoking and drinking, and child molestation. Two cases of that in the last three years. You'd think a man with four wives would be busy enough."

There were two thousand souls in Colorado City, governed by a patriarch whose authority came from God. He headed the Council Priestship. His own grandfather had been a patriarch. I asked how many children the patriarch had fathered. "I couldn't really say—he had over four hundred offspring. I don't think there's anybody around here I'm not related to."

We passed two teenagers in long dresses; their hair was parted down the center, the lacquered curls pressed to their foreheads. They ran along the red dirt road behind us, bound for graduation ceremonies at the school, it being June already. Laura Ingalls Wilder would have appreciated that scene, but not the fact that they were married and pregnant.

"We try to look modest," the deputy said, "and be modest. All we ask is that people try to live right, and work together." Everyone had pitched in to build the school. "I tromped them adobes all one summer."

The town had been raided back in the fifties by the state police, and the mothers and children taken to Phoenix. There, an attempt to "adopt them out" had been unsuccessful, and most ended up back in Colorado City in the same polygamous relationships. There was still a lot of bitterness toward the state authorities over that, he said, and more faith than ever in the institution of polygamy. As far as Colorado City was concerned, the Mormons in Salt Lake were apostate. "When they accepted the concept of monogamy, they lost the priesthood."

He had four children. I asked if he wanted another wife.

"You betcha!'

"What do you do to get one?"

"We don't believe in dating. Dancing is about as far as we go in that direction. The elders will decide when I'm ready, and who the celestial bride will be." There were enough females to provide celestial brides for Colorado City males because "more of the boys run off. There's Vernal now."

Vernal had a lantern jaw and three days of blond beard. His battered Bronco was full of the tools of his trade: Swedish power saws, calk boots, gas cans, a splitting ax, chaps, and ammo cans full of spare chains. He had cut eighty thousand board feet on the Kaibab that week, making close to a thousand dollars. His face, hands, and clothes were covered with dirt.

The deputy told him what I wanted; to my surprise Vernal said, "Want to see what I've got?"

He lived in a trailer on the edge of town. It had once been two-tone, but the colors had merged into a muddy approximation of the surroundings; the battered screen door hung limply. Vernal produced a key, although the thin metal barrier would have opened with a kick. He turned on the light, and out of the shadows leaped shapes of such beauty and sheer archaic richness that I caught my breath. Bowls, slender-necked ollas, ceramic canteens, arrowheads—Shoshone and Paiute points, some white, some of obsidian—Anasazi drills, manos for grinding maize, awls, dart shafts, flat turquoise beads, ax heads, stone knives, were all arranged on a plywood shelf next to an uncurtained window.

Vernal picked up a small pot with a spigot and matching handles, painted orange and black. I asked where he found it. "Somewhere," he said. He had been collecting since he was a child, inspired by the sight of the school principal's collection. Some of the things Vernal had found himself, others he obtained in trade. He figured the collection was worth upward of a hundred thousand dollars but wasn't sure. He dug for the pots—R and R after the rigors of tree-felling—and brought them back to his own little Smithsonian set amidst rabbitbrush and sage, where he mended the broken ones with epoxy, working deep into the night.

"Why?"

He slammed a muscular palm against the wall, rattling pots. "I love to hunt 'em," he said. "The shovel goes in, sometimes you feel something on the first stroke. You have to dig away real careful. They're wet, incredibly easy to break. You take 'em out and set 'em in the sun for a while . . ." The words trailed off.

He led me into the bedroom, where picture books about Indians lay on the floor. He reached under the mattress and pulled out Harold E. Driver's academic *Indians of North America,* then tossed it aside. "That don't do nothing for me." He opened the narrow closet, and a large olla rolled out. On hands and knees, he raked past lithic scraps, shards, pieces of bowl, and a Ruger rifle with a fifty-round circular clip before he found what he was searching for—a loose-leaf binder in which he had copied the name of every Indian tribe in America by hand. He was trying to match them up with the names of the chiefs, a homegrown anthropologist.

"I feel sorry for the Indian," he said. "The white man treated him bad, gave him smallpox and that."

His own ancestors were no exception. His great-grandfather had run Lee's Ferry on the Colorado after Lee. That stretch of the Strip near Short Creek had been in constant contention between Indians and Mormons, and a hotbed of polygamy from the time Utah entered the Union. Vernal belonged to a long tradition of church independence. He was twenty-eight and so far unmarried. I asked if the elders had a bride in mind for him, and he said, "Oh, you know about us. Well, I'm too busy to get married."

He had only recently heard about the existence of the Anasazi; he wanted to know more but was unsure how to proceed. Meanwhile the artifacts piled up. The same urge that drove kids all over the country to collect arrowheads had in Vernal's case gotten out of hand. He never dug in burial sites, he said, and disapproved of mechanized pot-hunting. The notion of the slit-eyed artifact dealer doing some dope on the side could not have been further from this reality: another American hunter-gatherer picking up scraps of previous cultures and trying to make sense of them.

He avoided public lands now because of the fines and jail sentences involved, but spoke wistfully of choice BLM sand just waiting for the spade. Artifact collecting had become a recognized outrage in academia, but many of those same outraged archaeologists had been inspired first by picking up something man-fashioned. Now they had job security in mind. How could anyone not pick up artifacts as Vernal had, when backhoes building roads had dumped colored pottery in front of him all his life, and exotic things protruded from the earth in every canyon beyond the narrow confines of his fundamentalism?

He had yet to sell anything. A dealer had come by once to look at the collection, but Vernal had sent him away empty-handed. "I can't stand the idea of getting ripped off."

On the way out he picked up a little corrugated bowl with a broken rim—an Anasazi porridge warmer. "Here," he said, handing it to me.

"I don't have money for pots."

"Take it anyway."

"Why would you give something so precious to a stranger?"

"Because you want it."

The breeze from the cliffs smelled sweetly of juniper; night moved on the sandstone hoodoos like a lover.

"If you come back through," Vernal said, "stop in. I'll either be cutting trees or digging pots."

I had come to the Arizona Strip in pursuit of the Anasazi on public lands; I found myself thinking about Mormons. Both cultures had flourished in difficult country; both were highly individualistic and imbued with an overriding notion of divinity. The Anasazi had dropped off the edge of the Colorado Plateau, a fate unlikely to overcome the members of the Church of Jesus Christ of Latter-Day Saints. Assimilation was more likely. Future archaeologists digging among Mormon genealogical records might well wonder what happened to these once exclusive, sometimes fierce, followers of a self-proclaimed prophet.

Mormon towns were built like medieval villages, centers of close-knit social and religious life from which radiated paths to useful employment. St. George, Utah, was a triumph of revealed religion over environment. Brigham Young kept a winter residence in St. George. Today the main drag is lined with symbols of American consumption—Chevron, Sizzler, Best Western, Montgomery Ward—and loud with the traffic of pickups and customized sedans. It was June when I stopped there, and half of St. George's blond Lotharios had discarded their shirts in celebration of summer. Broad side streets were set about with spacious lawns—Mormons have always been great waterers— and were full of kids on bikes.

An iron fence and well-watered trees surrounded the temple. I saw St. George burghers in business suits straighten their ties in the mirrored glare of their car windows before entering the temple. Some had removed Stetsons to reveal the rancher's white head and walked oddly in city shoes. They became something other than cowboys on the other side of the ironwork, but I wasn't sure what.

Mormonism grew out of the revivalist fervor of the early nineteenth century in the eastern United States. Its founder, Joseph Smith, Jr., a visionary New York farmboy, supposedly found gold plates bearing the text of Mormon scriptures after digging where an angel named Moroni directed him, and led the faithful west ahead of their persecutors. He was martyred by lynchers in Carthage, Illinois, in 1844, and Brigham Young took over. The murdering stopped at the Rockies. Young told his followers, when they came to the Salt Lake Valley, "This is the place."

The Mormons were hated in the West as well. No doubt horny outfitters, trappers, cowboys, and cavalrymen resented a man having several wives when there weren't enough women to go around, and making a go of it in barbarous country by the force of communal life. The United States acquired what the Mormons were to call Deseret in 1848, after the war with Mexico; Utah was granted statehood, in 1896, on the condition that the church give up polygamy.

The Mormons might have been cultish, but they counteracted some of the excesses that passed for individualism in the West. The word *Deseret* was coined in the *Book of Mormon;* the honeybee became the symbol of the Mormons. But bees seemed slovenly compared to Mormons and their accomplishments: the expeditions among the Indians by Jacob Hamblin, who assisted John Wesley Powell in making the first descent of the Colorado River; and the greening of canyon country that even the natives considered uninhabitable. The temple at St. George was built before the one in Salt Lake City, to bolster flagging colonists who had already made so many sacrifices. Newly married Mormons would travel hundreds of miles over the Honeymoon Trail to get "sealed" for eternity in the temple.

The Hurricane canal, which early settlers had dug by hand, was small potatoes compared to the transcolorado passage through the Hole in the Rock, when Mormons' wagons climbed onto the plateau over a road supported by logs driven into the cliff face by Mormon men dangling at the ends of ropes.

Nowadays Deseret unofficially includes Utah, Nevada, northern Arizona, northwest New Mexico, western Colorado, southwest Wyoming, most of Idaho, and the fringes of Oregon and California. The empire reveals itself in odd ways: the absolute order of cultivated farms and ranches, the tidiness of city streets, the hint of suspicion in otherwise guileless expressions.

The owner of the shop where I took my van to be tuned up had come to St. George by way of Los Angeles after marrying a Mormon and converting. His wife had since gone off with another man, he said, and he had fallen away from the church. He wanted to talk about that. "They chip away at you," he told me, while his mechanic poured dust out of my air filter. "They came around here and tried to set my prices." Customers wanted to pay him with little plastic vials full of gold dust. "I tell them, 'I don't assay, I fix cars. I want money!' "

He shook his head. "They say taxes don't exist because the Prophet never gave his permission. My wife's like that. She says the IRS don't exist because the president of the church in Salt Lake didn't give permission. She won't pay her light bill for the same reason—the power companies don't exist. You know what does exist, don't you? Alimony exists."

The manager of public lands on the Strip was Bill Lamb, a bishop in the Church of Jesus Christ of Latter-Day Saints. He had grown up in Cedar City, Utah, and had moved ten times in his twenty-two years with the Bureau of Land Management, including a stint in Washington essential to his career, before coming to St. George. Bishop Lamb looked like a professional

golfer: neatly combed black hair, good smile, striped sport shirt.
He sat on the couch facing his desk and invited me to do the
same. I asked if there were many Mormons in the BLM, and he
said yes. Most Westerners were interested in land use, and since
so many Westerners were LDS there were a lot of Mormons in
the BLM. Utah State University had developed one of the first
schools in range management, and over the years it had contributed many to the bureau.

I asked if Mormons were generally in favor of development in
the West. He pressed his fingertips together, a man divided
between secular and ecclesiastical duties. "You have to look at
the history of the church," he said, "and Joseph Smith. The
main idea was to *progress.* You don't sit idle, you continue to
develop—your mind, and whatever else you can."

The resources were here to be developed and used, but pru-
dently. The millennium would not be the end of the world. "The
millennium simply means a thousand years—the amount of time
that Jesus Christ will reign as king after the Second Coming.
Then there will be the final judgment to determine who will go
to the kingdom of glory. During that thousand years we will
need the resources."

"I thought the Second Coming meant destruction."

"There will be some, to purify the earth. There'll be a partial
judgment at that time, and some people, like murderers, won't
be resurrected. There'll be a big change, no doubt about it."

The murderers would go to the telestial kingdom, the lowest,
but most people would remain in the terrestrial kingdom—the
here and now.

"I think during the millennium you'll see a lot of people going
to the celestial kingdom, too, but they'll continue to develop.
They'll retain their physical being. Satan will be bound, and
there'll be a lot of righteousness throughout the world. A lot of
work will be done for the people who have already passed. It's
an American kingdom, all spelled out by Joseph Smith. Christ
will be very unhappy with anyone who has abused the resources."

The conversation turned to Indians. I had heard Mormons
refer to them as Lamanites, descendants of Old Testament char-

acters. I asked if Mormons viewed the Lamanite story symbolically, as some Christians viewed the Garden of Eden.

He shook his head. "We believe in the historical truth of the Garden of Eden, and the Lamanites. We know the Lamanites came over here by boat from the Holy Land, like the Nephites. That was before the fall of Jerusalem. I'm not sure exactly where they landed—somewhere in Central America."

They were all descendants of the sons of Levi and Sarah, he said. Christ appeared before them in Central America. There occurred two hundred years of righteousness during which time the Aztecs developed their calendar and other advancements were made. The Lamanites grew corrupt and began to disagree violently with their cousins, the Nephites. They migrated northward, the first people to enter what became the United States, fighting all the way.

"About 400 A.D.," Lamb said, "there was a big battle in the New York area. Millions were killed, most of them Nephites. The Lamanites wandered off in bands. They developed their own dialects, becoming what we call Indians today. Originally the languages brought to the United States were Arabic and Hebrew, but they were lost."

It seemed to me that the Mormons had a problem in the implications of carbon dating. I said, "Some anthropologists think the Indians came from Asia by way of the Bering Strait."

"Oh, I can't say the land bridge didn't bring over some Asians. They could have migrated there and *come back* again."

There was no righteousness left on the continent at the time, Lamb said. The Lamanites had fallen from grace, but that didn't mean they couldn't "progress" like everyone else. "The Indians should be proud—they have a great heritage. They come from the house of Israel, part of the chosen people."

He smiled, trying to help me understand. Here was an administrator of public lands, in charge of fifty BLM employees, twenty-three vehicles, and a $2 million annual budget. "They're Jews, really," he added.

He stepped to the bookcase and came back with a little blue volume, supposedly written by Moroni, son of Mormon. Gold leaf showed an angel standing on a globe, blowing a trumpet.

"The *Book of Mormon* is just an abridgement of what happened in the previous nine hundred years. There are thousands of volumes on gold plates still buried somewhere in the mountains of New York." He handed it to me. "It's all in there. Read it, and try not to fall into the same traps."

2

THE MOUNTAIN of Shiprock rears against the western sky near the convergence of New Mexico, Arizona, Utah, and Colorado. The old volcanic core, eroded into sharp spines and pinnacles, is the most famous landmark for a hundred miles around, including Sleeping Ute Mountain and the Four Corners power plant stacks. Some sentimental Anglo misnamed Shiprock. To the landlocked Navajo, it is a piece of natural sculpture left over from the creation—the wing tip of a primordial man-eating eagle, a much more evocative image than that of a frigate under sail.

The Navajo were the last Indians to arrive in the Southwest, at the tail end of the migration from Asia by way of the Bering Strait. They settled in high, arid country around Four Corners. Most enterprises in which other Indians were engaged, from weaving to agriculture, the Navajo mimicked and improved upon, including Hopi arrowheads. The Navajo language belongs to the Athabascan group—they could converse with Eskimos if they had to—but they developed their own linguistic anomalies. Navajo radio operators were used by the Allies in World War II, and the "code" was never broken.

From the Spaniards the Navajo got the horse and the sheep, and they converted the latter into ambulatory larders, which enabled them to move with impunity in large numbers over land where their enemies tended to starve. The Navajo kept the

Spanish out of the San Juan River basin and made guerrilla war on whites long after the conquest had given way to the United States of America.

At the time of the Civil War, Kit Carson was hired to round up the Navajo who would not submit to rule of law. Dealing with Indians was probably the first instance of governance in the West, and Carson was one of the better government agents. He makes an appearance in Willa Cather's novel *Death Comes for the Archbishop,* as an idealized version of the westering Anglo— slight, soft-spoken, courageous, humane. He lived in Taos with a Mexican wife, working as a fur trapper and as a free-lance guide and Indian fighter for the U.S. Army. He led Captain John Charles Frémont past Salt Lake and into California in 1845, to fight the Mexicans; later, he escorted Colonel Stephen Watts Kearny across the deserts of the Southwest and along the Gila River, and in 1864 led a company of soldiers and Ute and Jica-rilla Apache braves against the Comanches in the Texas Panhandle.

Carson became famous on the publication of Frémont's journals, edited by Frémont's wife, appealing to a public enraptured by Indians and the war with Mexico. Henry Nash Smith, author of *Virgin Land,* a literary interpretation of the West, saw Carson as the inheritor of the virtues of James Fenimore Cooper's heroes and other leatherstockings of the East. "The momentary effect was to make the fur trapper and mountain man just such a pioneer of empire as the glorifiers of Kentucky had tried to make of Boone in earlier decades."

Carson pursued Navajo relentlessly. He had been instructed to kill the men who would not go onto the reservation at Fort Sumner, in east central New Mexico, and take women and children prisoner. Some Indians agreed to transplantation but not the bulk of the Navajo. In the diaspora that followed, they spread south and west.

Carson and his men killed a lot of sheep near Window Rock, on the Arizona–New Mexico border, and piled the bones as a monument, but their primary offensive maneuver was burning cornfields. The Navajo, trapped in Canyon de Chelly, surrendered in the midst of a killing winter. That spring they hiked under guard from Fort Defiance, not far from Window Rock, to Fort Sumner, by way of Albuquerque. Four years later the Navajo signed a treaty. They got a piece of real estate the size of West Virginia on the edge of their old stomping grounds. The Navajo Indian Reservation was set up a bit west of the original settlement lands because these lands had proved productive enough to arouse the envy of white settlers, to whom Carson was a real hero.

Despite the sparseness of the land given to the Navajo, they have come to represent a Native American success story. At the end of the Civil War there were only about 8,000 Navajo; now there are 170,000.

On the reservation, Navajo willows stand like great green gum-drops over some houses, but most are exposed; some of the yards contain new Detroit iron, bright in the desert sun. The Navajo receive royalties from the oil, gas, and coal reserves under the reservation. The Tribal Council controls the revenues and also holds some lands outside the reservation in trust for expatriate members of the tribe. The council dispenses benefits and jobs, the proceeds of which occasionally become manifest in chrome roll bars and mag wheels on new Navajo pickups, a source of resentment among the underemployed Anglos in nearby Farmington.

The Farmington resource area is the largest in the BLM—1.5 million acres. Its administrators are responsible for energy development on the reservation and for all BLM land outside the reservation boundaries. Many Navajo families live outside the reservation. Some own the land they live on, but many plots belong to the BLM. Just locating these families living illegally on government land, amidst the confusion of desert boundaries, is difficult. Without someone who speaks the language and knows the country, the job would be impossible.

When I visited the area that essential person was a Navajo "Indian coordinator" named Danny Charlie. I met him in the BLM office, a utilitarian box on the edge of Farmington surrounded by a high cyclone fence and parked pickups and Suburbans. Danny Charlie wore a yoked shirt and cowboy boots, and when he spoke he rocked back on his heels, hands thrust into the pockets of his jeans, his big white teeth exposed.

We were introduced by his boss, Mat Millenbach, a rising star in the BLM. Millenbach wore tie shoes and a crewneck sweater— fast-track garb in an agency typified by carved elkhorn buckles and a round tin of smokeless tobacco in the back pocket. He said, "The regional office thinks I'm too big for my britches for counting the Navajo families living illegally on federal land. They wouldn't appropriate the money, so I took it out of another department. They said they were going to charge me with misappropriation of public funds, or some half-assed thing."

The Navajo were a ticklish subject politically. BLM careerists in Santa Fe didn't like to be reminded that some Indians were living on their land, but they couldn't stop Millenbach from dealing with the problem, since area managers had a lot of latitude.

Millenbach was anxious to show me how that system worked, and invited me to accompany him and Danny Charlie to Chaco Canyon, where the BLM and other agencies had become embroiled in a jurisdictional dispute over some coal. Also involved was the Nageezi chapter of the Navajo who lived off the reservation.

We rode south with a big, blond BLM engineer named Jim, across the San Juan River, which flows under natural sandstone pyramids, and past the De-na-zin and Bisti wilderness areas. Once the floor of a shallow sea, these areas are now a fantastic wasteland of earthen mushrooms with sandstone caps, and dark layers of shale in the sides of lunar ravines. There dinosaur bones abound; many were carted off in the early part of the century, like paleontological Elgin marbles. *Bisti* means "badlands" in Navajo, and *De-na-zin* means "standing crane." Both lay outside the reservation but were intimately tied up in Navajo history and myth, and should be an official part of the Navajo nation.

Danny Charlie had once taken a group of wives of visiting government brass to the De-na-zin, Millenbach later told me, to see the rock art. Then Danny had refused to explain the art because talking about creation was bad luck. Once Danny and a group of BLM technicians had come upon a rock with bits of feather tied on. Danny would neither touch nor discuss what was in fact a curse put on another Navajo: when the wind blew the feathers, an enemy felt pain.

We passed the Sunbelt Coal Company mine, sitting on the very edge of the Bisti—a political rather than an aesthetic boundary. The government wanted that coal mined, so there were no official objections. But the little bit of coal mined farther south by the Nageezi Navajo to heat their homes had caused problems. The Nageezi dug the coal with a crowbar, Danny Charlie said, and hauled it in a horse-drawn wagon.

Their lease covered about two acres belonging to the BLM. Any federal land in excess of two acres that was mined had to be the subject of an environmental impact statement, and this mining operation had expanded beyond the two-acre boundary. During a particularly cold winter the Park Service had gone in with a backhoe to break loose enough coal to get the handful of Navajo families through the freeze, and had taken some coal to use in the potbellied stove in the Chaco Canyon visitor center.

"Remember," Millenbach said, "this is *federal* coal."

The transgression had come to the attention of the New Mexico Bureau of Mines and Minerals. They called Jim and told him the site had to be cleaned up or they would prevent the Indians from taking any more coal. Jim got the Navajo and the Park Service to agree to work on the site, but meanwhile the state agency had issued a cessation order—the bureaucratic equivalent of a tomahawk in the back.

"There are three things going on here," Millenbach said. "The Bureau of Mines and Minerals has a legitimate concern about the violation. We were taking care of it, but the guy in charge lives by his little black rule book. And the state agency wants to be able to zing the feds because the feds are always pointing out how the state agency screws up."

There was a fourth factor, said Jim, driving with one hand through some spectacular ruts. The federal Office of Surface Mining, which had the same responsibilities as the state agency, was also involved. "The OSM's bitter because of budget cuts. The word is that they want to zing the BLM and the Park Service out of spite. They're also talking fines, to bring in revenue."

He turned onto a smaller road and broncoed through clumps of mustard weed. I could see hills of "red dog"—clinker coal—and berms of black rubble. "Not a pretty sight," said Millenbach, "but a pimple on a gnat's ass compared to the surrounding country."

We parked and got out and were joined by the state representative, a young man carrying a clipboard and clearly nervous. The Park Service had already arrived—three men in broad-brimmed hats with silver acorns attached to the bands.

"Would you look at those hats," said Jim, as they approached.

Another car arrived, driven by a BLM lawyer who had come all the way from Albuquerque just to be present.

"They worry that something might happen up here that they don't know about," Millenbach said, before they reached us.

We all looked at the mess. The state representative said he wanted the roads graded and topsoil spread around. "You're talking major stuff," Jim said. "How 'bout a road waiver?"

"If you were a company," said the state rep, "this is what we'd require. We'd also fine you the super maximum." The super maximum was five thousand dollars a day.

"We'd go to court over a fine," Millenbach said.

Yet another car arrived, and we were joined by a bearded representative of the Office of Surface Mining, who had also driven up from Albuquerque. He and his counterpart from Albuquerque BLM were receiving fifty dollars per diem, plus salary and gas. How everyone had convened on this remote spot remained a mystery to me. There were eight federal representatives, one from the state, and no Nageezi Navajo—the people most affected by the controversy.

"These little salt cedar water pockets will have to be preserved," the state rep was saying. "They're good for wildlife."

"How 'bout a hydrology waiver?"

Nine men crowded around a set of topographic maps, in the glaring sun, to negotiate the aesthetics. Millenbach agreed to smooth over the rough spots, with the assistance of the Park Service's backhoe. Everybody hoped the Nageezi would pitch in, too, but no one expected it. The BLM would have to stake out the area to be reclaimed, and make maps. Millenbach had to write a letter and send everything to the state agency and the

OSM. Once approved, the reclamation had to be done within ninety days or the whole process repeated. Then the BLM had to come back and stake out the parameters of the tiny mine, and write more letters. An archaeologist would have to inspect the site. If he found any significant artifacts, then everything relating to mining would stop and a whole new process of evaluation would unfold.

The state agent admitted, "This is a regulatory bureaucratic nightmare."

Driving back to Farmington, Jim said, "I've been talking to the Nageezi for weeks. I don't understand why they didn't send a representative. I swear, I think these Indians teach their children that white men—all white men—speak with forked tongue. Isn't that right, Danny?"

"That's what I tell mine," said Danny. If it was a joke, he didn't laugh.

The squabble over the coal symbolized a West crowded with rules and enforcers, where small transgressions often felt the full weight of enforcement. But large outrages like the Sunbelt mine were tolerated and usually encouraged.

Danny stared out at Huerfano Mesa, a vast tabletop that had usurped the eastern sky, with shadowed canyons seeming to hold it aloft. Huerfano was another holy place in a land full of them. I had been reading about Ever-changing Woman, heroine of the Navajo creation myth, raised there safe from evil monsters that were annihilating the archetypal forerunners of man. Ever-changing Woman had been found as an infant, wrapped in light; in adulthood she changed color with the seasons, and married Sun and Water, giving birth to the Monster Slayer and Sired-by-Water. Sun equipped them with flint armor and swords of lightning, and they set out like Navajo Jedi to rid Navajoland of the great bear at Chaco Canyon; the monster that hurled Earth People from the bluffs above the San Juan, known as Kicking-Off-the-Rocks; and the terrible eagle that became Shiprock.

Huerfano might have been a holy place, but it was also the highest point for miles about; and so it bristled with electronic gear and relay towers—a technological Parnassus. Huge sprinklers crept across the vibrant green of the Navajo allotments at the base of the mesa, watered with snowmelt from the San Juan

Mountains in Colorado. The water rolled down from Navajo Lake along canals that tunneled beneath the land.

I asked Danny if Shiprock carried the same spiritual freight for the Navajo as Huerfano Mesa. He said, "I don't know."

I saw Jim grinning at me in the rearview mirror.

I drove out to the western edge of the Farmington suburbs and sat watching the sun go down behind the Chuska Mountains, on the reservation. I thought I could make out Hogback Ridge where the San Juan flowed through, and Mount Taylor off to the southeast, although long shadows had created ever-changing landscapes where the Navajo believed their forebears emerged. It occurred to me that, for a Christian, it would be like sitting on a hill and looking out toward Eden. No wonder the Navajo resented a reservation boundary that fell short of Huerfano Mesa and the rest of the tribe's geo-mythic navel.

The brown haze of the Four Corners plant was just a mote in the arching sky. The plant had been in operation since 1963 and for about a decade pumped 320 tons of sulfur oxides into the atmosphere every year, fouling the sky for hundreds of miles around. Congress and Interior finally initiated studies and eventually issued operating guidelines to assure cleaner air. The Navajo received fewer jobs in the plant than they had initially been promised, but that was another matter.

Night fell, and Farmington seemed to undergo a change of personality. Indians and Anglos in low-slung cars and pickups sped out of side streets, made shrieking barrel turns in the intersections, and shot back the way they had come. Others went from blacktop to dirt at high velocity. Whether or not they were antagonistic, I couldn't say, but they sure didn't seem friendly.

I saw dust kick up at the foot of the hill where I sat, followed by the clap of a pistol. A second shot ricocheted off the metal electrical pole and whined away in the direction of Shiprock. The unseen gunman wasn't shooting at me, but he wasn't shooting away from me, either, and I decided to go back to the relative safety of the Village Inn parking lot.

* * *

Millenbach, Danny Charlie, and I sat in the tiny airport at Window Rock, capital of the Navajo nation, waiting for the arrival of a small airplane. It was a perfect day in the desert, and a pastiche of inadvertent patriotism: red rock, white snow on distant peaks, iridescent blue sky. The plane was to deliver their boss, the director of the BLM, Robert Burford, a rancher and politician appointed by James Watt, and husband of the former head of the Environmental Protection Agency, Anne Gorsuch.

Burford's visit to Window Rock, both rare and momentous, marked the official recognition of a land swap between the United States and the Navajo, and the unofficial fact that a piece of the federal kingdom was being given back to the Navajo. Millenbach, Danny, and others in the BLM had been working on this for years. Now arrangements had been made for cars to transport the dignitaries, speeches for reading before the Navajo pols, and a reception at the motel, with big boiled shrimp and Navajo tacos—spicy meat, onions, and tomato on fry bread.

The land in question lay just beyond the reservation boundary, in country much like that around the Bisti Wilderness. Two hundred families were about to be given land they had been living on illegally, some of them for decades, but their land didn't lie over a coal seam. In exchange, the Navajo Tribal Council was giving the BLM $3 million and several thousand acres of volcanic overflow to the south that would become the Maipai Wilderness. The United States would be richer in scenic lava and the Navajo would have marginal grazing land they had considered theirs for four centuries.

Since the deal had been made, Millenbach and Danny had found thirty additional families living on BLM land. They hoped to stop these incursions by negotiation rather than law enforcement. "We're haunted by the specter of a truck off-loading a Navajo and his family from land they consider theirs," Millenbach said. "Can you imagine what the media would do with that?"

A resplendent airplane — ironically, a Comanche — rolled across the tarmac, and out stepped the visiting BLM brass. Burford, a paunchy figure in gray pinstripes, blinked in all that light.

He had been a legislator in Colorado, part of a loose coalition of Sagebrush Rebels known as the Crazies by the opposition, and later was appointed BLM director. Burford and his friends had championed the Sagebrush Rebellion—the notion that federal lands in the West should be given to the states—and something called privatization, which meant selling government land to individual ranchers. But that inspiration had died after Westerners realized how much cheaper it was to let the feds own and maintain the range.

The crusade against government controls on Western ranchers and developers at the outset of the Reagan administration had lost momentum, and some soldiers. Burford's wife had been jettisoned, and so had Burford's benefactor, Watt.

Burford limped. His leg had been crushed under a falling horse in western Colorado, years before. His ranch included BLM land, and to avoid conflict of interest he had sold his grazing rights to his sons, a curious custom in the West, where people trade in real estate that isn't theirs. He shook hands all round. Then he and the BLM state director got into Millenbach's Suburban, and the public affairs people got into the other one.

Burford looked at Danny Charlie in the car next to him, and asked, "Who's that individual in that vehicle?"

Millenbach said, "Danny Charlie, our Navajo coordinator."

He started to explain, but Burford didn't appear interested. He slumped against the door, his body language suggesting that the BLM was a large and difficult agency in the grip of Washington bureaucrats and this Indian business was just another duty.

We had to make a stop to satisfy protocol. Danny led us across town to the Tribal Council headquarters, and we all trooped into the new office building. The BLM administered the oil, gas, and coal under 3.5 million acres of reservation land, no small source of income for the Navajo, and owned most of the land around the reservation. The arrival of the BLM director should be a big deal, I thought. But Burford stuck fast in the foyer outside the office of the chairman of the Tribal Council, for this was a foreign country and there was native business to attend to. Navajo with grievances and coffee cups passed in and out of doorways. There were introductions, hand squeezings, shoulder massages—all among themselves—while the Washington big shot and his entourage from Albuquerque waited to be recognized.

The young men wore short nylon Windbreakers and cowboy hats, their hair tied up in little pigtails with white yarn. The older men wore turquoise: three-inch stones on their fingers, and sprays of turquoise and coral in heavy silver bracelets that encouraged them to use the armrests on the benches. They watched Burford warily, wondering who he was. One old man got up and went out into the parking lot, and returned wearing even more turquoise, just in case Burford *was* important.

A ten-minute wait became twenty, then half an hour. Burford sat with his chin in his hand, staring into the middle distance. He was an unlikely proxy for the messianic Watt. I had interviewed Burford months before, in Washington, and found him willing to discuss the agency, if a little weary. He only warmed up with the telling of stories about fights between cattlemen and sheepherders in his grandfather's time. During a lull in the interview, he had said, "Shoot, coot, or give up the gun!"

"You need the patience of Job," said one of our entourage, a former teacher for the Bureau of Indian Affairs who had gone back to college to learn to be a football coach. "Nothing ever happens today, nothing is ever done about something the first time you discuss it. You rediscuss, you renegotiate. Then maybe . . ."

He turned and patted Danny Charlie's stomach. "I see you've wintered well."

Charlie smiled and rocked back on his heels. He had taken off his jacket and I could see the numbers tattooed on his arm when he was an infant, presumably by the federal government. The numbers had faded almost away.

A door opened at last. We filed into the office of the vice chairman of the Tribal Council, Edward Begay. Burford had an icebreaker ready. He smiled and said, "Why is it that every time I trade with you I give up something?"

Begay returned Burford's smile, as scrutable as a porcelain doll.

Another door opened, admitting the council chairman, Peterson Zah. He looked like a younger, Native American Lee Iacocca, in aviator glasses and designer jeans with a sunset embroidered on a back pocket. He had just come back from Maine, he told us, where he visited with other tribes. As chairman of the Navajo nation—the most populous—Zah was de facto leader of all American Indians.

Zah gave a speech about cooperation. Two years before, he said, the swap had almost been abandoned when the BLM told the squatters they would have to pay taxes on the land they acquired. They balked, and the council applied to Washington for a congressional exemption.

"I never thought they'd get it," Millenbach whispered to me, "but they did."

Across the street, where the Tribal Council met, a bell tolled to announce that the legislative session was about to begin. Council members had gathered outside, in the sunlight. We joined them, and followed them into the Navajo equivalent of the U.S. Capitol. The elected legislators sat in rows of desks equipped with individual microphones, inside a replica of an enormous hogan. The vigas were made of whole ponderosa pines, and the history of the Navajo was painted in the round on the wall, a continuous mural of earth colors on the white stucco.

The chairman began to speak in Navajo studded with Angloisms, "Washington" being the most frequent. Then he spoke in English, out of deference to Burford. Zah presented him with a tiny loom and a Navajo blanket the size of a pocket handkerchief, and told the assembly that the Navajo were getting more rangeland, while the BLM was getting lavaland.

That characterization brought discreet laughter, but Burford chose not to recognize it. The Navajo might be getting the better of the deal, but the BLM was getting rid of at least part of the problem of families living on government land.

Burford thanked the council for inviting him to Window Rock, and that was it. He and Zah signed the appropriate papers, and Burford said, *"Hagonnah,"* Navajo for "So long." He didn't get the pronunciation quite right but the council applauded anyway.

At the airport, Burford sat in the lobby holding the scale

model of a Navajo loom, waiting for the airplane to warm up. It was the end of the official process, one that revealed conflicting demands made on an agency bound up as much by history as politics. Kit Carson's men had piled sheep bones somewhere out beyond the tarmac. From that time on, the Navajo had been unwilling charges of a government that made occasional amends with land swaps and tried to apply regulations to attain its vision of empire. But no one seemed entirely happy with the outcome.

Burford stared at his pintsized Navajo blanket. He said wistfully, "The Zuñi gave Goldwater a beautiful bowl."

I later asked Vice Chairman Begay exactly what the Navajo wanted. They wanted the lands of Navajo legend to be included in the reservation, he said, and they wanted to control industrial and agricultural projects on their land, if there were to be such projects.

If it was up to the Navajo, I asked, would they have built the Four Corners power plant?

"Yes, but we would have cleaned it up sooner, and more Navajo would work there."

He paused and added, "We want thermostats in our houses, too. We want good roads. We want development, but orderly development. We want grazing, and farming, for individual families—everybody should have a vegetable garden."

The names of Navajo settlements suggest these concerns: Many Farms; Cornfields; Sweet Water; Birdsprings. People, place, and resources are intimately related. According to the book *Beautyway: A Navaho Ceremonial,* edited by Leland Wyman, the Navajo's universe, "viewed as an orderly system of interrelated elements, is an all-inclusive unity."

Wyman also wrote, "Place is of the utmost importance to the Navaho. The need is felt ritually to recapitulate mythical toponymy and topography in song and prayer. The geographical details of the long journeys of the protagonists of the myths almost literally bound the Navaho country."

Danny Charlie met me the next day at the BLM car barn in Farmington. Millenbach had told him to take me to a Navajo family living illegally on BLM land, and Danny wasn't happy about that. His cowboy hat was mashed down on his head, and he gunned the pickup mercilessly.

We shot backward into the lot, and took the same highway south, past Huerfano Mesa.

Finally I said, "Danny, I'm sorry if I offended you the other day when I asked about Shiprock."

He didn't respond.

"I was just curious," I added.

When he started talking, he couldn't stop: "Indians have been kicked around so damn long. It's still going on. We get no recognition for what we've done, like fighting and dying. The Navajo have fought in all the American wars. I did, my son's joining the marines. It makes me so damn mad. The Indian people are just for laughing at. I know it. I've lived with white people, I've eaten with them, and slept with them, and I know. The guys I work with aren't like that, except the new arrivals. You hear them talking . . ."

He pumped the gas pedal.

"These rednecks in Farmington are the worst. Four or five white kids go out on a Friday night, in a fancy car, looking for an Indian to beat up. You can see it in their eyes, what they think of us. They get a lot of it from the movies. They see John Wayne kill a hundred Indians with one shot, and they think, 'Hey, that's the way to go!' " He laughed, despite himself. "Those movies make me mad, but I watch them anyway."

He was born in White Rock, on a bleached bit of reservation just visible off to the southwest. His parents were uneducated. He learned to ride when he was five years old—"Nothing fancy, just Indian ponies"—and herded sheep most of his early life. He joined the air force and ended up in Korea, where he learned the language in a few weeks, presumably because it was similar to his own. He worked for the Bureau of Indian Affairs for ten years before joining the BLM.

He said, "People say Indians live off the government. Well, I work for a living, I always have, and there are plenty more like me. I came to Farmington the year a bunch of teenagers murdered some Indian winos. The courts didn't do anything about it, just slapped their wrists. Indians marched through town every weekend, in protest. It got real tense. I couldn't go out of my apartment at night. Then some of these redneck Texans dressed up like cavalry. It was such an insult—it almost caused a riot."

He felt hemmed in by two cultures. "At these hearings involving the BLM, people sometimes ask me why I'm on the white man's side. I have stayed with the Navajo way," he added sadly, "but I think it's dying."

I asked for an example of the Navajo way. He said he went to the white man's church, but also consulted a Navajo medicine man for physical ills. It was not an uncommon practice. The Navajo, he said, never claimed to have a monopoly on God. The people we were going to visit, for instance, were good Baptists, but they also collected plants of supernatural significance to use in Navajo rites.

We had arrived back on the edge of the Bisti, with its sandstone mushrooms and incalculable distances. I had wondered earlier who lived in the two old trailers sitting on hardpan, next to a flaking propane tank and a corral with old tires weighting down the fence posts in the rising wind.

A hand drew a curtain across a window. Danny stood in the dust and called out in Navajo, and the front door opened. We stepped up into a room that belied the sweep of monochrome desert at the end of winter, one wall covered with color photographs of children, a shrine for basketball trophies, and plastic horses in elaborate tack. Imitation Navajo rugs lay on the floor, but the real thing was spread over a makeshift loom made of rough two-by-fours—red, black, deep rich yellow. A fish tank bubbled brightly in the corner, next to the emblems of modern civilization—a Zenith television set and a tape deck.

The trailer belonged to John and Bessie Bunion, grandparents of most of the subjects in the photos. He looked much younger, despite the gold tooth; she wore a house dress over her massive frame, and a lot of turquoise, and after the introductions she moved with dignity into the kitchenette.

John Bunion began to speak in that soft, glottal, impenetrable harmony that is Navajo, with his wife interjecting from the other room, Danny translating.

"They say they had many things to do, but stayed here so they could meet with you. After all the letters they have had their children write to the federal government, at last someone has come from Washington to see them."

"I'm just a writer," I said.

It didn't seem to matter. We sat directly over a coal seam, on BLM land, and the Bunions wanted to talk about it with someone from the East. The land had not been included in the swap at Window Rock, because the coal was a valuable asset the United States government would not give up. The Bunions faced eviction if the coal was to be mined, and they faced eviction if it wasn't, unless Danny could negotiate a miniswap between the BLM and the Tribal Council.

John Bunion had grown up on the far side of the highway, part of a large family, but was forced to move by the Sunbelt mine. His grandfather's house stood less than a mile away, empty.

"Why can't the Bunions live there?" I asked.

"No Navajo can live in the hogan of a dead relative."

Bunion had moved his trailer into the middle of the BLM grazing allotment that had once been his grandfather's—three sections, or about two thousand acres, of sage and greasewood. He ran forty ewes, about fifty goats, and some cattle, and paid two hundred dollars a year for the privilege. The trailer site came rent-free, since in the eyes of the bureaucracy it didn't exist. Bunion hauled drinking water down from the mountains.

"Did he know he was moving illegally onto federal land?"

"Yes."

Bunion had been in the neighborhood all his life; he wasn't leaving. He and Bessie had started out in tents, because federal agents told them they couldn't build a permanent structure.

"She says they went through a lot of tents," said Danny.

Meanwhile they had watched other Navajo build houses, against the rules, and then be given the land. It didn't seem fair. Now if the coal was fully developed there would be another generating plant nearby, and a widened highway for better access, and a store, a gas pump, and eventually a bar—the ultimate neighborhood destroyer.

"What they want to know is, why is all this happening? Why,

when government agents come asking questions, do they never hear about what happens to the information? They lose a lot of sleep over this."

I didn't have an answer and felt uncomfortable in the role I had been assigned. For the Bunions this was sacred ground, a place of unmarked graves and locations called "offering points," used for launching prayers. The Bunions had told the government about the offering points, hoping they would not be destroyed by bulldozers, and now regretted releasing the information.

They had told the agents about crucial herbs used by Navajo families and medicine men, including yucca, blue grama grass, globe mallow, and even sagebrush. Dinosaur bones abounding in the Bisti were sometimes powdered by the medicine men and blown into the nostrils of the sick. Such things deserved respect in their eyes, but they had no idea what the politicians and bureaucrats thought.

Danny had seen a rainbow around the sun the day before and had predicted a storm. I could see haze moving on the Chuskas. The windows began to rattle, but that warm room seemed invulnerable. Bessie Bunion opened a drawer and withdrew twists of colored wool that she had cut, carded, cleaned, spun, and dyed with plants: boiled skunk cabbage root for the yellow, serviceberry for the red. She dug the plants in the yard, she said, pointing to something beyond the window I could not see. The wool she wove into blankets. There were Polaroids of those, too, in a scrapbook. She had sold a big rug to a man in Los Angeles for a thousand dollars, after working for three straight months, seven days a week. `

I asked what John Bunion wanted.

"That's easy," said Danny.

He wanted the coal mine to skirt his allotment, and a fence put up by Sunbelt to keep his sheep from falling into the pit. He wanted surface rights to the land he lived on. It seemed very little, and as a practical matter, too much.

Bessie beat dough in a bowl; she kneaded it with her knuckles and delicately draped a big pizzalike round over the back of one hand. A deep iron skillet sat smoking on the stove. She eased the paper-thin disk into the skillet, the hot grease spitting at her retreating fingers. A wonderful smell filled the trailer.

"Fry bread," said Danny.

It turned golden brown and puffy. She fished it out and slipped another into the grease. She dropped a bundle of herbs into an old enamel pot and poured boiling water over it. A few minutes later Danny and I were sipping deep russet Navajo tea, a hardy antidote to dehydration, and burning our mouths on light, flavorful crusts laced with honey.

Bessie Bunion watched us in silence.

"They'll eat later," Danny said, pushing the plate toward me. "Have some more."

I tried to think of something encouraging to say, some affirmation of the system. But all I could do was praise the fare.

Bunion said something in Navajo, and the three of them began to laugh.

"They want you to talk about fry bread when you go back to Washington," said Danny. No one could possibly disapprove of fry bread.

I left Farmington that evening, headed west. A Navajo man stood in the parking lot of the Turquoise Bar, just east of the reservation line. He looked stricken by some large, irreversible memory, his face upraised in spring snow flurries, drunk and bloated. Another Navajo from the bar walked beside the road, thumb out, his back to the traffic. His manner said pick me up, or don't; it makes no difference to me. I didn't.

Beyond Shiprock, I passed a Navajo boy on a pony driving a dozen more toward a hogan in a clump of willows. He wore a light jacket, and his legs banged against the pony's sides. In the angled light of the sun, set in lavender clouds, big snowflakes burned amazingly white against the deep green of greasewood. The boy grinned, whether at me or at all that unlikely moisture, I will never know.

3

BOB ZIMMER was a BLM ranger responsible for 2.5 million acres near El Centro, California, one of four such agents. He also supervised the three-wheeled all-terrain cycles, known as trikes, which tend to collide on a good weekend when ten thousand of them rush over the Imperial Sand Dunes. They devour the delicately precipitous slopes, rooster-tailing off hogbacks in showers of sand and sayonaran delight. Some riders wear plastic armor like samurais', with sculpted boots, grooved gloves, and gorgeous helmets with plastic visors to ward off the sun. Others wear nothing but acrylic shorts, and casts left over from previous accidents, their Playmate coolers bungy-corded to the seats.

Those same uncovered heads often come into violent contact with one another, and with handlebars and kickstands and the edge of Imperial Dune Road, a strip of tarmac laid down on the desert to provide access to its mysteries. It was there that Zimmer one day stared down into the dark crucible of a stranger's skull, while applying CPR—cardiopulmonary resuscitation. Every time he leaned on the rider's chest, a column of blood shot out his right ear. Zimmer knew the man was already dead. The rider's brother stood nearby, watching, as did several hundred more people. Some had left their trikes to gawk; others sped to a halt, took a look, and cut out again, engines revving, leaving a haze of dust. Zimmer had been trained as an EMT—emergency medical technician—and he knew how to concentrate on the task at hand, but sometimes he really got mad at the riders of ATCs.

Initials were a large part of Zimmer's life. He also checked out LTVAs—long-term visitor areas—when he wasn't dealing with the trikers. EMT and CPR proved essential on weekends like Thanksgiving and Easter, when more than thirty thousand people congregated alongside a road a couple of miles long, their trailers and motor homes parked so close together that Zimmer had to turn sideways to walk between them. Zimmer's gold and royal blue badge read "U.S. Ranger." He told people the initials stood for "Ultra Super."

Every evening he did pull-ups on a bar behind his house in El Centro until he dropped from exhaustion. The Imperial Dunes were included in his patrol sector because Zimmer could handle the stress better than his colleagues, although Zimmer didn't put it that way. He explained his assignment by saying, "It drives the others crazy."

He didn't call in a Lifeline for the severely injured man on the edge of Imperial Dune Road, because the man was beyond the need of a helicopter. Zimmer went with the brother to tell the victim's wife. He stood quietly by while the brother tried to coax her out of her trailer, while people partied all around them. "What's wrong?" she kept asking; then she said, "He's dead, isn't he?" She caught sight of Zimmer's tan uniform and his badge and began to scream.

He said later, "I felt like the angel of death."

We met on a Saturday morning in the El Centro BLM parking lot, toward the end of my trip. On his tooled leather belt he carried a .357 magnum, two "quick-loads" in leather cases, handcuffs, and a can of Mace for spraying dogs that charged him from beneath the houses of people living illegally on BLM land. He was thirty-seven but looked thirty, standing only five feet nine but squarely built, with a blond mustache and big, blue, close-set eyes revealed when he removed his shades.

We went for coffee at Denny's with two of his colleagues, one of them Zimmer's boss, a big ranger named Vernon. That was as close as they got to formal staff meetings. They took turns telling stories about their patrol sectors as the sun rose above El Centro—a kind of occupational therapy.

The week before, Zimmer had visited an old woman who lived in the desert in a discarded ice chest. She had apparently eaten her cats. "There were little strips of meat on this aluminum sheet," Zimmer said. "I told her she had to move, that she was on public land. She said her son had told her the land was hers. 'Tell your son he's mistaken,' I said. She said, 'Tell him yourself, he's right there beside you.' Well, he *wasn't* right there beside me, but what the hell, I told him anyway."

Vernon spoke of the man who lived in a bread van on the desert with five goats. Goat droppings had built up between the dashboard and the windshield. He and his colleagues referred to such people as fifty-one fifties, the designation in California's penal code for people of unsound mind. Fifty-one fifties included the old man who refused to wear clothes, and kept garbage on the floor of his trailer so long that it rotted through. "They always invite you inside," said Vernon.

Zimmer had an ongoing problem with a man living out there in a Toyota Corolla stuffed with newspapers. The man could barely fit in the driver's seat. Zimmer had found him standing with his feet buried in the sand, arms outstretched, face matted with hair and beard so that Zimmer had to walk around him a time or two to determine where to address his questions. "I said, 'Excuse me, sir, but you can't live in a car on public lands. This is a long-term visitors area only, which means you have to move after fourteen days.' I came back the next week and found that he had moved his car *two feet*!"

Fifty-one fifties living on federal land did not take up as much time as weekend visitors to the desert, who poured out of Los Angeles and San Diego once the temperature dipped below one hundred. Vernon kept a book of photographs in his office of the more gruesome manifestations of desert recreation, which covered an extremely broad range of human endeavor, including burning automobile transmission covers on distant dunes for the pleasure of watching the unearthly glow of hot magnesium, collecting explosive ordnance on bombing ranges officially off-limits to the public, and setting off homemade pipe bombs.

Getting drunk or stoned, or both, was usually a concomitant exercise, and sometimes the sole activity pursued on public lands. Many people out there were armed, but the rangers did not have shotguns in their pickups, a holdover from the days when the BLM was nothing but a clearing-house for commodities and had neither the authority nor the stomach for enforcing the law.

Zimmer and I went out and got into his new Dodge pickup and headed east. It was 8:00 A.M. and already uncomfortably warm. Furrows of deep black earth ran off to infinity on both sides of the highway, across the Imperial Valley, where alfalfa and sugar beets flourished on water diverted from the Colorado River. The river runs down through Yuma, on the Arizona-California line, into the All American Canal, and on into the fields of one of the grandest truck gardens on earth. Without irrigation, the Imperial Valley would be one big alkali storm.

A black stripe on a silo marked sea level—thirty feet above the ancient bed of Lake Cahuilla. Early in the century the Colorado broke through the embankments and flowed unimpeded into this vacuum, until the Southern Pacific Railway backed some of its boxcars, loaded with rock, into the rift. By then the flood had created the Salton Sea, a geographic anomaly and one more strange feature in a strange land, with no outlet to the Pacific. Every year it became saltier, less healthy, fed untreated sewage that flowed north in the New River from Mexicali into the United States, and the chemical runoff from the Imperial Valley's farms.

Beyond lay the desert. "It's unattractive from my point of view," said Zimmer, "but historically it has attracted people. Our LTVAs have no facilities, no water, but people like to stay there. They meet resistance and get pissed off."

His .357 was a potent little piece, but no match for automatic weapons. Zimmer also carried a "belly gun"—a snubnosed five-shot Smith & Wesson .38—in his cowboy boot. Those two pistols, a light bar on his pickup, and a radio were his only insulation against motorcycle gangs and desperadoes who built PCP labs in the desert out of old plywood and pallets used in crop harvests, equipped them with generators and exhaust fans to blow off ether produced in the drug's manufacture, and lay up behind boarded windows with AR-15's.

Zimmer divided desert humanity into serviceable categories: there existed good guys, turkeys, dirt bags, fifty-one fifties, and dangerous critters. Zimmer was himself a good guy, in my opinion. A turkey was stupid or incompetent, or both. Most tourists, and many long-term visitors, were turkeys. A dirt bag was sufficiently venal or uncaring to bring harm to others. It was a dirt bag on a motorcycle who had shot over a dune the year before and landed on an ATC, severing the trike rider's thigh with his chain. The man would have bled to death if Zimmer hadn't arrived in time.

Dirt bags smeared the walls of the toilets at the LTVAs with excrement, or doused them with gasoline left after a weekend of mechanized cavorting and set them off with their Bics. (Such behavior came close to the fifty-one fifty category.) Zimmer dealt with them all politely, with the exception of dangerous critters. One dangerous critter, he said, had fired a high-powered rifle slug through both walls of the Cahuilla ranger station, with rangers inside.

We crossed the East Highland Canal, a runoff from the All American. Shellaclike, reflective earth—desert pavement— stretched away toward the Chocolate Mountains to the northeast, a bombing range of daunting aspect and dryness. Creosote bush and tamarisk bordered the dirt road, offering the only amenities other than level ground at the Hot Springs LTVA— our first stop.

Zimmer eased up to an encampment of what he called rubber bums, a subcategory of turkeys, who bounced from LTVA to LTVA, without jobs or the intention of ever paying the twenty-five-dollar user's fee. A couch had been set in the sand, next to a panel truck without an engine and a structure built of pallets, full of old blankets. A fire burned in a metal milk crate, under a blackened pan of boiling water. A large woman in stretch pants sat on a discarded kitchen stool reading the romance novel *Black Swan.*

She glanced up as Zimmer approached.

"How's it going?" he asked. "Don't I know you?"

The woman shrugged and returned to her book.

"You can't leave this trash here," Zimmer said. He had already ordered a crew to come out from El Centro to remove the truck and the makeshift house.

A man came out of the shadows, tattoos up both forearms. He grinned crookedly.

"You can't build permanent structures on public land," the BLM ranger informed him. "You can't stay more than fourteen days without a permit."

"We're just hanging in 'til the SS check arrives."

That stood for social security. Back in his pickup, Zimmer said, "What do you do with folks like that?" He wrote in his log that he had contacted people in the Hot Springs LTVA. "Is that a grebe over there in the canal?"

He fished binoculars from under the seat. "It's a merganser. At Palm Oasis we get ducks, coots, hawks. A lot of passerine birds."

He carried *The Golden Guide to North American Birds,* which he preferred to Peterson. He had grown up in southern California wanting to be a game warden, and had a degree in wildlife management from Humboldt State. But everyone, it seemed, wanted to be a game warden, so he worked as a ranger, first for the Army Corps of Engineers in Montana and Oregon, now for the BLM in his home state. His wife was a bookkeeper. They had three daughters and would have another child as soon as they could afford it.

"I think kids are about the neatest thing going," Zimmer said. He happily baby-sat on his days off, he said, and dreamed of dove hunting in greener country.

The Coachella Canal cut close to the dunes. A few trikes from Gecko Campground were parked alongside, and their riders splashed in limpid green water from the Colorado. Some had strung ropes across the canal to hold them against the current. Swimming was illegal in the canals, but arresting swimmers was low on Zimmer's list. The bodies of drowned illegal aliens, known as floaters, regularly found their way into the canals. Decomposition and the desert sun blew them up to grotesque proportions.

"They're the most hideous things you can imagine," Zimmer said, screwing up his face. "The skin's all peeling off, the tongue's big as a baseball bat, and black. *Yuk.*" Occasionally floaters got hung up on swimmers' lines across the canals.

Tents stood at the end of a blacktopped loop. I could hear the snarl of motors and see distant plumes of sand spewed up by racing ATCs. It was still too early in the season for the mass of them. Some of the ATVs were ridden by children, who were often injured and sometimes killed. In death they took on the aspect of porcelain dolls, an image Zimmer had a hard time getting out of his mind. Their parents put them on trikes at five and six years old.

"Sometimes," he said, "their feet barely reach the pedals."

Zimmer asked parents why they took such risks with their children. "They say, 'After they break a leg two or three times, they'll learn.' *Learn what?*"

Some mechanized form of retribution lurked in those casual assurances. Scaling a dune at forty miles an hour and meeting a supercharged pickup on widetracks doing sixty was not a situation amenable to most six-year-olds. Zimmer had come upon just such a scene in the dunes, moments after the collision. A small boy lay in a jumble of apparently broken bones. The pickup's fender bore a perfect spherical dent, left by his helmet. Then, as Zimmer watched, the boy's eyes opened, his limbs miraculously realigned themselves, and he stood up, ashen but undaunted, and rode off.

One weekend 120 people went to the hospital in Brawley. A man broke a collarbone while riding a new ATC, got it fixed at the hospital, then came back to the dunes and broke the other collarbone.

"You have a lot of compression fractures," Zimmer said, "going over the washboards. You hit a bump and go up. The machine goes down. It hits another bump and comes up while you're coming down. Now you've got your basic compressed spinal disk."

There were no speed limits on the dunes. Collisions drew spectators who talked, smoked, revved their engines, and laughed. They pressed close to disaster, like visitors to an aquarium. Once while doing CPR on an injured motorcyclist, listening for the pulse, Zimmer had to call out for quiet. But the vital sounds of a dying human were no match for the idling ATCs. "I turned him on his side, to drain his fluids, and his face fell off. People started vomiting right there in the sand." It served the turkeys right.

He figured he lost about a dozen riders a year. Some died of the heat, like the boy who rode his motorcycle all the way from San Diego to the dunes on a July day, with no shirt. He bought a Coke at Glamis Beach, up the highway, crawled under a creosote bush, and died before he could get the can open.

Glamis Beach was a ramshackle mirage on the edge of the road—a deck with a view of sand waves was built over a sundries store full of cola and accessories for the internal combustion engine. A beach without an ocean. Trikers and buggyists hot from the dunes, wearing mirrored sunglasses and goggles, some wearing casts, sat at picnic tables, their machines drawn up to the periphery like horses at a hitching rail. Trikes needing attention could be taken to either Dirty Bob's or Clean Gene's repair shack. An ATC rental wagon, a gypsy on the shimmering sands, dispensed machines for twenty dollars a day, plus gas, doing a good business.

"You should see it during Thanksgiving week," Zimmer said. "Bonfires, thousands of headlights, big high-intensity illumination lights used on jumbo jets. They're bouncing all over the place—red, green, blue, white."

He shook his head in amazement. "Some guys come out here in trailers with complete machine shops—vises, acetylene torches, lathes. One guy has a semi, all chromed and painted with pictures of sand dunes, who only uses it for parking here. It cost him a hundred and fifty thousand dollars, at least. It has a shop, trikes, dune buggies, sleeping quarters, a bar, TV sets, an air compressor, refrigerator, blenders . . ."

At the beginning of a busy weekend, you couldn't get your rig out again until the holiday was over. One turkey had landed a Beechcraft on the tarmac, on a dare, to visit friends in the campground. He planned to take off again before the ranger caught him, but arriving motor homes cut off his runway and he had to stay in the dunes for four days.

*　＊　＊　＊*

I returned to Gecko Campground on my own. The dunes looked pink in the setting sun, and the smell of barbecue mixed with that of exhaust fumes rising from the mechanized encampment. A few trike riders moved like wayward cursors across a vast video screen, but most had come in for supper.

I wanted to meet some all-terrain cyclists on this ancient shoreline of the long-evaporated Lake Cahuilla. Its waves had beaten quartz and feldspar from the Chocolate Mountains into abundant sand during the Pleistocene epoch, and now towering mounds of sand run off toward Mexico for fifty miles, pushed one way by winter winds, brought back again in the summer. They lie across the San Andreas Fault like a sculpted Band-Aid and are the last remnant of a shift in sheltering sediments begun thousands of years ago and halted by a change in weather about the time of the Norman Conquest.

There are transverse dunes, longitudinal dunes, and barchan dunes in the shape of horseshoes. Just north of Highway 78 they support the yellow desert sunflower, found nowhere else, giant Spanish needle, desert buckwheat, and a parasite, *Ammobroma sonorae*—a saucerlike receptacle with tiny purple flowers concealing a massive network beneath the sand, sometimes with as many as a hundred five-foot stalks living off the buckwheat, creosote, and arrowweed bushes. *Ammobroma sonorae* could weigh fifty pounds; the Papago Indians once dug them up and ate them like giant yams.

Fingers of vegetation creep among the dunes, a phenomenon known to botanists and biologists in the desert as interdigitation. Microphyll woodland harbors the burro deer and the fringe-toed lizard, which has special feet for navigating hot sand and earflaps to ward off the sun; also the desert tortoise, kit fox, badger, and something called Couch's spade-footed toad, which spends most of its life underground, only to emerge after infrequent rains form shallow ponds against the dunes. Andrew's dune scarab beetle, a candidate for threatened status, emerges once a year and mates in lustful flurries before disappearing again beneath the sand.

South of Highway 78, however, there is no interdigitation. Broad, endless scars stretch to the bare horizon, as if left by the tails of supersaurians—the trails of ATCs. The dunes until fairly recently were considered a wasteland. The BLM let people do what people would on those soft slopes. Then the Federal Land Policy and Management Act forced the agency to set aside at least a portion of the dunes as habitat for rare and endangered species, a decision that enraged the mechanical warriors but maintained at least a part of the dunes as a refuge for plants and other nonmechanical life.

There are in the Southwest more than one hundred organizations devoted to off-road vehicular recreation; they want all public lands made available to them.

At nightfall, the lights and colored beacons created a vast electronic matrix of disturbing beauty. Zimmer had introduced me to a couple named Stone. They and their friends had driven out from San Diego the night before in a customized pickup with chrome rails in the back, and an electric winch for loading and unloading their dune buggy, their ATC, and their fat-wheeled motorcycle with two chains, designed for sand. The pickup pulled a thirty-foot trailer with a striped awning, a gas barbecue pit, deck chairs, a Coleman flare to act as night sentinel, special Cat hats with earflaps reminiscent of the fringe-toed lizard's, and an air spray for cleaning sand from their goggles.

The Stones had been using the dunes for years. Their dune buggy gave off a faint odor of gasoline and fresh paint. It had been equipped with airplane seat belts, a number of chrome gauges, and a turbocharged Volkswagen engine capable of 180 horsepower.

"The army's looking into these," Stone said. "They can mount a cannon on one and deliver a payload before anybody can figure out what to do about it. If Rommel had had these babies, World War Two might have turned out differently."

Stone worked as a projects engineer on military optics experiments set up in various parts of the desert. His eyes were red from the sun and flying sand. He ran a comb through thinning hair and invited to me "take a ride."

We strapped ourselves into the buggy and took off, hugging the ground, flag flapping from the long metal whip so approaching machines could see us over the crests. He had bought the frame and turned it into a four-seater. The first year he had discovered his mistakes and brought out tools and welding torches to fix them. The front tires had been buffed smooth, but the rear ones sported welts known as sand paddles. "It's kind of like driving on water. To go one way, you have to throw sand in the opposite direction."

It felt more like motorized sledding. We came up onto the rim of a dune and scooted along its sharp leeward edge, a "razorback." I gazed down at tiny creosote bushes at the bottom, and scour marks left by a legion of other sand paddles. "The front end has independent suspension," Stone was saying. "I call this baby the Wampus Kitty. The wheels pivot when you turn, to get a better bite. I never like to go straight over the edge . . ."

He angled off into thin air. I thought, *He's not going to do this,* but he did. I swallowed my breath in the descent, watching the sand rush up to meet us. "Most of the weight's on the back end," he was shouting, over the rush of wind. "When you take off up a hill, the wheels come off the ground, and the motor will almost touch. It has a low center of gravity. Instead of turning over, it just spins around—unless you hit a berm."

He braked with a lever on the driver's side; we spun out at the bottom. "That applies all the power to one side, if you're turning. The angles will be deceptive to you, will feel a little bit like a roller coaster."

A dune towered over us—a sand Matterhorn. Stone approached it at speed; instead of turning, he floored the accelerator and the turbocharger kicked in. Suddenly we were driving straight up, or so it seemed, a curtain of sand below us and the front end shimmering above us, wheels barely touching. It seemed that the Wampus Kitty would surely flip over backward and tumble to the dune's base, but instead we shot over the razorback in a gritty burst of glory. The engine screamed as Stone abruptly released the accelerator, "backing down" the rpm.

We bounced back to supper, my hands aching from gripping the bars. "Sometimes we take off for ten hours at a time, with food and water," Stone said. "We come out fifteen times a season, and I still can't get enough of it." They spent a week there at Thanksgiving, a week and a half at Christmas. "We bring our Christmas tree. The first time there was only one other couple here, way down at the end. We set up our CBs so we could talk to each other, and go out together when we wanted to putt." Putting was leisure riding, as opposed to "bowl running."

Stone was also an amateur astronomer and liked to set up a telescope on slow nights. He had come west from Providence, Rhode Island, twenty-six years before. His fifteen-year-old son had been riding trikes since he was six. As soon as he had finished his steak, he mounted the two-chain motorcycle and disappeared over a dune. The rest of us watched Stone's brother do jumps, slowing down only for the "whoop-de-doos"—washboard stretches that produced compressed spinal disks. In the gathering darkness the lights at the ends of the metal whips on other buggies began to blink on, tracing red, green, and blue lines in the clear desert air.

Riders came and went, leaving their machines for a time in a tight circle and then leaping from their deck chairs to trikes and streaking straight out onto the broad sand flat. The instant transition to motorized cavorting was part of the appeal, but mostly it was the absence of restraint.

"Theft has gotten to be a problem," Stone said, eating hurriedly from a paper plate. "Honda once had all the patents. When the machines got all piled up, you couldn't tell who owned what. Now we have to chain them up at night."

The machines had steadily evolved. Stone was most enthralled with his turbocharger, which recycled the exhaust gases and force-fed air into the carburetor at high speed. "I've got a waste gate, to prevent the engine from blowing up. Hear that?"

He cocked an ear toward a snarling engine in the next valley. "That's a Corvair. I used to use the old flathead Fords, chopped off and fully ported, but then the VWs came along. Now they're hard to find, so people are moving into Hondas and Pintos."

His turbocharger glowed in the dark—another wayward star. His pickup was powered by the largest V-eight engine made, for pulling his mechanized village, including the Komfort trailer with its shower, fifty-gallon water tank, kitchen and separate bedroom, air conditioning, and mechanic's shop. "Desert people are gadget nuts," he said. "Anybody want to go for a ride?"

By now it was a familiar refrain. Stone's wife, Deborah, finished dispensing chocolate chip ice cream to the sand warriors, and we joined Stone in his machine. "This'll be a putt," he announced, as another couple and several teenagers on ATCs lined up behind us. Stone didn't approve of bowl running in the dark.

Lines of trikes suggested electronic caterpillars bound for the dark wastes of the Chocolate Mountains. "They filmed part of *Return of the Jedi* out there," he said, "the part where sand creatures eat people. I don't know how they shot that without getting a single trike in the frame."

Even at putting speed we quickly entered the unknown. Great troughs of darkness lay between the dunes. Sand rose in the unblinkered headbeams, the grains seemingly aflame; overhead, the Milky Way spread densely across black sky. We paused on the crest of a dune for a cola—"We earned it"—and a view of the lights of El Centro and Brawley to the west, Yuma to the east. The kids soon grew bored. "I don't like to be settin'," said Stone's boy, "when I could be riding."

They took off one by one, their lights dropping into the abyss, appearing a mile ahead, then swallowed again in the immensity of the place. The night reverberated with the snarl of motors. Big winged insects swarmed in the buggy's bright beams, confused, clinging harmlessly to our clothes. Someone set off a flare far to the south, and we watched it descend like a bright lavender parachute.

"I love the desert," Stone said, groping for some appropriate image. "I like the . . . scenic aspects."

Back at camp, they drank more cola and lounged in the deck chairs. "The night's young," Stone said, but I felt the effects of sun and sand. One of Stone's friends, also a defense contractor, sat silently under the trailer awning, while his son navigated the whoop-de-doos. Stone asked if something was the matter.

The man said, "The bushes are coming back."

"What?"

"The bushes. They're growing back."

It was a serious allegation, however far-fetched. Creosote and other bushes had been almost eradicated from this part of the dunes; evidence of regeneration lay entirely in his imagination. But even the possibility depressed him. Bushes made trike riding more exacting and in some curious way represented a threat to the supremacy of his machine.

Stone assured him that the bushes were indeed not coming back, and his friend went off for another ride.

Zimmer waved to the driver of a green border patrol Suburban the following morning. The Suburban was packed with dark faces behind wire mesh. Zimmer raised his binoculars, following the railway spur into the haze under the Cargo Muchacho Mountains. He was looking for lone figures in dirty clothes, hiking in the middle of nowhere.

"The giveaway is the plastic water bottle," he said. "They try to look casual, which is hard to do when you're lost and dying of thirst. Last week we had six go down on us. Found one hanged in a tree." The corpse was six months old. "Also a pile of bones. One under a creosote bush, and three women dead, left behind by a bigger group. We don't touch the bodies— they're the coroner's property."

Once he rounded up twelve Salvadorans in a single day. They were low on water and wanting to get caught. Resources were his main priority, he added. He didn't search for drugs or aliens in car trunks, but since he was a federal officer he didn't like to pass up the obvious. He carried two jugs of water at all times, one for himself and one for strangers—good guys, turkeys, dirt bags, fifty-one fifties, even dangerous critters.

The road, a dry streambed, led past ocotillo and paloverde. A board driven into the sand provided cryptic information to coyotes bringing aliens across, but we could see no one on the shimmering land, and no fresh prints. Those of mice and other nocturnal creatures crisscrossed the sneaker prints left by some earlier incursion.

Zimmer got out of the pickup and surveyed his domain— desert pavement, barren mountains where the air force dropped live bombs and flares. Turkeys occasionally kicked unexploded bombs and died because of it. Other turkeys in motor homes dumped their waste in the sand—probably Zimmer's biggest complaint against the transitory humanity with which he dealt daily. He enjoyed chasing trailers with dangling rubber hoses, and issuing citations to the drivers. "One turkey dumped his oil right in the sand," he said, "and a burrowing owl died a horrible death."

The desolation of the country, like its beauty, overwhelmed; my head swam. Zimmer lived and worked at about fifty feet below sea level, occasionally getting up to two hundred feet above it. In summer the desert was simply too hot to patrol and almost devoid of human life. A few die-hard ATCs came out in motor homes, slept all day under high-intensity air conditioners, and triked all night. Soon Zimmer wouldn't have the luxury of cruising the rest of the desert, inspecting the elaborate graves people built there for their pets, and the hovels they lived in on public land after digging a ditch outside so they could claim to be miners. He seemed amused by the more blatant idiocies, without condemning them.

"Why do people torch public toilets?" I asked.

"How do I know? Why do they burn up saguaro cactus, steal our signs, and shoot automatic weapons through each other's motor homes? Why do they sleep in junk piles?" The desert was fifty-one fifty country; they went with the job.

We ended up in the shadow of Pilot Knob, on the edge of the All American Canal. Mexico lay on the other side, beyond the fence, a welter of sun-bleached fences, garden patches, and the isolated encampments of the *paracaidistas*—squatters who might have dropped from the sky. We bumped along the dirt road above the canal; the water was fast-flowing, wide and deep.

"A lot of floaters here," Zimmer said, checking the road for fresh prints of live aliens. There were none, but black plastic garbage bags lay discarded in a willow grove, left by those who had packed their clothes in them before the plunge.

"The smart ones use inner tubes," he said. "Kids on the other side rent them out, then swim across and bring the tubes back."

We turned around at the dead end. In the ten minutes it had taken us to travel the road, wet footprints had been left in the dust, over our tire tracks. But there was no one in sight—just green willows and the reflection of sun on desert pavement.

▪ 4 ▪

In 1985 the Forest Service spent $166 million fighting wild-fires, most of them in the West. Seven thousand fires charred half a million acres, leaving a haze of smoke in Western skies. Some of the fires were allowed to burn for a time, a strategy known as confinement. Indians in the Southwest had used grass fire as a weapon against their enemies; those fires, and the ones set by lightning, had traveled through dense understory and burned off sage and greasewood, permitting grass to grow back more densely. Fire also benefits forest in higher elevations, if the fire is neither too hot nor too extensive.

Confinement is one of those aggrandizing management terms assigning human intent to natural processes. Confinement is ecologically sound but politically risky. In addition to providing trees, the national forests attract tourists, and those who depend upon tourists. These people don't like confinement fires. As Stephen Pyne wrote in *Fire in America,* "Smoke is an ugly public relations message to send to the source of that revenue."

In the summer of 1985, one such fire burned in the Okanogan National Forest—2 million acres up along the Canadian border in the state of Washington. Lightning struck a snag in a remote section of the forest in July, kindling a sleeper fire that was not discovered for almost a week. A lookout saw a plume of smoke rising from the Wolf Creek drainage, in newly designated wil-derness, and radioed the fire dispatcher in the town of Okanogan. That set in motion a complicated process with an outcome no one predicted.

Washington's Coast Ranges wring moisture from the ocean air. Wind that reaches the east slope of the Cascades between spring and fall is hot and often ungodly dry. It fans some ferocious blazes and sears a landscape that has more in common with Arizona than the fog-drenched peaks of the Pacific Northwest.

I went to Okanogan looking for the fire. I had trained with a hotshot crew in New Mexico, and obtained a pink card from the Forest Service entitling me to earn seven dollars an hour for some of the grubbiest and most dangerous work imaginable. Fire fighting closely resembles a war in the large-scale mobilization of fighters and equipment, the maintaining of a "front" where both offensive and defensive maneuvers are essential, and in the general drama of people caught up in something larger than themselves. There are base camps and aerial attacks, even correspondents with cameras.

What I discovered in the Okanogan National Forest was not a fire in the dangerous phase, but one that had already peaked, threatened to go out, and then continued to burn. It was not being fought by people, but by a computer.

Formerly the Chelan National Forest, the Okanogan is part of the original Washington Forest Preserve established by President Cleveland in 1897. *Okanoga* is a Northwest Indian word meaning, roughly, "rendezvous"—a reference to potlatching and the gathering of fish for winter that took place before the white man moved in. Okanogan County is agricultural, with a powerful overlay of cowboy ethic: so many sheep were killed by angry cattlemen in the 1903 Curtis Slaughter that a visitor to the site claimed to have walked for miles on sheep bones.

The town of Okanogan bills itself as "Sunland City and Eastern Gateway to the Northern Cascades," as geographically precise a promotion as I had seen, and a bit of a tease. Big humps of glacial till sit on the horizon, and sprinklers sucking on the Okanogan River lay down swaths of chlorophyll in sharp contrast to the burlap-colored land beyond. Ten inches of rain fall annually. Without irrigation, the orchards would have turned to kindling, and the supermarket and stores along the main street to dust.

When I arrived at the FS office in Okanogan, I asked about the fire and was taken to Phil Gum, the fire and aviation staff officer. Gum was remarkably hirsute for a career manager in the Forest Service. His sideburns were long and full, and his full gray mustache drooped at the ends. However, his desk and floor space reflected an ordered mind and a sense of humor. His paper piles looked mitered. A sign above his desk said, "Hark! I must hasten after them, for I am their leader."

Gum explained to me how the fire had become one of the most expensive in the region. He provided me with copies of his daily reports, written over a period of several weeks. From these Confinement Fire Summary and Decision Documentation Sheets emerged a picture of a fire that refused to comply with the program.

The Okanogan National Forest is divided into a grid with eighty-two-acre cells, so that fires can easily be located by longitude and latitude—"longs and lats"—with alphabetical and numerical coordinates. The location of this fire was established as Delta Echo Zero Five Alpha Delta Five. When the fire was first reported, the dispatcher in Okanogan contacted the North Cascades Smokejumper Base over in the Methow Valley. As it happened, the smokejumpers' Beechcraft was already in the air, with the management officer aboard, and it swung over to take a look.

This fire, as yet nameless, was number 122 in the driest year in the last sixty. It burned on a slope above Hubbard Creek, in aspen, alpine fir, and Engelmann spruce, miles from the nearest road—steep, rugged "no-go" country, in FS fire-fighting parlance.

Gum met with his boss, the forest supervisor, to discuss the characteristics that lead to fire categorization: slope aspects in the Wolf Creek and Hubbard Creek drainages, weather forecasts, the fuels involved. They also discussed the implementation plans for three possible responses to the fire. The most extreme response—control—simply meant going in and putting out the fire, at whatever cost. But dwindling funds, and the realization that all fires are not critical, made another category, containment, more popular.

The *Appropriate Suppression Response Implementation Plan,* a yellow-jacketed manual on most shelves in the Okanogan FS office, stated that containment was "to minimize suppression costs and reduce resource loss." In other words, save money that might be spent on the extra firefighters, aircraft, and aerial retardant required to put a fire out cold, and instead restrict the fire to existing parameters. Containment was still traditional fire fighting, but less than an all-out assault.

The third possible response, confinement, was the newest and most controversial. The growing popularity of confinement was directly related to cost and the emerging notion that some fires were actually beneficial. Fire opened up forage areas for wildlife and allowed the growth of healthier trees. Periodic burns in seral forests strengthened old growth and eliminated deadfall that, if allowed to accumulate for decades, eventually burned with such intensity that nothing was spared.

Since confinement meant doing nothing, it provided less work for seasonal firefighters, less hazard pay for smokejumpers, fewer requisition slips for FS regulars to fill out, less money in the pipeline in general, and less of the appearance of control so important to any bureaucracy.

The management officer at the smokejumper base recommended that the fire be contained, i.e., fought with limited manpower. The forest supervisor, Fire and Aviation Officer Gum, and the district management officer all flew over the fire together in the FS reconnaissance Cessna. The supervisor, acting on Gum's recommendation, ordered confinement—the "let-burn" strategy—and the beginning of the trouble.

"It was a gutsy decision," Gum told me. "The fire had the potential to come outside the wilderness area, and our implementation plan said we didn't want it to do that. It had the potential to be one hell of a fire."

That night Gum filled out his first Confinement Fire Summary and Decision Documentation Sheet, including precipitation and wind forecasts, possible threats to populous areas and the southern border of British Columbia, smoke tolerance levels, monitor team availability, regional preparedness, suppression resource capability (people and equipment), and minimum cost predictions. Under the decision tree criteria that Gum helped develop, the wrong answer in any category would trigger a different, more aggressive response to the fire.

Decision trees are paper outlines largely comprising arrows pointing to seemingly inevitable decisions, like confinement, containment, and control, developed at considerable cost in money and computer time. Gum was proud of the ones he'd helped put together. The Park Service in neighboring North Cascades National Park used the same decision trees to classify and track its fires. Decision trees were an essential part of modern fire management, but the FS sometimes found itself dealing with the unmanageable.

The fire still had no name. Gum estimated that it had consumed twenty-five acres eight miles from the nearest trailhead, and was subject to winds of five to eight knots coming down Hubbard Creek. Then he went home to supper.

Gum owned the orchard next door to FS headquarters. His commuting time was about a minute. He and his wife both came from Pennsylvania. Gum had worked on the Okanogan for ten years, an unusually long stint for a career officer in one posting, after working for several years in Alaska. The Gums liked the country and the town and the river. They grew top-quality red and golden delicious apples, and during picking season depended on seasonal workers. At night, Phil Gum could hear the whisper of water jets against the apple trees a few feet from his bedroom window.

The 1976 National Fire Management Act directed the FS to develop so-called integrated land management plans, including fire strategies for designated areas such as wilderness, recreation, winter range, and so on. Responding to this directive, Gum had prepared a report, "The Computerization of Fire Dispatch Utilizing Satellite Imagery," known as the Okanogan Project, which earned him praise.

In it he wrote, "Traditional data bases and decision processes were incapable of fully supporting fire management direction. . . . Therefore, new natural resource data bases were acquired utilizing Landsat multispectral imagery, digitized terrain data, and ancillary information. . . . These data bases are a key component of a fully integrated real time computerized fire dispatch system."

Of such computerized fire dispatch, he wrote, "It was obvious to us that traditional data bases and decision processes were unacceptable for implementing the new fire management direction. . . . The system was to be designed to handle logistic questions and to allow for alternate strategy selection."

"Phil's known for his analytical ability," a colleague told me later. "And his can-do economics. He's great at cutting things out of a budget, great at computer stuff. Like vegetation models. But he's not a people person."

The day after the fire was spotted it was named the Hubbard Fire. Gum wrote on the Confinement Fire Summary and Decision Documentation Continuation Sheet, "Yesterday's decisions look even better today. . . . Now estimated size come snow fly 2000 acres." The Hubbard Fire had consumed fifty new acres overnight.

For three days it smoldered and flared, and then on July 26, five days after its discovery, it burned a hundred additional acres. The smoke was clearly visible from the populous Methow Valley and the tourist town of Winthrop, where local promoters staged mock gunfights for tourists coming in over the North Cascades Highway.

On July 27 valley residents woke up to a huge column of smoke rising from the wilderness. It eventually blotted out the sun. The Hubbard Fire grew that day to a thousand acres. It rained hot ash on houses ten miles away. Calls came in continuously to the North Cascade Smokejumper Base and the Okanogan FS office from people who didn't understand confinement fire strategy. The publisher of the *Methow Valley News* flew over the Hubbard Fire and came back to the smokejumper base to tell the manager, "The Forest Service better do something about it."

That decision still lay with the Okanogan office. Most of the smokejumpers and local FS employees thought Gum and the forest supervisor were suppressing information about the seriousness of the fire. In the last five years there had been more than fifty confinement fires on the Okanogan, but only recently had the FS admitted it. Now confinement was a hot item. Washington, D.C., liked confinement fires because they were cheap and incidentally improved habitat. The regional office in Portland liked confinement for the same reasons. A fire and aviation staff officer could do well for himself with confinement strategy, and Gum's ability to remain on the Okanogan, avoiding transfer, was due in part to successful confinement fires he had supervised.

Fire fighting was no longer a glorious occupation within the FS, which had turned its attention to the engineers. The chief of the FS in Washington, D.C., was an engineer. Engineers built roads. "It used to be that everybody in the Forest Service talked about fires," Gum said. "Fire was very much part of the culture, something people had in common. Now people talk about timber sales.

"We have people in top management who have never worked a fire. You say, 'We have to scalp the edge of the clear-cut,' and they don't know what you're talking about."

People began to say that Gum wanted to prove that confinement would work in a record dry year, as a kind of professional grand slam. Gum said he was just following the criteria he had helped develop, ascending the decision tree a branch at a time.

By the following day the Hubbard Fire had become the largest in Washington State, but the Okanogan public affairs officer was unable to interest the media in it. "It had no sex appeal," he said, "because we weren't fighting it. The media is only familiar with control. A reporter said, when I mentioned the Hubbard Fire, 'Oh, that's the one you're not doing anything about. If you're not putting it out, there's no story.' "

The fire grew. By July 30 it covered more than fifteen hundred acres and seemed to be moving toward Milton Mountain. That ridge had been designated in the fire strategy as a barrier the fire would not be allowed to cross. Methow Valley residents were still treated to spectacular night skies, but Gum's reports remained optimistic. "Fire very quiet today," he wrote on July 31, and on August 1, "Fire really looked inactive today."

Each time Gum flew it, he reported what the fire was doing by radio, adding, "just like I said it would." "Just like I said it would" became a stock joke around the smokejumper base and among Gum's growing number of critics within the FS.

Gum's subordinate at the smokejumper base, Bill Moody, was a veteran with 499 jumps to his credit. Moody started when he was seventeen, and now managed the oldest jumper base in the United States. He opposed the original confinement decision on grounds that the fire did not really meet the confinement fire screening criteria he had helped Gum develop, because of something called the severity index, a measure of rainfall.

"The *Appropriate Suppression Response Implementation Plan* was based on the probability that an event will happen, given certain parameters," Moody told me. We were sitting in his office with a view of smoke still rising from the Hubbard Fire. "In this case total accumulative rainfall, by month, is used to predict future fire season severity."

The severity index did not include winter precipitation, which had been unusually light. "If those figures had been included in the equation, the Hubbard Fire would not have met the confinement criteria. My gut feeling was that this wasn't a normal year, that we couldn't count on nature to bail us out."

The confinement strategy decision, once made, was not officially open to debate. "We've got people," said Gum, in his own defense, "who have spent twenty-five years being paid and rewarded—all positive strokes—for immediately controlling all fires. They say, 'Why the hell are we doing this?' It's like going up to them and saying, 'The sun rises in the west.'"

On August 3, the fourteenth day of the Hubbard Fire, Gum wrote, "Flew the fire today and it really looked cool."

That night the wind came up. The following afternoon a new column of black smoke rose from the wilderness, and on August 5 Gum saw from the air the beginning of the end of confinement. "Fire is burning the slope below Milton Mountain," he dutifully wrote. "Good threat the fire might cross. . . . Will need to review the necessity of possible containment."

The forest supervisor, still acting on Gum's advice, put off the decision another day. By then the fire had crossed the ridge, exceeding the confinement fire screening criteria. The implementation plan stated that such a development was undesirable, as if that wasn't already obvious. Gum wrote, in what must have been a galling moment, "Dropping 6 SJ [smokejumpers] as monitoring team on Milton Mountain and to take containment action on spots."

Smokejumping is a dying profession, according to most experts on the subject, a vestigial link to the Forest Service's past. However, when the computers fail, the FS infantry—the hotshot crews—still climb out of trucks and choppers dressed in boots and helmets, wearing seventy-pound packs, and carrying water, a Pulaski (an implement named for a famous firefighter which is a combination ax and grub hoe), a shovel, a chain saw, and chaps, all for digging line in air as dense with smoke as with oxygen.

According to the master decision tree, the Hubbard confinement fire had become a de facto containment fire. "We decided to contain the northeast flank," Gum said, in retrospect, "knowing that all the Monday-morning quarterbacks would have a field day. That in a way was a gutsier decision than the original one."

Twenty-five smokejumpers went in, and two twenty-person fire crews. From the beginning the effort seemed jinxed. One jumper badly bruised his shoulder and back. Another broke an arm, dislocated a shoulder, and severed a radial nerve and had to be medivacked. A woman on the fire crew was hit by a falling snag, and another broke her ankle. The fire had consumed the two thousand acres Gum had predicted.

On August 9 the "long line," the 150-foot cable attached to the helicopter for lifting equipment and for bucket work, apparently became entangled in the rear rotor of the chopper. It crashed in a wooded canyon, killing the pilot.

"That took the wind out of us," Gum said.

The fire seemed finished at last, after burning for almost three weeks. Gum took two days off and worked in his orchard, aware that he was being criticized throughout his district. The wind began to gust out of the northwest, and on August 16 the fire blew up again. Four new crews were committed to the fire, and three choppers dumping retardant.

The next day the Hubbard Fire was declared contained once

more, although it was still officially a confinement fire that had cost a life, numerous other injuries, and from $300,000 to $1 million, depending upon whether the estimator was a confinement advocate or a Monday-morning quarterback.

Gum maintained a professional demeanor, but his entries were by now plaintively familiar. August 18: "Fire really looks good." August 19: "Continued mop up. . . . Fire showing very little smoke." August 20: "Fire really looks super cool today."

A "hot fire analysis" had been scheduled for key FS personnel, including the forest supervisor, Gum, the district ranger, the district fire manager, the jump base manager, the fire behavior officer, and the air attack boss. Gum would be in the hot seat during the analysis.

An internal meeting of all FS staffers was to follow, so the smokejumpers and anyone else could ask questions if they desired. In addition, the newspaper publisher had organized a meeting at the chamber of commerce in the town of Twisp. The word was, if you wanted government blood, go to that meeting.

None of these was as important, however, as the regional review organized in Portland. Every year the head office analyzed the expensive fires in the region—"broke down the big-dollar expenditures," as Gum put it—and the Hubbard Fire was a prime candidate because of cost and the death of the chopper pilot.

The Washington, D.C., office was likely to review it as well, on the basis of "process and procedure." None of the principals in the Hubbard Fire was willing to speculate about the professional consequences of what, a month before, had been a snag burning in a little-used wilderness in a remote part of the public forest.

I asked the forest supervisor if the fire could adversely affect Phil Gum's career. The supervisor said, "There was a time when losing a fire meant losing your career. I think the Forest Service has matured beyond that."

That evening I stopped by the Gum place. He was soaking boards in creosote, getting ready to build another shed in the orchard. Pennsylvania Dutch hex signs decorated his barn. Inside, it was as neat as his desk, with bundles of spreaders—wood used to keep the apple branches apart—stacked beneath tl e workbenches.

His wife, Audrey, picked a cantaloupe and handed it to me without ceremony, saying, "It's small. Seems this year nature's just against us. First it was the drought, then the wind."

"We underjudged it," Gum said. "But the original decision to make the Hubbard a confinement fire was the right one. It burned only a hundred and fifty acres beyond the barrier. I'd have to ground-truth it to get the actual acreage, but it's not really very much."

The next morning Gum and I drove to Twisp. He was to take the county commissioner up in the North Cascades Smoke-jumper Base helicopter to look at the fire's remains—a public relations gesture. The commissioner was waiting near the Bell Jetranger; he was a determined-looking fellow in bifocals and a baseball cap.

Gum helped him into a fireproof Mylar jumpsuit and fireproof gloves, and I put on the same gear. Once in the air, the helicopter tilted over the rugged terrain of the broad Wolf Creek drainage. We could see stumps still blazing, and the charred course of the fire. Gum explained how it had made its runs in Hubbard Creek, and why it had never represented a threat to the commissioner's constituents. Then the interlock sound system on the commissioner's headset malfunctioned, and he lost most of the explanation.

Gum just shook his head when he got back to the smoke-jumper base: one more snafu on a snake-bit fire.

Driving home, Gum instinctively checked the orchard to see if his sprinklers were running. "You know," he said, "a lot of people make a living on thirty-five acres of orchard." He might get a chance to try if his supervisor was wrong and the FS did blame Gum for the failure of confinement.

He let himself into the empty FS office and sat down at his desk, still wearing the garish yellow fireproof shirt. "It was an interesting fire," he said, "when you look at it. She'd lay down for a few days, then she'd run. She'd quiet down, wander around. Some places she'd burn hot, some places not at all. A lot of variety."

He picked up the Confinement Fire Summary and Decision Documentation Continuation Sheet and his ball-point pen. It was August 22, the thirty-third day of the fire.

"There's nothing to write," he said.

The wind came up over the weekend. When I left the next day, smoke was again rolling out of an area now well known as Hubbard Creek.

▪ 5 ▪

WEST OF THE Missouri River, in western Montana, lay blond fields full of wheat stubble. Huge rolled hay bales cast knife-edge shadows in the late afternoon, and irrigation ditches ran like lush green piping along the edges of parched rangeland. Beyond the browns and burnt sienna, buttes the size of counties hung isolated in the sky, against a backdrop of what I thought were thunderheads.

I continued westward for another hour, and they became mountains, devoid of sharp peaks and alpine detail, just massive escarpments along the horizon. There the Great Plains run slam up against the Rockies in a celebrated collision known as the Rocky Mountain Front. If you believe the hunters and the environmentalists, wildlife spills out of it and onto the flatland like progeny of the infinite Ark.

The town of Choteau lies in the Front's long rain shadow. Arriving there I found a plains settlement typified by concrete silos belonging to General Mills, a Sears outlet and one for State Farm Insurance, a beauty shop, two sporting goods stores, an American Legion post, and a solvent Roxy Theater. The public pool sat behind a fence made of wire on whitewashed posts, the sandlot full of bicycles. At five in the afternoon, when kids in wet bathing suits trailed towels through the streets, bound for supper, they were accompanied by the carillon bells of the Choteau Methodist Church.

I ate a breaded veal cutlet in the Log Cabin Drive-in, while people at the counter talked about the governor as if they knew him personally. Many of them did—one of the advantages of living in an underpopulated democracy.

Lately, a new component had been introduced into the political and imaginative life of the town: grizzlies. One had been sighted on the western outskirts the month before. Since then the banks of Spring Creek, a local trout stream reserved for kids, had been deserted. Wrecked beehives lay about the countryside, a sign of bear. A rancher had tied his goat to a post one night and returned the next morning to find the goat eaten and its head still tethered in the dust.

Reports of grizzlies on the flatlands had brought me to Choteau. I had been dealing with people supposedly in control of their pieces of the kingdom—a BLM ranger, an archaeologist, a firefighter—but here was an animal that lorded over the realm by virtue of strength and tenacity.

The Montana Department of Fish, Wildlife, and Parks had "handled" an unprecedented number of bears that year near Choteau—an indication of a healthy population looking for spring forage, and possibly for trouble. A MDFWP biologist in Helena had told me, "A certain aura builds up in people's minds about bears. A grizzly represents the pinnacle of so many things. The Indians had it in their religion as a symbol of power. The grizzly's the most challenging animal for the hunter to find and harvest. For the person who wants to experience wilderness, the grizzly is the best sighting. A lot of people lie awake at night, listening for griz."

Grizzlies are protected under the Endangered Species Act and so cannot be legally blown away, as has been done in the past. Ranchers who lose property or stock to grizzlies feel themselves hamstrung by a law giving rights to recalcitrant bears. One rancher near Choteau stood up at a meeting of the Environmental Committee on Public Works convened to look into the grizzly problem, and asked his senator, "How would you like it if the federal government allowed a burglar on your block to rob you of your paycheck every night?"

In campaigning for office, Choteau's mayor ran against grizzlies. Some Choteauans think grizzlies should be shot on sight when they leave the wilderness. Bears belong in the woods, although in fact grizzlies and other big game have ranged down out of the mountains for as long as anybody has taken notice of such things. The mountains run up into Canada and have remained a natural preserve.

Today what is called the Northern Continental Divide Ecosystem by the professionals contains the largest population of bighorn sheep in the country, as well as moose, elks, mountain goats, mountain lions, peregrine falcons, grizzlies, and black bears. That is due in part to the fact that the state of Montana had the good sense to create its own Sun River Game Preserve in 1913, and partly to the ruggedness of the country.

When game leaves the wilderness for the flatlands its mortality climbs steeply. In the 1940s ranchers advertised for machine-gunners to help push elk herds back into the mountains. The federal government had for many years been an extirpator of grizzlies, treating them as vermin. In the early years of the century there were grizzlies in Colorado, New Mexico, Utah, Arizona, California, and Oregon, as well as Montana; now they exist only in Yellowstone National Park, parts of the Cabinet and Yaak mountains, and the Northern Continental Divide Ecosystem. Homesteaders, and strychnine put into sheep and deer carcasses by herders and ranchers, almost annihilated the grizzly in the Dirty Thirties.

Later, Compound 1080, a virulent pesticide ostensibly used by stockmen against coyotes, ended up in many a grizzly maw. The government had done so much poisoning on its own over the years that statistics were impossible to extract from the agencies. Conservationists finally had 1080 banned in the early 1970s, and the government that had once killed bears was telling people to let them be.

The unspoken objection to grizzlies is that they cost ranchers and other landowners money in the form of royalties on oil and gas exploration. By law the habitat of endangered species has to be protected. That means closing some areas to seismic blasts and chopper flights needed for exploration. The presence of grizzlies means putting light brakes on the development of the Rocky Mountain Front.

*   *   *

In recent years the FS has metamorphosed from a conservation-ist enclave run by silviculturists to a developmental engine driven by road engineers. Since the Rocky Mountain Front offers no prime timber, the FS in Choteau depends upon oil and gas to justify its new pay scale. Most of the Front, including half the Bob Marshall Wilderness and all of the Scapegoat Wilder-ness, lies within the Lewis and Clark National Forest.

At the time of my visit the district office in Choteau had re-cently been upgraded—the GS ratings of employees raised—on the basis of the discovery of some oil and gas in the Lewis and Clark. Laws protecting grizzlies hampered an all-out assault on these resources. The Endangered Species Act required what was called sufficient mitigating measures to protect the habitat and prey base of threatened or endangered species, known in the environmental and forest management trade as T&Es. Biologi-cal evaluations had to be made to determine "may affect situa-tions"—how a project like seismic shooting could affect a T&E, for example—followed by consultations with the Montana De-partment of Fish, Wildlife, and Parks, which was responsible for animals roaming federal lands.

Then there were the environmental evaluations (EAs) and environmental impact studies (EISs) that required public hear-ings. The process could take years. Oil company executives were saying in private that the grizzly was a large pain in the ass; some FS personnel were saying in private that they hoped the last grizzly would choke to death on the last woodland caribou.

Something called the Interagency Grizzly Task Force had been established—a sufficient mitigating measure to protect the habitat and the revenue base of bureaucrats, although it did some good for grizzlies, too. The task force agreed on inter-agency guidelines to end seismic activity in grizzly habitat dur-ing mating season, and to designate helicopter corridors into the Front.

I went to see the district ranger, a career man named Lloyd Swanger who had lived in Choteau for years and was enthusias-tic about oil exploration. His people, he said, were busy with a habitat component mapping project from which they would con-struct a computerized "cumulative effects" model, i.e., a fast way of determining the theoretical effect of choppers, underground explosions, Caterpillar exhaust, and drill pad operation on grizzlies.

This was a joint effort with the BLM and MDFWP, and would include information about food sources, denning, and travel areas. "We'll be able to be right on top of this," Swanger said. "If a company wants to drill, we can run it through the cumulative effects model and let them know immediately if it's a go situation."

"I've heard that you allow helicopters and seismic crews into areas where they're not supposed to go."

"Guidelines are just that," said Swanger, who was unperturbed. "You can't violate them because they're not binding in the first place."

I drove up onto the hill behind town, to watch a storm roll in from the west. The country was powder dry; some of the farmers to the east had been pushed into Chapter Eleven by the worst drought in half a century. Now a mass of slate-colored cloud came straight out of the Front, with bright sunlight to the north and south and darkness behind. A lavender bruise extended downward—heavy showers blocking the view—and long, febrile streaks of lightning bounced off the range or leaped parallel to it, angling back into the sky. The storm was probably twenty miles across, cyclonic in shape, with wispy clouds at the periphery and a frightening concentration of power and moisture in the center.

The dry grass around me clattered in the breeze. Without rain to quench them, lightning fires would have risen all along the storm's path. The first drops were few but enormous, splattering on the windshield like broken eggs. Thunderous wind hit with hail behind it, bending the grass double and raising hell on the van until I thought the glass would break. What began as sightseeing became a rout; I fled downhill, watching lights come on all over town and big hailstones splash in the road like jumping trout. I stopped under a sycamore and, incredulous, looked back at blue sky stretching east, where parched farmland still lay under the sun's unblinkered eye.

Drought was one explanation for so many grizzlies on the

flatland that year. In swampy willow bottoms they found food that had disappeared higher up the water table. Another theory held that because grizzlies were more numerous, the young adults came down seeking uncontested territory. According to yet another theory, the bears had grown accustomed to living off human resources like cows and sheep and trained their young to do the same, and so perpetuated a strange and increasingly perilous cohabitation of man and grizzly.

The government agent dealing most closely with that cohabitation was a wildlife biologist who worked for the state, Keith Aune. I had telephoned his home several times, but he was always fifty miles out of town. I tried again from the John Henry, a bar that filled up with rain revelers. Aune's wife said her husband would be home late. It didn't matter when I called, she added; he never got to bed before midnight.

I went to see *Rambo* with half of Choteau, and when I came out the rain had stopped. On impulse I drove to Aune's house. A pickup sat out front and a light burned in the living room. Aune padded to the door in sock feet—habitual attire in country where wet and muddy boots stay on the porch. He was thirty years old but looked forty, with gray hairs amidst a darker mop, and bookish spectacles. He had been out on a stock kill and had not eaten yet. "In the bear business you never know when something's going to happen," he said. "Come on in."

The telephone rang. The ensuing conversation between Keith and a colleague with MDFWP made them sound like lawmen: "Seen any bears? . . . Number 326 came down to the crick to get a drink and went around our camp and kept heading east. I took a shot at him with some birdshot but it didn't do any good. . . . I think they were into chokecherry and got a chance to corner this little Holstein. I hope it's 326 and not 316. . . . I think he's gone, and not legally. I think there's foul play."

Grizzlies apparently had personalities, just like people. The bear 316 was no threat to people: more like a teenage vandal in the late blush of puberty. "It's rare for a bear to kill livestock," Aune said, hanging up. "No animal takes on a steer, and says, 'That was fun, I'm going to do it again.' But the old myths seem impossible to get around."

A Holstein calf had been killed the night before by a grizzly.

Keith had spent part of the day setting a snare to catch the bear, using rotten meat from road kills that he kept frozen in a walk-in refrigerator next to his house. His clothes smelled of road kill and his eyes were full of fatigue. "It's incredible what people are starting to believe," he said. "They think the bears are all drug-crazed. They're so paranoid they won't go jogging, when the possibility of conflict is extremely remote. Yet they'll drive when they're drinking, and let their kids drive ATVs when everybody knows they're death traps. There have been only fourteen deaths by bear this century. It's a psychological problem, really."

Bear management revolved around habitat zones, or "situations." Situation One was prime habitat, an area needed for the recovery of the grizzly, where bears were often seen. Situation Two was an area used occasionally, but not essential to the bear. Situation Three included FS campgrounds and other areas of relatively high human density. Situation Four meant suitable grizzly territory where there happened to be no grizzlies—most of the intermountain West. Situation Five meant no bears and no suitable habitat.

"We zone bears away from people," Keith said. "It's a gradient of acceptable social tolerance. Trouble is, the bears don't recognize the lines. Here it's socially intolerable for people to see bears, so we zone it Situation Five. By biological definition we could make it Situation One all the way from the Front to Choteau."

The telephone rang; he answered and exchanged a few words with his colleague. "There's a grizzly in the snare," he said. He then called his assistant in Choteau. "We have to get up at four o'clock again. . . . I hope it's not 316. . . . We'll need a scale, a weighing tarp, and some Rompun. Throw a pistol and a shotgun into the truck. The drug kit. A capture form. Anything else you see, throw it in."

The bear lay on its back amidst scattered branches, under a cottonwood tree in the middle of the pasture. I thought it was asleep, or dead, but as the pickup stopped it twisted its head to look at us, revealing the radio collar. It stretched out a hind leg bound by the steel cable. "It's 316 all right," Keith said. He and his straw-haired seasonal assistant, Bart, walked around to the back of the pickup to prep for the main event. They had both attended Montana State; they worked so closely that they shared the smells of rotted elk and deer carcasses.

It was a clear morning, but cool. The rancher in whose field the bear was trapped stayed in his pickup with his wife and two grown daughters. They watched Keith open the drug box and take out a syringe, and then they stepped tentatively to the ground and stood in a tight group. They were not hostile to 316 but neither did they consider him joyous proof of grizzly regeneration. They had lost a calf to the bear, and had their sleep disrupted. "I thought I wouldn't be bothered too much by the noise," the rancher said. "But when I heard that bellowing, the hair stood up on the back of my neck."

Keith said, "Most of the problems around here are connected to the murder of a mother grizzly with three yearlings. Now they wander around like abandoned teenagers, getting into trouble."

Bear 316 was one of the yearlings. He had been trapped and moved once already; if he returned to delinquency a third time, he would be killed. Now he watched us like a large, recalcitrant hound, aware that something unpleasant was about to happen. Keith put on rubber gloves, loaded a syringe with Rompun, a tranquilizer, and transferred it to the metal dart. He cleaned the tip with alcohol. Bart opened the breech of the .22 caliber dart gun loaded with a blank, and Keith slipped the dose inside.

Keith walked toward the cottonwood with the rifle. The bear rolled over onto his stomach and backed into the broken timber. Keith had tranquilized many bears; those determined to kill him threw their five hundred and six hundred pounds against the cable while he stood there with a pop gun. But 316 did not want a fight. The dart struck his radio collar and went off into the brush, which meant Keith had to go through the whole process again. He did so methodically. This time the dart struck home, and 316 clawed the cottonwood, sending bark flying, then subsided into an exhausted heap, his chin resting on a paw.

The eyes never closed, but his breath came in long, sonorous wheezes. Bart photographed him for the record; the rancher's wife, emboldened, took out her Instamatic. "People are fascinated by bears," Keith told me, laying out a tarp with heavy brass rings in the corners. "There's a big discrepancy between what they say and what they really feel. They say they hate bears, but they can't wait to stroke them and be photographed with them."

Bart had disengaged the steel cable from the hind leg of 316. Keith rapped the bear sharply across one shoulder with a stick, testing the drug's effect. Then everyone did in fact go forward to touch the broad, woolly head. The fur felt impermeable, the claws too long and graceful to survive the power that ordinarily drove them. On the black market the claws would bring a hundred dollars apiece, a complete grizzly rug, five thousand. The demand for griz parts was great enough for the feds to conduct sting operations aimed at poachers.

I was touching something out of my childhood: an outsized stuffed animal on a carnival shelf; a dream of warmth and ferocious friendship in a dark and distant wood. We lifted 316 onto the tarpaulin and hoisted the scale on a tree branch. He weighed 260 pounds, down 10 from the previous capture. "He doesn't look too good," Keith said.

"Poor baby," said the rancher's wife.

Keith squeezed salve into 316's eyes, to protect them from dirt and to blur his vision when he came awake, thus softening the shock. We hauled him toward the culvert trap, a huge piece of pipe on wheels, with grates at both ends, in which he would be towed ninety miles to the edge of the Bob Marshall Wilderness. After much heaving and pushing, we got the bear loaded, and Keith rolled up a gunnysack for 316's pillow.

The rancher said, "I think bears have a place up in the back country, but this is too damn close."

He offered coffee, the social glue of the West, and we hauled 316 back toward Choteau. "We don't want to run out of gas with a grizzly," Keith said. "Nobody would pick us up."

" 'Specially when we smell so bad," said Bart.

They laughed with the abandon of exhausted men. We stopped at a gas station, and a dozen people gathered around the culvert trap. "Somebody ought to do a behavioral study," said Keith. "If I could spend half an hour with each one of those people I could do a lot to straighten things out."

The median habitat on the Front supposedly could support only one bear for every 16 square miles. He estimated the total at one hundred bears on 180,000 acres, around 280 square miles, and about 15 percent of those had been marked or collared. "People just don't understand that a bear reported in different places is often the same bear. They look at you like you're crazy. Then the finger comes up, and they say, 'I've been in this country for forty years, and I can tell you . . .' "

The game warden arrived. He got out of his wagon, his gun belt creaking, and knelt beside 316. "You dumb son of a bitch," he said.

We drove on to Choteau. "They're just great animals," Keith said. "Sometimes when I'm working alone, putting on a collar or an ear tag, I look up and see a jet headed for Seattle, full of vacationers or people going to see their relatives, and I think, 'There's a whole load of folks up there who don't know I've got a grizzly in my hands.' "

An entirely different sort of grizzly expert lived on the other side of the Rocky Mountain Front. He wintered in Tucson and spent summers up against the Canadian border, spotting fires for the Park Service and tracking grizzlies and photographing them for no particular reason. He liked fine cooking, or so the stories went, and was a fair cook himself. He liked to drink, and had lost the hearing in one ear in a barroom brawl. His nickname was Arapaho, although no one seemed to know why. He was the inspiration behind a major character in Edward Abbey's *The Monkey Wrench Gang*, a man of large appetites named Hayduke.

Twice in different parts of the West I had seen bumper stickers that said "Hayduke Lives." I knew it was true, but finding him was another matter. The telephone numbers I had been given rang funny bells in cabins and throbbing taverns set up on those slivers of mountain fastness between larger chunks of public land. People had seen him here and there, always bound for somewhere else, wife and children in tow. He was in the area, they said; it was the best they could do.

In truth, I didn't want to find him. His real name was Doug Peacock and the area was Glacier National Park and the Flathead National Forest—prime grizzly habitat. To find Doug Peacock was to risk going into the woods with him. For ten years he had studied and then photographed grizzlies with varying degrees of intimacy. He knew where they swarmed in season, and had collected grizzly footage unlike any other. The seral scrub fields were utterly neglected by hikers, and by Forest Service rangers. Peacock had been relieved of his fire-spotting duties because he criticized their handling of grizzlies. The officials didn't want Peacock at large in their woods, which already had a bad name because of human death by bears.

"I give Peacock more space than my 'learned' colleagues," said a wildlife biologist working for Montana Fish, Wildlife, and Parks a month before. "He's an old-style naturalist and may be the best source on grizzly behavior. It doesn't take a lot to determine what's in bear shit, but Peacock approaches the question with a philosophical as well as a biological concern. I wish I had his passion."

Peacock had last been sighted in Polebridge, a tiny community up the North Fork of the Flathead River, thirteen miles of serious washboard culminating in a scattering of cabins, the Northern Lights saloon, and a general store with a barrel nailed to the wall containing a telephone. Polebridge conveyed the gentle shock of recognition—a reliquary of imagined Western virtues in a charmed state. The Coca-Cola sign on the roof bore an ancient patina of rust, and facsimiles of old Burma-Shave signs beside the dirt road read, "Inconsiderate . . . sons of bitches . . . throw their beer cans . . . in the ditches."

Pickups eased onto the grass here so as not to raise too much dust, and men drank at the tiny bar and looked out the window through the fine Montana weather at snow hanging on the escarpment of Starvation Peak. The whiskery bartender had heard that Doug Peacock was in Missoula, attending a convention of grizzly experts, information that secretly pleased me: no one could blame me for eating the Northern Lights' taco salad and moving on, without having to go looking for bears.

The convention was sponsored by something called the Great

Bear Foundation. Grizzlies have become the seminal environmental issue in the mountain West, and a symbol of the last truly wild and unmanageable aspect of primeval America. People tend to locate themselves among the political megafauna by their attitudes toward grizzlies. Grizzly habitat also supports woodland caribou and wolves, but big bears cut across every environmental issue, and so it was little wonder that a bear convention had filled up Missoula's Village Red Lion Inn. I telephoned there, and to my surprise soon had Peacock on the line. "I'll ask you to cover your pack if it's a bright color," he said huskily, with a slight stammer, "and to wear camouflage clothes. Sometimes they fly that area in a helicopter."

He and a friend had a trip planned and they didn't want to be spotted by the FS—Peacock's avowed enemies. They would camp in dense bottomland forest less than a football field away from a major grizzly highway, and spend the days photographing. "I don't know how dangerous it is," he added.

He made his living photographing and writing about grizzlies; only three times in his life had he grossed as much as four thousand dollars. Occasionally he hired himself out to television crews needing grizzlies in their telephotos, but mostly he wandered unassigned in the best and really the only unspoiled grizzly habitat in the Lower Forty-eight. "I had to borrow a grand to get up here from Tucson," he said. "We call it migratory poverty."

Grizzlies were a disturbing phenomenon to contemplate. The stories of deaths, maulings, and lesser grizzly misbehavior carried mythic overtones, which did not keep 2 million visitors a year from coming to Glacier National Park. In the last decade or so, well over a hundred people had had their gear damaged by bears. One notorious grizzly ransacked cabins up and down the North Fork valley and even broke into a U-Haul trailer before he was finally shot. Twenty people had been injured by bears in the same time period, and four killed. One killing had involved a man named Laurence Gordon, who hiked to Elizabeth Lake with several religious books in his pack. A bear ate most of him, and left tooth marks on one of his scriptural texts.

We were to meet at a cabin set among lodgepole pine, in

grazed-over meadow. I got there early and to pass time assembled my fly rod and struck a half-mile through the woods to the North Fork of the Flathead. A semblance of civilization lay just upstream, but the water had that deep green, uncluttered power of wild rivers anywhere. A downed fir took me across to a rocky spit in the middle; I waded in jogging shoes, pushing an old Cahill toward the far bank, hoping a trout would rise. I switched to a wet fly, but it was a difficult stretch to fish in the best of moods. The water ran fast and clear, with dense forest on the far side. I lashed the water. It was not the streaks of cloud across the sun that distracted me, but the prospect of encountering bears the next day in Peacock's company. Finally I put the rod down and took off my clothes and got into the river, which seemed to help.

Peacock arrived in late afternoon, in a small car packed with disposable diapers. His wife, Lisa, drove their two small children like turkeys toward the outdoor privy. Peacock reminded me of an aging tackle at summer football camp; he was wearing shorts and boots and had legs like hairy telephone poles, a slab of chest, a grizzled black beard. He shook my hand and began doing back exercises to relieve the pain from an injury picked up in one of a variety of violent encounters. "A goddamn front's coming in," he said, looking west.

Another car arrived, driven by his friend and photographic assistant, Dan Sullivan. He also had a black beard, and considerably more hair on top. Sullivan lived outside Chicago and owned part of a company that cleaned up toxic waste sites.

We set our packs up under the pines and spread gear on the grass: sleeping bags, sweaters, film in plastic canisters, two camera bodies, a telephoto lens the size of a small cannon, lots of garbage bags. "I don't know how Lewis and Clark did it without garbage bags," Peacock said.

He held up a Bic lighter. It was to be used in case grizzlies came marauding, to light a stash of kindling kept dry at all times in one of the garbage bags, close to a can of lighter fluid. "One night I listened to bears walking around all night, before a sow and her cubs got real close. It was my first time to use fire as a deterrent, and all I had brought was a *Newsweek.* It didn't burn worth a shit."

We would take along only granola bars and homemade trail mix, which had no scent. We would eat huckleberries, bear fare and a good source of sugar and vitamins. If you ate what the bear ate, so the theory went, you might smell a bit less human. Peacock had occasionally conducted sweats to purge himself of human odors, and stored his clothes in bags with dirt and leaves before putting them on, but there was no time for that now.

"It's a calculated risk," Dan said, carefully wrapping the telephoto in a sweater and the sweater in a garbage bag.

Peacock scratched a biceps when he talked, or beat himself around the shoulders with sticks, blinking furiously. There was something ursine about him. "Grizzlies should be listed as endangered," he said. "Poaching takes a lot of bears, and managing them. They die after being tranquilized, and while being moved. But if the managers stopped, people would be put out of work. We have a bureaucrat for every bear out there."

He blinked some more. "What it does, really, is create more specialists to study what's already been studied." Bear counts, he said, were highly extrapolative; no one really knew how many bears there were in the Glacier-Flathead complex, or in Peacock's chosen spot. "We might well not see a grizzly."

He opened a canteen full of Wild Turkey. "Everyone to his own narcotic. Mine happens to be alcohol."

Dan said, "You wacko 'Nam vet."

It had the ring of something private and long-lived. Peacock had studied Vietnamese in Hawaii before they met, and ended up a medic in the Fifth Special Forces, running a military hospital near Mylai. He was captured by the North Vietnamese but wouldn't bear much questioning about that experience. They released him, he said, because he ate too much.

Lisa assembled chili on the butane stove, unconcerned about the next day's mission. "I don't worry about him up there," she said. "He's at his best then. I worry about him in the bars."

She set a chunk of cheddar on a stump and we cut hunks of it with my Buck knife. The question of tents arose, and whether I should sleep alone in mine. "Can three people fit into our North Face?" Peacock asked, and when Lisa said yes I wanted to hug her.

Her husband owned a .44 magnum, bought from a friend who

acquired it from a Blackfoot; Peacock suspected that the pistol had quite a provenance. He didn't carry it when he was working, and he didn't allow those traveling with him to arm themselves. The presence of a gun changed the relationship between people and bears, he said, and offered false assurance. For months I had been surrounded by guns and now when I wanted one, they were disallowed.

We ate supper from paper plates.

"Why do you like bears so much?" I asked, hoping for some reassurance.

"They don't reduce to the idea that we have a dominion," Peacock said. "They're old-time outlaws and sons of bitches. They can kill and eat you. It's a contradiction to say we can manage such a critter. We should just back off, but we've never been able to do that—it's part of our Manifest Destiny not to."

And then, "Bears represent a domain where man isn't king, a magic place—our last chance to take a walk in the big woods."

That night I woke up to the howling of coyotes, an ethereal yapping that echoed through the valley of the North Fork. It made me shiver but also thrilled me. I was afraid of morning but at the same time driven toward it, and was up at dawn, lacing my boots. A light came on in the cabin, and soon we were tossing packs into the back of a pickup. Lisa and the kids would travel with us to the jump-off point, and she would drive the truck back.

The four adults piled into the front seat, our laps full of cameras, sweaters, and children wrapped in blankets. The little girl threw up after a few minutes of the washboard road, eliciting from her father a profane condemnation of microorganisms in the drinking water. Lisa took care of it, commenting on the beauty of morning sun on mountains knitted in granite, heavily firred, with elephantine rocks amidst the greenery. The Bob Marshall lay miles to the south and east, beyond the stately, cerulean cadence of the Flathead River, and beyond that the Rocky Mountain Front—one enormous conduit for things wild, and imagined.

A few miles away lay the Great Western, the ag center, the

acupuncturist's, Montana Earth Pottery, Retiro Cabins, and the used car lots of Kalispell—what Peacock called Cowsmell, in another century.

On a deserted road on the valley floor, Peacock pulled over and he, Dan Sullivan, and I bailed out like a helitack team and hauled our packs from the truck. As Lisa drove off, we scrambled through scrub aspen and into the woods by way of an abandoned trail, careful to stay out of sight of a passing car that might contain a government ranger.

Within half a mile we came upon dry grizzly scat, crumbling and full of hawthorn berries. We crossed a terrace of ferns and, traveling in single file, entered a stand of huge climax larches. Thorny devil's club raked our packs, but otherwise we moved silently. More scat, very fresh, lay like a loaf of black braided bread in the middle of the trail. Anything capable of such a spectacular dump deserved respect. Peacock picked up some, examined and sniffed it, the naturalist in search of components. He passed the specimen along; it smelled like smokeless tobacco to me.

Glacier grizzlies were smaller than those in Yellowstone but could still weigh close to six hundred pounds. This one had left a print in the bed of the stream where we filled the canteens; it was a broad dish with the crown of claw marks that distinguishes grizzly tracks from those of the black bear, as if there could have been any doubt left by the size of the print.

After an hour we emerged into sunlight, facing a mountainside covered with ruddy shrubs. "Huckleberries," Peacock said. "The leaves have already turned."

We stashed the tent and sleeping gear in a side valley and bushwhacked up near-vertical slopes thick with the huckleberry bushes. Within minutes our shirts were soaked with sweat. Peacock stopped to wring out his camouflage bandana and picked some berries—fat, glossy nubs of flavor better than anything I had experienced from a supermarket. Centuries of cross-hybridization had produced hues from black to crimson, tastes from tart to sweet. The bears gorged on the berries in season, sweeping the mountainsides until the first frost killed the fruit.

The huckleberries thinned out as we climbed. Fewer shrubs

and more sunlight meant even lusher crops, however, skirted by elk and deer trails converging at the ridge's rocky spine. Scrub fir afforded some cover. A towering snag leaned out starkly against the gathering cirrus, and behind us the mountains reared like upended funnels, snow tight in the crevices. Heavy timber lay below, on both sides of a ridge, in landlocked valleys.

Nothing moved among the deadfall or around the muddy melt ponds in the valleys' end zones. We took off the packs and covered the brightly colored cloth with garbage bags. Peacock unlimbered his tripod. From the stand of larch directly below came the staccato call of a shafted flicker. "Something's bothered it," he said, maneuvering his good ear in that direction. "I can hear them breathing."

Bears slept a lot, lying on what he called day beds, a ludicrous description when applied to anything as large as a grizzly. It was not a good idea to disturb one on a day bed, but then it was a worse idea to disturb one feeding or drinking or caring for its young. "I think it's a sow with cubs. Sometimes the cubs get up and want to play, like kids, and she has to slap 'em down."

Powerful inferences, I thought, from nothing more than a bird call in a shadowy clump of trees. I sat on a rock, my shirt gone clammy in the wind. Dan knelt beside me, a pair of heavy tank-spotting binoculars dangling from his neck. He pointed to the slope opposite and said softly, "Look, there's a grizzly bear."

At first I couldn't see it. Then a small piece of the mountain lurched, and amidst the huckleberry bushes honey-colored haunches took shape, then the hump between the shoulders that makes grizzlies so different from other bears: muscle that drives the powerful forelegs. The bushes shook as if in an earthquake. The bear turned and gazed speculatively down toward the pond. It resembled several animals in one skin, each doing its job while the whole supple contraption loped downhill, the contrasting gold hair and black undercoat adding to its fluidity. It stopped at the water's edge and stared vaguely in our direction. A grizzly's eyesight doesn't amount to much if you compare it with the extreme acuity of its ears and nose.

I could feel the cold wind on my damp shirt. Peacock had the bear in his telescopic lens and began to pump the shutter. We stood two hundred yards above the bear but he heard the clicking. He could have reached us in half a minute but wheeled and lumbered into the larches, out of sight, breaking large limbs along the way. Miraculously, a smaller grizzly ran out the other side of the woods, frightened by the bear we had frightened. "They're constantly displacing each other," Peacock said, "like a game of billiards."

I could hear them breathing now. "They're more wary than I expected. Must be a big son of a bitch around here somewhere."

Dan pointed again. "There's a grizzly bear," he repeated.

This one was hugely black, and untouched by fickle breezes that had taken our spoor into the valley. Peacock needed something more than photographs of bear asses to sell, and this one was not cooperating. He and Sullivan watched it with hands on hips. They had worked together for eight years, the master and the willing disciple. It seemed a curious relationship based on little money and much trouble, not to mention risk. Peacock had seen his first grizzly in the Brooks Range, in Alaska, while on a University of Michigan field trip as a major in natural sciences, but that experience didn't take. Then he saw another one in a meadow in Yellowstone and never got over it.

I pulled on a wool shirt and crawled over the ridge, to check the other basin. A bear stood directly below me, on the shore of the melt pond, white in the sun. Lewis and Clark had encountered many blond grizzlies and had given their reputed whiteness worldwide notoriety. Aldo Leopold wrote a century and a half later, "Each generation in turn will ask: where is the big white bear? It will be a sorry answer to say he went under while conservationists weren't looking."

This bear waded into the shallow water and lolled on an elbow. I motioned to Dan, and he and Peacock scrambled over and set up the tripod among scrub pines.

"I think that's Happy Bear," Peacock said, grunting as he wielded the big lens. He had names for a few regulars. This one concentrated on swirls of mud rising from the bottom of the pond, pawing with curled claws, motions of great delicacy.

Happy Bear pushed his nose under the surface and came up with a tree in his teeth, twelve feet long and water-logged, held by one end in apparently effortless perusal.

Bears are built like medieval catapults, all internal straps and pulleys. The sloped shoulders and oracular head conceal more force than would seem necessary for the needs of an omnivore that often grazes like a cow. Bearbaiters in New Spain had turned wild steers loose on chained grizzlies that broke half a dozen bovine necks before a horn found home. Grizzlies were as unpredictable as they were versatile and preferred corms, sedges, and berries to red meat; but they were prepared to move boulders just to get at a chipmunk.

Trees as an escape route were not recommended by Peacock. Bears could cover a hundred yards faster than a linebacker for the NFL, he said, and pull you down again. His favored defense was talking to bears, and moving his head from side to side—peaceable ursine body language. "It's best to stand your ground and reason with them."

His dreams of bears were full of carnage and death, he said, which made the waking moments less fearful. "I don't plan to get mauled," he said, "but you never know." Dominant grizzlies chased and killed full-grown bull elk just for the hell of it, when there was abundant food elsewhere. They could be almost artful. The grizzly that ate Laurence Gordon, according to one writer, peeled Gordon's booted feet like bananas.

Wind tore at the pages of my notebook; Happy Bear seemed to hear it. He dropped the tree and ambled from the pond. He shook himself, a six-hundred-pound golden retriever, and climbed up onto a toppled Doug fir. He ran up and down the log with comic grace, rocking back and forth. He gazed in our direction, then turned his attention to huckleberries and fed slowly out of sight.

We sat down to eat trail mix. "This is a loveless place," Peacock said, "kind of ugly, with no macho peaks to climb. Fortunately, it's not everybody's idea of an alpine holiday. The fact that grizzlies use it shows how adaptable they are. They only come here in late summer and fall, and they'll go back up there"—he gestured toward the mountains to the northeast—

"and dig dens on north-facing slopes, to get the warmth of the snowpack."

He liked Glacier grizzlies because they had not been trapped and tinkered with like those in Yellowstone. "Benign neglect is best, but wildlife biology has become the new cottage industry. How often do you have to perform an experiment to learn the same thing? Biologists are intrigued by computers and technology, they prefer collaring and tracking with a helicopter to sitting on a ridge looking at bears."

The assertive, or dominant, bear—what Peacock called the old-time outlaw—was systematically being culled from the population. They tended to get into trouble and eventually found themselves at the wrong end of a .30/06. Managers favored the shy bear that avoided man, thereby contributing to the deprivation of the gene pool. When all grizzlies became shy, according to Peacock, they would be less than grizzlies.

He stretched out in the intermittent sun. Dan did the same. I was too exhilarated to sleep and began to browse on huckleberries, on my hands and knees, looking down into the east basin. Two elk cows had appeared in the lower valley, and a big buck mule deer lay in the shadow of mountain ash, uneasy amidst all that grizzly spoor. What had earlier appeared to be lifeless burned-over second-growth timber had come alive now that bears and men had taken to their day beds.

Peacock slept, murmuring, "Dance! . . . Dance! . . ."

A sow and a cub moved down the far slope, followed by a young adult. Peacock woke up to watch. "I think it's an atypical grouping," he said. "Sometimes young bears will hang around their mother when she has new cubs, and she'll tolerate them up to a point." He had seen as many as eleven bears at once in a basin. "I've seen them put on as much as hundred and fifty pounds in six weeks here, just on berries."

Berries had stained our hands and mouths purple; drops of huckleberry juice punctuated our shirts like bullet holes. "The most dangerous time is late September, when the berries fail. There's about a week of stress, when bears are competing, and changing territory, looking for new food. Two of the six deaths in this park have occurred then."

We were to sleep in the valley, which had more cover than the ridge. Of the seven grizzlies we had seen, five had gone off in the general direction of our camp. Bears migrating down from the higher ranges, where the huckleberries were less plentiful, also used that trail. We wanted to pitch the tent as far from it as possible. There was no reason the bears should get off the trail, Peacock said, sensing my reluctance to see the sun leave us. It was descending through broad banks of gray nimbus riding in from the west—heavy weather on the way.

We packed the cameras and trail mix and started down, leaving a full canteen so we would have to pack up less water the next day. A flock of buff-colored Canada jays drifted silently overhead. Where the trail dropped steeply we paused to watch another bear nosing about in ruddy shrubs on the far side of the drainage. That made eight.

The woods lay in shadow. We crossed the trail without encountering bears or bear sign, retrieved the tent we had stashed coming in, and moved on. Then we came upon a second bear highway.

"Shit," whispered Dan. We were running out of places to sleep.

"We don't have a lot of time to screw around," Peacock said. "It's getting dark. Go another fifty yards, and set up." Beyond that, another mountain rose.

He walked off alone, to fill the canteens. We were camping, I realized, in the midst of huckleberry bushes. Evergreens kept out the sun, so these didn't bear fruit. The thickly interwoven branches snared our legs, and Dan and I ripped them out by the roots and kicked up centuries of decayed deadfall to make an island amidst the hummocks. We worked quickly, with wonderfully concentrated minds.

"Sometimes bears just go crazy," Dan said. "Like people." In 1967, after fifty-seven years during which no one had been killed by bears in Glacier, two campers perished on the same night, in different campsites, in the grip of different grizzly bears.

Peacock returned with the water. We ate granola, then

wrapped it and the trail mix in a garbage bag and suspended it from a snag fifty yards from the tent. Peacock assigned me the task of kindling the fire, should we need one; he handed me the Bic. "Don't worry," he said, "you'll have plenty of time."

That was not reassuring. We blew up our mattresses and spread our sleeping bags inside the tent; I made sure I was between Dan and Peacock. Peacock had once taken Arnold Schwarzenegger into the woods to look at bears, for a television special. Dan did a good imitation of the muscle man in the wild. *"Peacoke, Peacoke,"* he whispered now, in an Austrian accent. *"Dese bears are hooge, Peacock! Dey gonna make me fweak out!"*

I lay there, exhausted, wishing we smelled a little less anthropoid, and that the walls of the tent were made of kryptonite.

Peacock yawned. "After a couple of weeks in here I'll be able to sleep through the elk and just wake up for the bears."

Impending rain seemed about to break over the night range, although no drops fell. I thought perversely of food—thick burgers, Pralines 'n' Cream. If a bear came, the fire—presuming I had time to light one—would simply put off the inevitable. I had heard stories of people hitting bears with packs and sticks and surviving; others played dead and in fact did not end up that way.

After an hour, Peacock said, "I'm going under now. Sleep light."

He snored softly, twice, before some self-regulating mechanism shut him down. A few minutes later he snored twice more and then lapsed into silence again. So it went. I imagined a bear approaching, parting the reinforced nylon with dextrous claws, and the heat of his huckleberry breath.

I dreamed I was riding a train across a strange and sullen landscape, telephone in hand, trying to make a reservation at a restaurant the name of which I had forgotten.

Silent dawn, and the smell of rain hanging above the forest like something thwarted. The other two slept on. Cautiously, I crawled out of the tent, laced my boots, and stood up under the still, green canopy. The absence of birdsong could not dampen the exaltation I felt at simply being alive and bathed in light, such as it was.

I navigated the surrounding shrubs, moving carefully down-breeze, until I reached the edge of the clearing. On the far side and a quarter of a mile up the slope, a grizzly took his breakfast with stately deliberation, a magnificent Rorschach blot on autumn reds and golds. Watching him, I felt a kind of postcoital sadness, as if I had outstripped imagination and was left with a large, primal force as mysterious as it had ever been. That raw piece of burned-over, undevelopable mountain where he browsed was his salvation, and maybe mine, too.

We saw four more grizzlies that day, in the east basin, too distant to be photographed. Our presence had roiled the air currents, sending them rippling like the water in a good fishing hole. Then the rain came suddenly in the late afternoon. Big drops rattled against the garbage bags and the hoods of our ponchos, making hearing difficult and rendering the descent from the ridge treacherous. On the trail beyond the stream we found grizzly tracks over our bootprints from the day before. "Let's make a little noise," Peacock said, his fierce bearded face running with water.

I whipped my poncho and drummed my Vibram soles on the springy earth, and a red-tailed hawk screamed at us from the larch tops.

At last I saw the road glistening through the gathering mist. We skidded down the hill, and Peacock scattered leaves over the asphalt—a signal to Lisa, who was scheduled to come looking for us. We hid our packs and set out toward town, soaked and cold. A valiant young couple in an old Volkswagen bus picked us up, and we listened to James Taylor over the knock of the engine.

In West Glacier we found a tavern where Peacock was known and the barmaid gave us free beer. I bought rounds of Stolichnaya—his favorite vodka—and we knocked them back. It was happening too quickly, something precious was slipping away: thirteen grizzlies in thirty-six hours, leaching into puddles about our boots.

Lisa arrived with incredible dispatch, hugged her husband,

and told him they had only a hundred dollars left in the bank, and the rent yet to pay. "Shit," he said, "down to the wire again."

She touched his cheek.

Holding a Stoly in one hand and a can of Rainier in the other, wearing a tattered green sweater and sopping cords, Peacock looked older than he had on the mountain, his thinning hair in disarray. Members of the Sierra Club were coming up to have Peacock show them grizzlies the following week. Then Peacock wanted to fish the Yellowstone with a friend. Then the friend and his friend wanted Peacock to show *them* grizzlies in Glacier. He belonged to a large informal net where one needed an independent income; Peacock had none.

We drove north through the dusk, the car full of groceries, children, camping gear, and anxiety. Somewhere north of the ranger station Dan put on the brakes and Peacock leaped out of the car. He ran through the woods, stooping and pulling things from the wet earth. The berries are failing, I thought.

"Chanterelles!"

He displayed a dozen in the lap of his poncho. "I'm going to make chanterelle soup!"

And he did, too, using powdered milk and loads of garlic, in the cabin on the North Fork. There we drank a bottle of Bordeaux I had carried for thousands of miles amidst clothes and gear, and then another. The kids hung happily on Peacock's legs, while Dan took turns tossing them into the air.

In the dry heat of blazing aspen logs, with four hard walls around me, I remembered a dark, majestic creature browsing contentedly on a mountainside.

· IV ·
VISIONS

Go west, young man, and grow up with the country." Horace Greeley first used those words in an editorial in the *New York Tribune*. Greeley, an idealist and the newspaper's editor, might seem an unlikely advocate of the limitless and the unsettled. Short, potbellied, bespectacled, he perfected that august institution, the editorial, and through it championed the landless, the Homestead acts, and a transcontinental railroad to carry resurgent humanity into the wilderness.

Greeley traveled west by stage before the Civil War and wrote about the trip in *An Overland Journey from New York to San Francisco*. He lost his trunk in the swollen Sweetwater River, and got sick drinking from it, without complaint. A town in Colorado was later named for him, a utopian endeavor that became just another metropolis.

The West has long been a resting place for notions of the perfect human community. But most experimental communities in "the West" failed: the Millerites in the upper Hudson Valley, Robert Owen's followers in New Harmony, Indiana, and disciples of Charles Fourier in the Midwest. Some French utopians ended up on the banks of the Red River, in Texas. The socialists didn't do any better. Theodore Hertska's colonies in Washington State failed, as did those in California's Sierra foothills. Joe Harriman's followers planted fruit trees in the Mojave Desert in the early years of the twentieth century, and succeeded for a time, in retreat from the press of urban existence then making itself felt throughout the country.

The communes of the 1960s—supposedly harbingers of a glorious return to the land and biocentric politics—proved dystopian. They left little more than abandoned geodesic domes in remote corners of the American West.

· · · · ·

▪ 1 ▪

NORTH of the San Juan Mountains, in southwest Colorado, the road snakes up along the Dolores River and then the South Fork of the San Miguel. The mountains roundabout stun with their depth and diversity: massive granite peaks, sawtooth ridges, cirques and cols and high, new-green meadows.

Telluride, up the valley, has a reputation as a soulful spa with the collective aim of not becoming another Aspen. The actuality rises out of a welter of new plywood and old clapboard, and an alpine traffic jam. A bluegrass festival was in progress the day I arrived. Amplified guitar and banjo bounced off as impressive a backdrop for a town as existed.

Telluride was a mining town before it became a resort, part of the San Juan Triangle, which also included Ouray and Silverton, silver and gold mining centers that burgeoned after the Civil War. Butch Cassidy reportedly robbed his first bank in Telluride. The Wobblies' push to unionize the mine was bloody and unsuccessful. The medley of gamblers, whores, and speculators characterizing any boom town had moved out before the 1920s, and now as I drove into Telluride giant sprinklers wetting down the bulldozed tailings were the only reminder of that lost bonanza.

Sturdy brick emporiums on Main Street had been repointed, and the Victorian houses on the hill were trimmed in pastels. Still, the town reflected the seediness of its origins—structures thrown up a century ago, during the short span between spring and winter at nine thousand feet, and a current boom fueled by Easterners and other outsiders. An awesome winter landscape was easy enough to envision; the bones of developing ambition showed well enough with the snow gone.

Big Hondas and Harleys lined a full block of Main Street, and young men and women in shorts and declarative T-shirts walked up and down between the municipal park and the storefronts carrying beer and bedrolls. Umbrellas shaded the more affluent residents, whose dogs sat in parked Japanese pickups with bandanas around their necks.

I checked into the Best Western, for want of a camping space, and walked around town. The Sheridan Hotel and the opera house resonated with vague Western reminiscence, stately piles of decorum in the storm of Telluride's tumultuous history. The town was called Columbia until 1887. No one I spoke to knew what Telluride meant, just that it resembled the name of an ore, tellurium, found in a few mountain crevices. By the time tellurium was discovered, Telluride already had a couple of gold and silver mills and a newspaper and a bank. The hotel and the opera house came later, but no matter. The Rio Grande Southern Railroad arrived in 1890, a boon that pushed the number of souls to five thousand, including two hundred whores with names like Diamond Tooth Leona, twenty-six brothels, and as many bars.

The collapse of the metal markets in the twenties turned Telluride to the manufacture of whiskey, with the raw materials brought in by railroad. Prohibition shut down that industry. The town limped along, feeding sporadically off the mines, until the bounty of deep powder was discovered by skiers around 1970.

Telluride was for all practical purposes a company town, with TellCo being the company. In the dark days a few skiers had been hauled up the mountain in a Sno-Cat, but there was no money to build lifts and runs. Then a southern California investor named Joe Zoline came to town because of a tip he had picked up on an airplane. Deep in the mountains of southwest Colorado, the story went, existed a town of spectacular beauty and impoverishment, surrounded by Forest Service mountains aching to be developed.

Zoline bought some property snuggled up against FS land,

then took FS officials up the mountain to view the part of the forest that Zoline wanted to carve up. Early development brought in freaky hot-doggers who could rampage in bottomless powder for very little money; après-ski included Acapulco Gold and some stronger chemical substances. Visitors from far away had to fly over the Continental Divide from Denver to Montrose in a commuter plane known as the Vomit Comet, and then thread narrow, icy roads. But once they got there, Telluride was cheap, beautiful, and turned-on, and provided just enough amenities for good countercultural R and R. The hippies who stayed all turned into capitalists.

There were about fourteen hundred people living in Telluride. From the onset of development, Telluridians cited Aspen as an example of what their town should not become—overdone, precious, expensive, foreign. One doesn't hear much about that nowadays. Eighteen million dollars have been invested in the ski operation and a new development including restaurants, condos, and a subdivision with one-acre lots called "ski ranches" starting at $160,000.

The previous winter, 150,000 skiers had come to Telluride. An airport is going in at Deep Creek Mesa, just down the road, which would boost the occupancy figures exponentially. Tourists already pay a dollar for a tiny cup of frozen yogurt on Main Street, two dollars for a long-necked Coors, and seventy dollars for a motel room—steep rates in the West.

All that prosperity is directly attributable to the Uncompahgre National Forest. The FS has been the most understanding of landlords, allowing the company that became TellCo to develop public land without paying the government anything until profits started to roll in. An FS computer assists ski operators in the West in designing runs and lifts, all in the interest of recreation, although the economic spinoffs are enormous.

I visited TellCo headquarters in an old pharmaceutical building on Main Street, renovated at great cost. The sign outside said, "Drugs." A cunning interior decorator had left many of the old apothecary utensils in place. The receptionist came out from behind the soda fountain and took me upstairs to meet one of the corporate officers, Brian Rapp, a Yale graduate and former

White House executive fellow who had worked as city manager of Flint, Michigan.

Rapp had a red beard and an easeful air of command. Khaki shorts were unusual executive garb even in the West, part of a bicoastal image that includes a Ralph Lauren polo shirt, discreet Navajo bracelets, and frequent references to Washington, D.C., and southern California.

"I came here because this is a soulful place," he said. "I had been thinking a lot about how resorts are changing. If done right, Telluride could be one of the best resorts in the world, like Saint-Moritz, Zermatt, Sun Valley, and Aspen. I wanted to implement something other than the single activity," the single activity being skiing.

Now the move was toward "significance," as well as fun. "If you go back to the Greeks . . . a spa was a place where people went to be renewed. It wasn't just recreational, it was also cultural, spiritual, if you will. Now when you look at the cost of spending seven days at a resort, you want something more than skiing. On a given day in winter, sixty percent of the people are *not skiing*."

Telluride offered a "smorgasbord" of alternate activities, including the bluegrass festival, a mushroom festival, a film festival. Someone had come up with the notion of an ideas festival.

"The theme is 'Reinventing Work,' " he said, shaping the air with his hands. "It will add another dimension to the smorgasbord. People learn when they're relaxed—if we had people talking about interesting things all the time, that would set us apart from other resorts. Yes, I think a menu is the best metaphor. You might be able to go rafting on a Thursday, listen to a string quartet on Friday, and on Saturday learn about the geology of the San Juan Mountains."

I said, "It sounds a lot like Aspen."

"We're more . . . accessible. There are fourteen hundred very above average people who have found this valley."

History repeats itself, but often in odd ways. The West is full of examples of drifters who have made money with the cooperation of the federal government and wrecked the place in the process. I didn't mention it to Rapp, but I could imagine Telluride becoming a ghost town again, down the road. Foreign oil embargoes could well make travel too expensive for even well-heeled hot-doggers and ski ranchers. A more likely cause would be competition—the overproduction of ski resorts—or the simple fact that people would go elsewhere because they grew sick of the developmental foreground in Telluride's view.

Meanwhile, there was always money to be made. The daughter of Joe Zoline, the original developer, lived in Telluride. Her name was Pamela Lifton Zoline, and I was told she had created an artistic salon, and that her husband was writing an opera about Houdini. She wore knee socks and a straw hat when we met—the picture of rural ease. Her husband, she said, was English. "We go back and forth rather a lot. I live here because Telluride's a place of great beauty, and power. I don't want to see happen to it what's happened elsewhere on the West Slope."

That was not preventing her and her husband from developing West Meadows. "Some of it may not seem appropriate in a mountain setting," she said, "but people in the future won't identify with teleported European villages. We want to position our development appropriately vis-à-vis the information revolution. Telluride is really going to be one of the first places for information revolution people to live."

Telluride would appeal to very above average information revolution people who occasionally skiied but were also interested in what Zoline called "an edible landscape—a mountain garden that will eventually include sculpture and a formal element."

The town of Ouray, only eight air miles over the mountains from Telluride, was sixty miles distant by looping road, and about half a century away in social development. Incorporated in 1876, a few years before Telluride, Ouray fed off the same veins of ore, and shared a colorful and cyclic history, though one without Telluride's glitter. Theoretically it was possible to walk through the mountain between the towns, if one knew the maze of deserted shafts and sealed tunnels. Ouray was set in a valley narrower than Telluride's, and slightly less spectacular—a quibble—but its population had remained roughly equal to Telluride's in the early sixties.

Ouray was proud to be a teleported European village, calling itself the Switzerland of America. The mountains seemed smaller—a diorama of the unscalable, with plenty of metamorphic geology. The steep, sunlit main street had an Alpine Café, an Alpine Motel, and Alpenhair for unisex cuts; the hot springs on the edge of town served as community swimming pool, full of local kids and tourists from Texas to California.

I found a copy of *Mountain Mysteries* in a shop. According to the book, "Ouray" was the first word out of the mouth of the child who became the Ute chief, and had no meaning. One of the authors, a retired contractor and aspiring journalist named Marvin Gregory, lived in Ouray. "The difference between us and Telluride," Gregory said when I visited him, "is skiing. We don't have it, or the kind of people who hang around skiing. People come to Ouray because there *isn't* any skiing. Instead they hike, jeep, take photographs, sit in the hot water, or do nothing at all. Mostly that."

I had a Coke in the Apteka Pharmacy down the street. It was crowded with sundries in gentle disarray, and original wire-backed chairs and marble-top tables. The only other customer was a divorcée from Houston. She had left her husband of fourteen years to live in Ouray after coming there for a winter holiday. "I couldn't stand Houston any longer," she said. "I wanted a place with a soul, where we wouldn't get lost in the shuffle. My kids have the run of the town, I don't worry about them. We never lock our doors, and there are no drugs."

The winters were tough. She had worked as a short-order cook, a waitress, a maid. "People really have to scrape to get by. I like that." She lit a cigarette, staring out at the popcorn machine on the sidewalk. "I know you've heard it all before, but it's hard to find a place like this, that still has a soul."

The co-author of *Mountain Mysteries,* P. David Smith, had an office just up the street. He was a county judge and a real estate salesman, an unusual combination. "Ouray is a family town," he told me. "We don't like drugs, nightclubs, or single people living together."

Ourayans also disliked too much building, he said. "More than half the county is public land. We're dependent on it, and don't want to do anything to destroy the natural beauty." He paused. "Many people think we should be able to do what we want with the public land."

It happened that he represented a Houston developer with an eye on Ouray County. He handed me a color brochure for something called Enchanted Mesa Ranch. "Five hundred acres just north of here," he said. "A two-hundred-and-fifty-unit hotel, three hundred and ten condos on a hundred and thirty-five one-acre lots. It'll cost eighty to a hundred million to build." The zoning variance was already in the works. "There'll even be a golf course."

"What about skiing?" I asked.

"As a matter of fact, two potential ski areas have been iden-tified, just outside of town. But we're going to be careful. We don't want this to turn into another Telluride."

▪ 2 ▪

ECONOMIC DEVELOPMENT in the West, and the recognition that man's needs were altering what was out there, led to attempts by conservationists to declare some of the land inviolate. Early in the century, Aldo Leopold, who worked for the Forest Service, proposed that the headwaters of the Gila River, in southwest New Mexico, be administered as a primitive area. His superiors agreed, setting a precedent that eventually led to fierce legislative battles over wilderness.

Today the Gila Wilderness is contained in the national forest of the same name, in what was once Apacheria—wild and varied canyon country at the bottom of New Mexico, close to the Arizona line. Spring thunder shook the earth the night I arrived, over the blacktop leading from Mimbres to the south Gila trailheads. Stray cattle stared into the headlights with a stupid approximation of savagery, and lightning violently partitioned the sky.

The morning broke clear, with a warming sun. Mexico lay not too many miles to the south, and to the north rose the wall of the Mogollon Mountains. I spread my hiking equipment in the parking lot on the West Fork of the Gila, as did a couple from Los Angeles, their compact car full of dry desert flowers and bits of dead ocotillo. Preparations for backpacking always resemble the wreck of a small aircraft: scattered tents and sleeping bags, a pot and a stove, the litter of freeze-dried food in bright foil, progeny of the space program.

Gear has become a significant factor in contemporary nature appreciation; you are what you wear. I was an electric blue Kelty pack, badly scuffed; a Camp Seven down bag; a SierraWest Skylighter tent, lovely for stargazing and useless in a thunderstorm; a Permarest self-inflating (ha!) mattress; a Coleman one-burner stove, heavy and stinky but a blowtorch when you needed one; an L. L. Bean shirt; Hudson Bay Gore-Tex; Buck knife; Fabiano boots shedding their soles; and Mountain House lasagna.

We hikers were all after a "wilderness experience," as if it could be had like a dose of Benzedrine. Every time I swing into my pack I wonder why; fifty pounds of temporary furniture, and the prospect of ten thousand footsteps before I can stop and eat hydrated mush.

On that particular day, my first steps led directly into the river. I had to change to jogging shoes and lash my boots to my pack. The water was clear and very cold, forcing in the gut and leaving me pensive on the far bank. The pretty forest ranger in her drab green shirt had given me some advice with my wilderness permit, a contradiction in terms: there would be fordings. There would indeed. About twenty fordings, in fact, between that apron of civilization and the needled understory where I would finally collapse, just short of Hell's Hole.

The West Fork cut through canyons with sheer walls. Occasional sandstone hoodoos stood like wind-carved columns under the headlands, or isolated in bowls of fir and ponderosa pine. Plants and animals of seemingly exclusive domain flourished here in what was a kind of biotic Babel, including cacti and Engelmann spruce, yucca spikes and huge Douglas fir, and aspen. I had read that the Gila contained desert lizards and the banded rock rattlesnake, ospreys, golden eagles, and mountain lions, and endangered peregrine falcons and Gila trout.

Two white-tailed doe clattered up a scree slope off to the left, flashing their bar towels, not particularly concerned. Wolves had been their main predators before the wolves were wiped out. Aldo Leopold had himself shot a wolf close by, in the early years of the century. "I was young then," he wrote in the oft-quoted essay "Thinking like a Mountain," "and full of trigger-itch." He saw a green fire in the eyes of the wolf, or so he claimed. "I thought that because fewer wolves meant more deer, that no wolves would mean hunters' paradise. But after seeing the green fire die, I sensed that neither the wolf nor the mountain agreed with such a view."

His point was that the upset balance of nature would mean trees and shrubs grazed to the point of extinction, which is what happened. Leopold's writings, and those of John Muir, a founder of the Sierra Club, brim with suggestions of imparted natural wisdom, as if these men sucked some ineluctable knowledge from the earth both edifying and too mysterious to question.

The Gila National Forest contains some of the roughest country in America, more than 3 million acres of it, where fires spring with such regularity that a permanent fire-fighting force has been developed to deal with them. Stephen Pyne, writing of the Southwest in *Fire in America,* might have been describing the Gila: "Its fuel complexes range from desert to grassland to chaparral to pine and finally to taigalike tangles of spruce and fir. It harbors one of the heaviest concentrations of lightning fire in the world." Pyne makes a case for the Apache as an unwitting environmentalist who kept the southern grasslands from being overgrazed by preying on cattle. He cites Leopold's essay, adding, "The virtual extinction of the Apache had an effect similar to the eradication of the wolf. . . . What Leopold failed to realize . . . was that the problem involved an interaction among peoples, not merely between people and wildlife."

I didn't get back into my boots for five hours. During that time I took off my Levi's and hiked in my underwear; the day before it had been snowing. I put on wool socks that insulate even when wet, and cut a staff for purchase in rushing water. Suckers darted along the bottom and trout kept their counsel under overhanging ledges and in pools formed by drowned cottonwoods jammed in the riverbends. I was grateful for having left my fly rod behind: I was not obliged to catch a trout.

A green kingfisher scolded me, moving from snag to snag. A great blue heron rowed his way westward, neck folded like a jackknife. Coming out of the shadow of a sycamore, I jumped two turkeys. The enormous gobbler ran up the opposing bank like a fat old transvestite in a black Victorian gown, his beard flopping. The hen took off, beating air with broad wings toward a wooded ledge. At the last moment she flared and vaulted over.

I crossed and recrossed a horse trail, as much of a shock as the discovery of a Jeep track. I knew an outfitter who ran a string of twenty-four horses on the West Slope of the Colorado Rockies, taking hunters up through ponderosa and aspen to base camps. His were corporate customers he courted after watching a Louisiana oilman write out a single check for a party of hunters in his employ. They paid twenty-five hundred dollars apiece for at least the proximity of big game, and scenery as far from sales meetings and computer terminals as they could get. The outfitter's teeth were broken—the outcome of numerous fights—and the patches showed when he smiled. His eyes reacted painfully to too much sunlight because he had once fanned a .22 magnum slug into a pack rat's hole, where it struck a cache of dynamite and blew up his cabin, deafening him in one ear as well.

Outfitters' hoof-carved ruts lace the national forests; pack strings are the hallmark of high stands of ponderosa and Engelmann spruce. They share the trail with backpackers, an uneasy accommodation going back to the animosity between cowboy and sodbuster. The view from a saddle affects people in strange ways, bringing out fatal arrogance in some overweight men with guns strapped to their legs, their pack horses loaded with collapsible boats, electric motors, cases of beer, acres of plastic sheeting to protect themselves and their clients from the outdoors, and an occasional cast iron stove for baking biscuits and preparing Irish coffee. Some of that junk is left in the woods for unfortunate Forest Service volunteers to haul out, when the FS should hire gunslingers to go after the offenders.

I camped under an isolated sandstone pinnacle, a delicate variation on an Easter Island monolith, part way up the slope. Cold air would sneak along the river at night, and more cold air would sit like a cap on the canyon walls, trapping what warmth there was in between. Evergreens softened the view of red sandstone, and provided a backrest and a carpet better than the mattress. The sun drew from the pine needles an exotic fragrance that lingered after the sun was gone. Stellar's jays paused overhead to see what I might be eating, and painted redstarts flitted among the shrubs.

I had been reluctant to subject myself to backpacking's discomforts, but now the stove began to hiss and the water to boil, and a change occurred. It is a mistake to try to quantify, but something does transpire in one who makes the passage from pavement to leaf rot, a burgeoning sense of possibility being the most important. Public lands accommodate a lot of wish fulfillment. They derive from conquest, purchase, and the plain fact of occupancy. After independence, seven of the original states ceded surplus territory to the new federal government under the Articles of Confederation, as an equalizing measure and a means of raising revenue. This was the "public domain," frontier lands given in payment for military service and others sold in speculation, and states carved out of it entered the Union on an equal basis.

"Westward the star of empire takes its way," said John Quincy Adams at Plymouth Rock in 1802. The Louisiana Purchase, the Oregon Compromise, and a victorious war with Mexico added new possibility for the landless willing to risk; that daring, individuality, and optimism melded in a national character trait. The impulse still exists in the West, as I was learning, thanks largely to public lands. They have harbored certain quirky, unruly, even dangerous states of mind; they remain a large pocket of innocence that has been lost elsewhere, a focus of infinite variety, and finite means, full of contemporary refugees who are not much different from the first ones.

I had a paperback copy of Leopold's *Sand County Almanac*. In his essay "Wilderness," he described his subject as "the raw material out of which man has hammered the artifact called civilization." Wilderness should be preserved, he said, for those "who may one day wish to see, feel, or study the origins of their cultural inheritance."

I had brought along Leopold's writings but had forgotten my spoon. I carved one out of a willow bough; it was spongy in the middle so I ate wood with my lasagna, with satisfaction, watching violet-green swallows dip to the river. I pitched the tent and spread my artifacts as a barrier against the unknown—dry socks, poncho, flashlight, water bottle. There was not a grizzly within a thousand miles, but there was a large darkness coming on.

The sleeping bag decadently swallowed my exhausted self. A three-quarter moon appeared between the hoodoo and the mountain, reminding me of a parachute in a solar wind, or a luminous jellyfish drawn along by the dark tide.

I found the legacy of Leopold and Muir in the canyon country of southern Utah a month later, in June. Professional environmentalists were gathering in remote country to shape a debate on wilderness in our time. There was nothing special about it—the same sort of meeting occurs hundreds of times every year in various parts of the West—but in the process I hoped to learn something about their methods and motives.

I had been invited to attend by a stranger named Clive Kincaid, who was something of a legend among environmentalists in the East. Kincaid lived in a cave, I had been told, so great was his love of the land; he had been shot at by locals who wanted untrammeled development, and hung in effigy in a little town near his wilderness retreat.

From the southwest, the road to Bryce Canyon passes through the relatively lush valleys of Kanab Creek and the Sevier River, where green meadows run up against the base of sandstone cliffs, and ranch houses with neat picket fences are oddly out of scale with the surrounding country. John Wesley Powell called it the Plateau Province. "It is scenically the most spectacular and humanly the least usable of all our regions," wrote Wallace Stegner in *Beyond the Hundredth Meridian.* This arching shield of eroded rock and lava extends from the Grand Canyon to the Wasatch Range, most of it as daunting as it was in 1871, when Powell set out to map it.

A band of his men passed between Kaiparowits Plateau and the Sevier Plateau. They were looking for the Dirty Devil River but found another one entirely. They called it the Escalante, after the first white man known to have passed through. Today the town of Escalante ("Esca*lant*") has about seven hundred inhabitants and remains almost as isolated as it was then, surrounded by lofty forest, flaming rimrock, and canyons of "unmitigated stone"—some of the last country in the United States to feel the impact of tire treads.

I arrived at Deer Creek, on the Burr Trail, a dirt track passing through one of the wildest parts of the West. Kincaid had a cabin nearby, without electricity. He and others like him lived in a curious way at the behest of public lands, working to have them set aside in wilderness preserves. Within minutes Kincaid came rolling down Deer Creek, which he used as a driveway, water up to the axles of his dilapidated green pickup, in a fresh T-shirt admonishing all beholders: "Don't Waste Utah." He had studied anthropology at UCLA and had gone to work for the BLM before making a profession out of opposing it.

"You've come at a good moment," he said after we shook hands. He was to be the host at the environmental conclave the next day, with representatives coming in from as far away as Washington and San Francisco to thrash out strategy on the eve of the Utah Wilderness Review. Other lead players belonged either to the Wilderness Society or the Sierra Club—both among the largest environmental groups. Only the National Wildlife Federation and the Audubon Society exceeded them in numbers of members, and it was Wilderness and Sierra that often led the fights over wilderness.

Kincaid had founded his own, smaller organization, although he worked in concert with the others.

He had not been shot at, I discovered, but he had been threatened. One night in 1981 he walked out of the only and now defunct restaurant in Boulder, Utah, and found four flat tires on his pickup. He asked the driver of another truck in the lot if he had seen who had let the air out of his tires, and found himself looking into the barrel of a .357 magnum resting on the windowsill. The driver cocked the pistol, a simple metallic sound that stayed with Kincaid long after he walked back into the restaurant and called the sheriff.

Two weeks before that, Kincaid and two friends had been hung in effigy in Escalante. They had filed an appeal with the Forest Service to prevent the cutting of timber on Boulder Mountain, a standard procedure in most of the West, but not in the Plateau Province. A lot of people in Escalante worked for the sawmill. The operators had sent out notices with the Friday paychecks stating that a bunch of environmentalists were tampering with their livelihood, and young men had taken turns dragging the effigies up and down the main street behind their pickups.

Kincaid's organization, the Southern Utah Wilderness Alliance (SUWA), was a local group with ties to the national wilderness movement. He had been flown to Washington by the Wilderness Society to testify before Congress on the BLM's wilderness proposals. He had accused the BLM in Utah of slovenly and maybe fraudulent procedure that excluded prime areas from consideration. "Clive was the star," said a Wilderness Society representative at the time.

As a BLM employee in Phoenix ten years before, Kincaid had "inventoried" 6.5 million acres of potential wilderness. The Federal Land Policy and Management Act had just been passed by Congress, making the BLM responsible for the condition as well as the disposal of its lands, and the even distribution of them among many competing interests, including recreation and users of pure, unrepentant wilderness.

They were heady times. FLPMA brought in new blood and new programs; the BLM had officially come of age. Young careerists started to exercise their environmental sympathies, only to see the possibilities dwindle with the election of Ronald Reagan and the ascendancy of James Watt.

Some of the BLM resource people, like Kincaid, had left the agency and formed a government in exile. Reagan's reelection had put a crimp in the plans to recover power; the pendulum was bound to swing back again. Meanwhile, there was testimony to be given and lawsuits to be filed, all by people who knew one another, some on the payrolls of the environmental establishment, others, like Kincaid, free-lancing their knowledge and contacts and building up their own organizations like any entrepreneur.

Kincaid was eager to talk about his problems in Utah. "Robert Redford was hung in effigy in Kanab," he said, establishing that tradition during the fight over construction of a power generating complex on the Kaiparowits Plateau. "Backpackers' tires were slashed. For years the people around here have treated outsiders badly."

He was putting up, stone by stone, a dairy barn that he and a friend had bought in northern Utah and moved down by semi; and he was trying to put SUWA into the black.

Kincaid's vision for southern Utah, he once told a colleague, was to sit on top of the Aquarius Plateau at night and be unable to see a light in any direction.

Kincaid had a prospective donor in a Colorado rancher named Greg, who had also stopped by for the meeting. His green Opel was parked by Deer Creek, with a kayak paddle locked inside. We found the kayak leaning against the cabin and Greg waiting in canvas pants, fresh from a descent of the Colorado. He had short black hair and what I thought was a born-and-bred Western accent, but he came from Vermont, a product of the Putney School. At age thirty-two he owned two ranches in Colorado, one in Arizona's Coronado National Forest, some land near Escalante, and a lot of land near Phoenix, where he spent the winters working the telephones, selling real estate.

"I'm a go-getter," Greg said. "We've got to hash out this BLM wilderness acreage and write a bill."

Greg had gotten involved in the earlier fight over the Kaiparowits because the high-tension lines were supposed to pass close to one of his houses.

We loaded pots and pans into Kincaid's pickup and headed for the confluence of the Escalante River and Calf Creek, where the meeting was to take place. Greg put on a pair of sunglasses with rainbow-colored rims. He said, "I'm trying to get a balance here between development and preserving a way of life. I'm not a strict wilderness fanatic—I see it as a dollars-and-cents issue. I'm a business guy."

The house on the Escalante belonged to a cofounder of SUWA named Weed, a New Yorker who had come to southern Utah at Kincaid's suggestion and bought a five-acre in-holding surrounded by BLM land at the mouth of Phipps-Death Hollow. His land had a spring used by the Anasazi a thousand years before and petroglyphs on rocks behind the house—all for twenty thousand dollars. The well had been salted during the effigy-burning time, and a board full of nails buried in the sandy driveway had punctured the tires on his car.

That didn't prevent the house from filling up with environmentalists. The two Wilderness Society representatives wore khaki shorts and button-down collars. They had driven in that morning from Colorado. One, Mike Scott, had come all the way from Washington, D.C. The society concerns itself solely with public lands—BLM and FS lands, wildlife refuges, and national parks. It hires resource specialists and "issues people" away from the agencies to counter those same agencies' initiatives when it deems them harmful or unworthy. It makes decisions quickly, and depends upon large and small donations from almost 200,000 members. The Wilderness Society's board is self-perpetuating; the working members lobby effectively from spacious glass offices in downtown D.C. hung with original prints by Ansel Adams.

The Sierra Club members in Weed's house preferred sandals and didactic T-shirts. Their organization is looser and relies more on local chapters and volunteers. They seem to reflect Leopold's view that ecologically all things are linked. The Sierraites tend to argue from a holistic point of view: clean air and water, and even an absence of nuclear devices, are prerequisites of a sound environment. The Sierra Club's board is popularly elected by the membership; Sierra's scruffy Washington offices near Capitol Hill abound with people and hand-lettered signs, but the power lies on the West Coast.

A lanky, dark-haired woman named Maggie Fox said, "Let's put together an agenda. We should start with the cosmic issues—when do we want to release our wilderness proposal, and how many people want to get involved?"

In addition to Wilderness and Sierra there were other, smaller groups represented, some with overlapping affiliations. Greg and I were the only ones who didn't belong to something.

He plumped down in a dilapidated rocker and set it in motion.

The coalition wanted about 5 million acres in Utah put into wilderness, whereas the BLM had proposed only a million or so. Kincaid said the BLM had drawn straight boundary lines without regard for the beauty or remoteness of the country, in an attempt to exclude resources so they would be available for future development. Criticizing the BLM wasn't enough, however.

"We have to have *reasons* for our proposals," said Mike Scott, "so we can tell the press."

Maggie Fox agreed. "We have to order the universe for the public."

Ordering the universe took twenty minutes and consisted of dividing southern Utah into two parts: the Colorado Plateau and the Basin and Range, geologic divisions between canyonland and desert, red rock and sand.

"That's just going to confuse everybody," Greg said. "It should just be the Utah bill. Nobody outside this area knows what the Colorado Plateau is. And your support's gonna come from out there."

He had a point. Congress, not the people of Utah, would make the final decision on the state's wilderness. Utahans wanted to get at the resources and, through them, the jobs. Both senators favored development, so the coalition would have to go over the senators' heads for broad public support.

Someone proposed a glossy brochure showing the wonders of Utah. Also a media kit with maps, "themes"—verbal descriptions of the areas in question—and stunning photographs of wild beauty. A number of such photographs circulated about the room, preserved in plastic wrap: reefs and washes, water pockets and lava folds, upthrusts and hoodoos and hondos, and occasionally something growing—a cottonwood or tortured P-J. A press conference had to be set, preferably on the eve of the secretary of interior's congressional testimony, forcing him to address the Utah problem. Another press conference must be held in Salt Lake.

"Let's do Washington first."

"No, the Utah press will hang us in effigy."

Food appeared—fresh fruit from the Sierra Club; Doritos and cookies from Wilderness; Tab, beer, crackers, and cheese from elsewhere. Mike Scott's Wilderness Society colleague stationed himself at the table and began to deal seriously with these resources.

The debate returned to local support. Sponsors were needed in Utah among ranchers and other prime users of the public lands.

"Let's talk AUMs for a minute."

"Only two percent of the beef in America gets onto public lands."

Greg's eyes fell open. "That's a trap," he said. "Two percent total, maybe, but twenty-five percent of the breeding stock goes on the public range. Make the point that wilderness and cattle are compatible. Keep it simple."

"We've got to stop saying they're compatible," offered a visiting member of Sierra. "We—"

"Goddamn it, don't pick a fight with the ranchers. I want some mileage out of this bill."

No one wanted to fight with Greg. There were bigger things at stake, and I realized that the professionals were used to accommodating a wide range of difficult and outspoken people. Often those people had their own, hidden agendas.

The Sierra representative from Phoenix asked how to deal with the mining issue.

"What's the standard slop you dish out?" Greg asked.

The Sierraite said a small percentage of recoverable minerals lay beneath proposed wilderness. That didn't include coal, tar sands, and uranium, all of them contained in the lands the environmentalists wanted protected.

"We don't have to emphasize those," said Maggie.

She made a list of Utah media markets that read like a history of Mormon settlement: Salt Lake, St. George, Monticello, Blanding, Bluff. They would all be notified of the press conference.

"What we have to do," Kincaid said, "is decide what we want to *accomplish* by a press conference."

Make the point, someone suggested, that their wilderness proposal included more acreage than any other in the Lower Forty-eight.

No, Idaho environmentalists had proposed 9 million acres.

Well, then make the point that Utah's were more important. Bring in the national directors of Wilderness and Sierra to say so.

"Get David Brower up there," Kincaid said of the former head of Sierra, "and let his heart bleed."

Diplomatic forays would be made into the ranks of the sometimes-allied—the Audubon Society, Friends of the Earth, the Wasatch Mountain Club, outfitters, fishermen, duck hunters.

"What about celebrities? What about Abbey?"

"What about *Redford*?"

Three hours passed. It was raining up on the Aquarius Plateau; the Escalante River had gone from near-clarity to something resembling chocolate milk. But the sun shone over Phipps-Death Hollow and orioles flitted among the cottonwoods. Virgas—isolated clouds dropping rain that would evaporate before it touched the hot earth—drifted southeastward.

Greg told me, "This is all small stuff. The important part will come when three or four of us sit down in private and talk funding."

Late arrivals brought armfuls of rolled maps, and cardboard tubes full of documents showing potential wilderness that had been walked and measured and photographed from the air. As the maps and surveys were spread on the floor, a welcome breeze moved through the isolated house, thunder riding behind.

A list of possible endorsements was made up: the Torrey Chamber of Commerce, provisioners to tourists bound for wilderness; Marmot Mountain Works, maker of sleeping bags; Peregrine Press, publisher of the ecologically sound; Kelty, maker of backpacks, and a manufacturer of pitons used in mountain climbing.

"Pitons?" said Maggie Fox, eyebrows going up. "Aren't you a clean climber?"

A fire had been built under the eaves of a cave facing the Escalante, a natural sauna to which everyone was invited before supper, but the virgas had reached us now, and rain splattered on the dusty windowsills. When it had passed Maggie put on her jogging shoes and loped down the sandy drive with Sierra's Phoenix rep, recently out of college. I joined them. They seemed to represent a new class in the West, but I couldn't figure out where Greg fit in.

"Neither can I," said Maggie. "Greg's an unknown."

"I thought he was a big donor."

"He's a baby donor, and potentially a big one." She speculated that his contribution would cover the cost of the Utah wilderness brochure—a few thousand dollars.

She was a teacher in Outward Bound, as well as Sierra's emissary from San Francisco, and ran on ahead.

"Environmentalists out here don't have any role models," said her colleague, out of the blue. He added, "Nobody stays around for more than a few years."

They went on to administrative jobs, or to Washington to lobby for wilderness, and more young people filled the ranks. They felt remote from early idealists like Muir and Leopold, and even from the professional conservationists like Bob Marshall, Benton MacKaye, and Howard Zahniser, who symbolized earlier stages of the environmental movement. Still, they operated from a premise that they could change things. Because change came slowly, there was little instant gratification in the profession, and people burned out quickly once they doubted change was possible.

The environmental movement has deep roots in the West; it was once closely linked with the government agencies responsible for the country. Then conservationists were more concerned about animals, hiking, and hunting than trees, giving rise to the considerable power of the National Association of Audubon Societies, the Isaak Walton League, the Appalachian Mountain Club. The need for enduring animal and human habitat seemed a given, but in the twenties the American Forestry Association turned from conservation to corporate strategy, and various government agencies, including the National Park Service, began to show more interest in developing their domains.

A relatively gentle, highbrow reaction set in. As Stephen Fox, author of *The American Conservation Movement: John Muir and His Legacy,* has written, conservation was first a Waspy Republican reaction in the mold of Teddy Roosevelt and his appointee Gifford Pinchot.

The original founders of the Wilderness Society and the

Sierra Club wanted something more than managed resources. They met at the Cosmos Club in Washington in 1935 "to save from invasion . . . that extremely minor fraction of outdoor America which yet remains free from mechanical sights and sounds and smells."

Sierra shared some interests with the Park Service; the Wilderness Society found the Forest Service less development-minded, although neither of those affinities would last. Bob Marshall, a founder of the Wilderness Society, went camping with a prominent member of Sierra, and they were soon sharing mailing lists, the ultimate environmental test. In 1955, the Wilderness Society and the Sierra Club teamed up with other conservation groups to oppose the Echo Park dam proposed by the Bureau of Reclamation, which would have flooded Dinosaur National Monument. David Brower was the head of Sierra when it became a political force rather than a collection of California mountaineers. Echo Park was a watershed victory. It put Wilderness and Sierra in the vanguard of "the movement" and set the agenda for battles to come.

The Wilderness Society's proposal in 1955 for 50 million acres of de jure wilderness to be enacted by Congress forever divided the environmentalists from the government agencies and the organizations dependent upon public resources—lumbermen, miners, developers, even stockmen. The Wilderness Act of 1964, creating a wilderness system, was a reflection of public sentiment for wilderness. Twenty-two new units were added to the system in 1970. Emphasis moved for a time to Alaska and the Native Claims Settlement Act. Five years later both FLPMA and the National Forest Management Act passed, requiring the BLM and Forest Service to manage the public lands with regard to all uses, including wilderness. The outcome rested, as always, with the people actually engaged in carrying out these directives, and their perception of what mattered and what did not. The people gathered at the confluence of Cow Creek and the Escalante River were professionals working within the system in an attempt to alter the official perception by altering the public's.

Tents were rising in the cottonwood bottom when we returned; the smell of clams in tomato sauce had entered the environment.

The next morning Greg sat on a rock with Maggie Fox for half an hour. Then he sat on a rock with Mike Scott. Then he collected his gear. "We've planted the seed for an Alaska-type coalition," he said, "right here this weekend. There'll be a staff position created in Salt Lake just to handle it." He grinned. "This is no different from what you'd do on a golf course."

He drove off in the Opel with the kayak on top.

I asked Mike Scott how much of that office in Salt Lake Greg would pay for. Scott said, "The funding will come from a number of sources, maybe including him. It's hard to tell with Greg. He could get halfway down the Burr Trail and change his mind."

Kincaid had not sat on a rock with Greg, but that didn't bother him. "He'll fund us," he said, and if Greg didn't Kincaid would get the money elsewhere. Kincaid would also get his stone barn built, but now there was important work to do.

▪ 3 ▪

THERE WAS another side to the environmental movement, I knew, one unconcerned with "the system." Its members would have scoffed at the orderly meeting on the banks of the Escalante, and such civilized objectives. They favored something called ecotage—ecological sabotage, a leafy version of bomb-throwing.

I heard about ecotage first from the Western writer Edward Abbey, a former Forest Service employee. In 1968 Abbey had written a book called *Desert Solitaire*, which found a wide audience. The book was an evocative narrative of canyonland life in the service of the federal government, and it aroused my interest in the arid West. The author seemed fractious but informed, moved by an old sixties countercultural élan. He had greatly augmented his following with a subsequent environmental thriller, *The Monkey Wrench Gang*, which was an inspiration for ecotage—uncivil disobedience that included shooting holes in the radiators of FS bulldozers, all in the interest of the untrammeled land.

I telephoned Abbey when I was in Tucson, where he lives. We made arrangements to have lunch the next day at the Holiday Inn. It seemed odd to meet one of the foremost advocates of the undeveloped West in the symbol of instant American ease, but Abbey liked the stir-fry there, and the Holiday Inn was convenient.

The restaurant was deserted when we arrived together. I had expected a brawny embodiment of the voice of *Desert Solitaire,* not a rangy fifty-eight-year-old in a Cat hat and wrinkled cords.

The waitress appraised Abbey's beard and rubber sandals but showed us to a table anyway. I had heard stories about Abbey: he was a hard-drinking, four-square extrovert with four wives and five children, or five wives and four children; he hated cities and Eastern reporters and refused to be interviewed; a bleeding pancreas had almost killed him a few months before.

That last story was true, he said. "Too much booze, too much aspirin."

He lived with his fifth wife and two of his four children, one of them a baby girl. He was writing a novel and teaching part-time at the University of Arizona. "It keeps me from becoming a hermit," he said. "I'd prefer to live out in the country, but my family likes it here."

From his back yard ten miles outside Tucson he could see plenty of public land; its development had been the focus of most of his writing. "The public lands have been exploited and continue to be. It's important to resist, to slow it down, hoping against hope that people will change their views, or that we'll have an economic collapse. I'm counting on biology to bail us out—famine, plague, anything short of nuclear war."

Desert Solitaire had made him slightly famous; renewed movie options on *The Monkey Wrench Gang* kept him slightly rich, at least by the standards of retired seasonal rangers.

In *The Monkey Wrench Gang,* a group of ecotagists attempt to destroy a dam on the Colorado River. "I wrote it to vent my spleen and indulge my fantasies. It's a funny book, but I'm serious about ecological sabotage. At readings I advocate illegal action, and catch hell from editorial writers.

"Politics isn't enough anymore. Our representative democracy has broken down, the politicians represent only those interests that finance their elections. You must have some recourse— free-lance sabotage is the only thing left."

I asked about what seemed to be a violent aesthetic.

"I see it as a force against violence," Abbey said. "I've attacked machines in the national forests threatened with logging.

I've spiked a few trees offered by the Forest Service to the highest bidder—a commercial buzz saw can be ruined with a single heavy nail. After you spike trees, you call up the logging company about to bid on the timber and tell them about it. That way we save both the buzz saws and the trees."

The Forest Service then had to go around with a metal detector, trying to find the spikes. "We have a little war going on out here between the preservers and the developers. Sugar and sand in crankcases, handgun blasts to radiators. I wouldn't urge anyone to do what I wouldn't do myself."

He asked the waitress to warm up his stir-fry.

"I think of the public lands as a whole, administered from Washington," he went on. "I wish a century ago we had had enough sense to set aside the entire West as a wilderness preserve. I'd move back east right now if everyone else would. I'd go back to Europe if the Indians would go back to Siberia."

He came west from a hardscrabble farm in western Pennsylvania forty years before, hitchhiking, and fell in love with the country. With money from the GI Bill he studied philosophy at the University of New Mexico, Yale, and Edinburgh University, and he worked summers for the Park and Forest services. "I had academic ambitions, but I gave them up when I realized I could make a marginal living as a seasonal ranger. I used to be able to pick my park out of half a dozen choices every spring. It was a good life, and a good life for a writer."

The journal he kept, which became *Desert Solitaire,* carries the immediacy and detail of something written quickly, in the heat of discovery; in fact it took ten years. "I've been a welfare case worker in Brooklyn. I lived with a painter once in Hoboken, and New York. I've seen the bottom side of the urban world. We should limit our numbers and demands, and let half the planet remain undisturbed—a fifty-fifty split. We should reduce the population of the United States to, say, fifty million through incentives and tax bonuses for fewer children. But we'll keep drifting from disaster to disaster, as humans always do."

"You haven't set much of an example of population control."

"Four children by five wives is a modest rate," he said. "Every woman is entitled to one child. If she's able and willing to be a full-time mother. Women who prefer other careers should not have babies."

The waitress was pouring more coffee; Abbey's comment sent her eyes rolling back in her head. "We're trying to close," she said.

"I don't want to leave you with the impression that life is all gloom and doom," Abbey told me. "Personally, I'm very happy. I have a good life, I make my living as a writer, and I don't work too hard. I'll be a father to a teenager while in my seventies—a fantastic prospect."

I had met the priest in southern Arizona; the ceremony took place two months later on the Uncompahgre Plateau, dry, remote country in southwest Colorado. *Uncompahgre* is Ute for "red water springs" and refers to the higher, snowy ranges in the same national forest. Tourists are still something of an occasion along the plateau's western edge. Those I saw on the eve of Independence Day wore shorts and headbands and drove motorcycles or beat-up Saabs and other foreign machines piled high with camping gear and water jugs. They took a dirt road looping up onto the Uncompahgre, strung out for miles in a kind of migratory homing. I followed them, bound for the annual convention of something called Earth First!, ecotagists of record.

Our destination was a high meadow strewn with blue lupine. Cars and vans filed in and parked in the shade of aspens; dust rose from the groups gathering for what had been advertised in the EF newspaper as "personal interaction and communication" in the interests of the ecosystem. Anyone could attend, for free.

The high, cool air was no match for the July sun. The array of head coverings was devoid of those imprimaturs of Western values, Cat hats and cowboy hats, and rich in misshapen straws with feather-stuffed bands, camouflage deerstalkers, boating caps, upside-down canvas buckets, floppy-brimmed bush hats, miners' caps, and weathered tweed anomalies.

Save the Earth First! read a banner strung between two big aspens, above the working seminars on nonviolent prep and media manipulation. Participants were the friends of many rivers, judging by the messages on their T-shirts. One shirt, worn by a young woman with a knife in a beaded scabbard and lace-up boots with studs the size of silver dollars, said "Eat the Rich."

Brightly colored tents going up among the aspen; stacks of canned food, beer, and backpacks; scattered chairs and tables; children playing in the mottled sunlight, eating Doritos and live-culture yogurt, and drinking pop—the occasion had all the makings of a grand July Fourth picnic. License plates from every Western state, as well as Ohio, North Carolina, Maine, and Australia, passed in the haze of drifting dust.

The smell of cooking rose in the evening air from camps as various as the people tending their Coleman stoves. I made supper. The lushly darkening sky of the high mountain West was reflected in the lupine out in the meadow.

Later, a bonfire drew everyone into its bright radius; the night bloomed with serapes and suede jerkins, embroidered coats, great hoods, turbans, and slouch hats. The moon was rising. Two guitars spoke to each other across the fire pit, through the skunky haze of sinsemilla. I moved around, trying to find out who made up the ranks of EF, and found to my surprise a physics teacher from Houston, a biologist from Hawaii, an instructor in wilderness values from Yosemite, and an astronomer from southern California. "You basically get the professionals," this last explained, "and then you get the hippies."

The Fourth broke hot and clear. The steady beat of a tom-tom announced the beginning of orientation in the meadow. Dave Foreman, a hulking New Mexican in a red beard, told the assembly, "Five years ago when we founded Earth First! in a bar in Sonora, we never dreamed it would come this far. We've become a national and an international force. Deep ecology, and biocentrism, is more than loving aspens and butterflies. It requires effort, and courage. If it isn't a driving force in your life, it doesn't count."

Foreman introduced a teacher of ecology from southern California who was wearing a red baseball cap and hiking shorts. The teacher told us, "I see two circles working here. They are interconnected, and they fluctuate. The first is everyone around this fire pit. It feels good. But there's another circle. . . . Take yourselves analogously out of the big environmental group networking, and put yourself here. That calls for a different response—a *deep* responsibility, not the same thing as attending a workshop." He leaned over and picked a spiderwort. "The responsibility for picking a flower—I haven't killed it because it's a perennial—is important.

"The second circle is the things that grow here—the flowers and aspens. It would be irresponsible not to respond to this circle, a response you can't have in San Francisco, or lobbying in Washington, D.C. Let the circles interact. Deep ecology is more than direct action."

I asked the ecology teacher later about deep ecology, and a message I thought ran counter to EF's ethic of direct action. In fact, he said, there was a sharp division of views in the meadow. The "redneck" wilderness advocates preached ecotage, but the college professors favored a more orderly approach. "Some of us see ecology as the whole earth and its interrelationships. We have to think deeply about the state of the human race and other critters."

Earth First! was the first organization of its kind to look at all the questions, he added, and to try to rise above the needs of man alone. "We're dealing with the here and now. Thoreau started off as a transcendentalist but went beyond it and saw himself as part of the whole. He saw that man had to get away from manipulating the earth for his own ends, and tried to impress that upon his fellow Concordians. They took him for a kook, just as some would look at the people here."

I finally caught up with Foreman. He was a busy man but took time to sprawl in the shade of an aspen. "The West is under absolute assault," he said, "and nothing's stopping it. The dead flesh of the livestock industry has begun to stink, but a bigger threat is road-building in roadless areas that are the real wilderness today—not those created by Congress, full of backpackers, but the unofficial wilderness."

These wild lands lay in remote sections of the national forests; bulldozing made them ineligible for consideration as official wilderness later. Worse, roads let in people with guns and chain saws. "The roadless areas are all that's left of old-time America. Developing them will destroy the ambience of the West, the lifestyle and the wildlife habitat. We're trying to stop that by the only means left.".

He excoriated the Sierra Club for going hat in hand to Congress and requesting a couple of million more acres for wilderness designation in the West, when EF demanded 14 million new acres. "The Wilderness Society and Sierra can't sue on every timber sale and seismic permit, so we take direct action. We try to differentiate between sabotage and vandalism. We try to be thoughtful, deliberate, responsible. If you wipe out a snowmobile, say, for defiling landscape or running down animals, you think about the distance from a road and the age of the man riding it who has to walk out."

Foreman's great-grandparents had homesteaded in eastern New Mexico. He called himself a desert rat, but his voice rang with the conviction of a man who had stood up before many a gathering, in settings far more conventional than this one. Foreman had dropped out of mainstream conservation after working for the Wilderness Society on the Roadless Area Review and Evaluation process, which was still going on. He gained a deep pessimism about the trading of roadless areas for designated wilderness areas, and about the ability of conventional environmental groups to deal with development. "The Forest Service has become much more sophisticated, with good PR and 'people process.' We're the last line of defense." He seemed resigned to the inevitable demise of the West, but not without a fight.

A conflict of workshops developed between Guerrilla Theater and Toxic Waste; Foreman wisely settled it by allowing both to be conducted. Chanting would be done at sunset, next to the tepee on the hill. Two sweats would be held in the sweat lodge that day, and a spiritual sweat the next. Earth First! T-shirts were available for a price at what Foreman called "the snake-oil table." The T-shirts printed with the message "Fuck Bechtel" had sold out, but more were on the way. There were bumper stickers: "Bio-Centrism," and "Subvert the Dominant Paradigm."

A forty-eight-star American flag hung from a tree over the snake-oil table. It had been flown during EF's first bit of civil disobedience five years before, when Foreman and a few others dangled several hundred feet of black plastic down the face of Glen Canyon Dam, symbolizing a crack.

The list of seminars nailed to an aspen included Citizen Activism, FS Issues, Guerrilla Theater, Rain Forests, and EF! Image. I was intrigued with the latter and joined a dozen people settling uncertainly amidst the lupine. The leader was a teacher of psychology in Santa Cruz—another professor. He said, "This workshop will revolve around the questions: What are your and others' feeling about Earth First!? And what do you want it to be?" He added gravely, "There's a lot of possibility for controversy here."

"I want to discuss the hard-ass aspects of Earth First!" said a fellow Californian in a carrot-colored goatee. "Hard-assedness could get us out of favor with the public."

"Excuse me," said the girl with the beaded knife scabbard, "but I thought this was Toxic Waste." She walked off.

"I'm delighted there's a place in Earth First! for monkey-wrenching," said a young Vermonter in a red bandana who had ridden a bus all the way out West. But he was not pleased with what he referred to as "Montana cowboy environmentalists"— the redneck wilderness advocates. Their women did the cooking, he said, while the men talked about fights they had seen in bars between the locals and the developers, and between themselves and the developers, and themselves and the locals. "They started drinking here last night," he added, jerking his head in the direction of the Montana camp up in the woods.

A woman in a serape said, "I've seen Earth First! referred to as eco-terrorist. In my opinion, moving a survey stake is a high act. I like the Montana redneck, shit-kicking, beer-drinking image. They make up myths, and the West is a mythical land. But eventually somebody's gonna get killed on one of these monkey-wrenched machines."

It was Santa Cruz's turn. "What attracted me to the Earth

First! image was that it was *fun.* They did neat things, like rolling
plastic down dams, and getting on TV. I'm from Santa Cruz, a
liberal town aware of feminist issues. We don't all go along with
the Montana image."

That "image" made trouble for him at home, where he
couldn't get tables at conventions of nonviolent political groups
because people thought Earth First! blew things up. "I decided
Earth First! had an image problem. Instead of ecotage, we're
going to demonstrate at Burger King against destruction of
Central American rain forests."

Throughout the discussion a skinny old man sat propped
against a tree, arms folded. When he couldn't stand it any
longer, he said, "The reason I'm not in Sierra or Friends of the
Earth or any of the others is because *all* they're concerned about
is image. I don't give a fuck. You do something because it's
right."

Water was a problem on the high plateau. Most people had
brought their own, and a plastic container for emergencies sat
next to the snake-oil table, but there were no rivers or streams
within striking distance, just a spring a mile away, down a trail
strewn with hot, dusty people in various stages of undress. A tiny
pond had formed at the mouth of the spring, and people stood in
the weeds and in the shallows, their bodies stark in the sunlight.

I took off my clothes. The pond looked like a biopeptic soup
but proved to be icy and wonderfully refreshing. A school-
teacher from Reno was washing her friend's hair with biode-
gradable shampoo. She introduced me to Wildcat Annie, a ro-
bust woman ruddying herself with a towel, who worked for the
BLM. Wildcat Annie was an alias she used in what she considered her real life. She worked as an outdoor recreation planner
in a Western state but asked me not to mention which one, since
belonging to Earth First! could cause her problems in the work-
place. "Morale has plummeted since the 'eighty elections," she
said. "The BLM has become a lot more political. There are less
people at the top who have worked their way up. Now even the
associate state directors are being appointed. They're changing
the agency."

She had given Earth First! three thousand dollars, an impressive piece of her salary, to combat the practices of her employer—e.g., chainings; tolerating trespass by ranchers, timber cutters, and pot hunters; and ignoring environmental regulations. "Right now I can do more good staying than leaving," she said. "At least I can see what's going on, and try to change things."

I got dressed and walked back to camp. The Santa Cruz contingent had hung a poster on the big aspen. "Oppression of wilderness is the same as oppression of people," it began, and went on to champion feminism and equate civil rights with wilderness values—a blatant effort to improve the EF image.

The professors were making other efforts to enlighten. The chanting session had been scheduled by Santa Cruz himself to counter less uplifting behavior by the Montanans and other rednecks. At dusk a steady drumbeat drew me into the shadows, where he had constructed an Indian medicine wheel out of fir branches, moss, a rock, a flickering candle, a plastic bowl of water, and four woodpecker feathers. He sat cross-legged before it, holding the drum.

"Choose the sign that suits you best," he said, as a dozen of us settled in a circle. "It's appropriate to begin with the Air Chant." He beat the tomtom, and began:

> Fly like the eagle, flying so high,
> Around the universe, on wings of pure light.
> *Hey hunga ho hunga hey yung yung.*

We repeated it several times, holding hands and swaying. We chanted the Fire Chant. Before the Water Chant, Santa Cruz said, "Water is a little bit sensual. You may squeeze hands."

> The earth is our mother,
> We must take care of her.
> Her sacred ground we walk upon
> With every step we take.
> *Keya wate lenya lenya ma mate*
> *Hi yano, hi yano, hi yano.*

Guitars were warming up in the meadow. A few verses of extemporaneous scatology reached us, deepening the mood. "Sage is a purifier," Santa Cruz was saying, holding some in a dish, which he tried to light with a match. "Usually I have a propane lighter."

He passed the dish around. "As you breath in the smoke, let all tensions go. Let the hurts go. Let today go. Let tomorrow go. Let those intellectual pretensions go. Stop trying to figure out intellectually how sage can purify you and let it work on your energy."

He handed the tom-tom to the widow in a serape. "Say a prayer and send it along with four beats of the drum."

Her prayer was silent, but the young man in camouflage said, "Heal the earth, and stop the oppressors."

"Nourish Mother Earth," said the journalism student from Columbia University.

Thump, thump . . .

I was passed the drum. I prayed silently that this would soon end, but it wasn't answered. Santa Cruz launched a prayer of stunning duration: "Grandfathers, help us. Some of our brothers have become confused." He meant the redneck environmentalists. "Others do not know how to treat the Earth Mother. Help them understand that the Earth Mother sustains us. Some of our brothers and sisters have attacked the Mother. They have cut her trees and torn the rocks out of her. Help them see the error of their ways, Grandfathers. They are many, and we are few . . ."

The mosquitoes were many, as well. It was getting cold. Santa Cruz was breathing now, great sonorous exhalations we had to emulate. This was the man who had joined Earth First! for fun.

"Feel your power," he moaned. "Feel it flowing through your inner selves. Feel it spreading around the circle. Feel it flowing back inside you. Now we're going to get physical."

We danced around the fire wheel. The chanting switched from Native American to Japanese, then back to English. "You are an aspen tree," Santa Cruz told us, when we came to a halt. "Close your eyes and wiggle your fingers, feel the wind in your branches. Feel the animals around your thick trunk.

Sense the deer running past, the wolverine digging a nest at your roots, the gophers eating—mostly forbs and sedges. Feel the sap running into you. Feel the water deep in the earth. Sense the glimmer of the stars. Sense the moon that will soon be rising . . ."

I stumbled off into the darkness. I had yet to meet the redneck environmentalists, but by now was firmly on their side. A big crowd had gathered around the fire in the meadow. Figures drifted between the light and the collective domicile of cars, vans, and tents tucked into the woods. I could see a wilder array of caftans and elaborate hats, and a woman with a white dove tied to her shoulder. A rail-thin figure in handmade leather boots, with beads and leather tassels, circled the group like a coyote, beaded leather pouches and a broad-bladed knife on his belt. The line between reality and parody has always been thin in the West. The real cowboy becomes the drugstore version with ease. Easterners take up Western crudeness like college degrees; mountain men buy their cocaine and *TV Guide* in shopping centers.

The Montanans were raising hell, off by themselves. I followed their shouts of "Rednecks for wilderness!" to a bunch of buckskin and leather, even Cat hats, gathered round an illegal campfire. Steam rose from a pot of vegetables. The women were not cooking but drinking beer and singing raucous songs and eating home-salted salmon out of a Mason jar.

"What's the slant of your book?" one asked, as soon as I had stated my business.

"I don't have a slant."

"Bullshit!"

"What do you know about public lands?" asked another.

"What do you know about *Montana*?"

"Do you like to fish?"

"Do you like tequila?"

What began as a fight became a determined effort to make me understand the beauty and importance of Montana, both considerable. "Montanans are different," one kept saying. He was runty but fierce, with a black beard. "We're conservative, determined, and we're going to stop the bastards from killing the griz and destroying the most important ecosystem left in America. Period!"

"Fuck Senator Melcher!" someone shouted, and the others took up the theme.

"FUCK SENATOR WALLOP!"

"FUCK SENATOR McCLURE!"

The Montana women sang of the sexual inadequacies of their state's congressional delegation; the men shouted "Drunk and sensitive!" in an attempt to improve their image with the rest of the camp, but that soon changed to "Drunk and ignorant!"

Walking back to the van, I passed a couple intertwined in the bushes, their clothes in a puddle beside them. The fact that they made love in the cold was not as remarkable as their uninterrupted laughter.

The next two days ran together in a stew of deep ecology, green politics, ecotage, and dwindling food and water. The Santa Cruz statement was ripped down, probably by the Montanans. Phrases drifted up like ecological blimps from gatherings on the grass: glamour species, bioprostitute, Civil Disobedience (CD), Direct Confrontation (DC), animalist, specist. A specist was someone tolerant of the extinction of lesser species in the interest of glamour species like griz and woodland caribou; an animalist condemned owning and eating animals, but sinned against plants by owning and even eating them. A bioprostitute performed biological assignments for the FS and had to be subverted either through CD or DC. There was hard DC and soft DC. Soft DC was planned in Yellowstone later in the summer, when EFers would appear in the park hotel in grizzly costumes and sit around the lobby eating huckleberries. A large woman from Oregon offered to make five bear costumes if EF would send her the material; it would be made of synthetics, admittedly a mineralist action with animalist and specist overtones but directed toward bio- and other prostitutes in the machinist continuum . . .

I bought a copy of *Deep Ecology* off the snake-oil table. The two authors were present, taking part in workshops. I read during the heat of the day, propped against an aspen. The book was a compendium of thought on the subject, most of it from the Norwegian philosopher Arne Naess, who coined the phrase *ecosophy*—a process through which profound questions could be put about nature and man. The phrase *deep ecology* had a pedantic ring; but the notion that humans must practice self-denial, and that the human fate was directly related to that of grizzlies, and even spiderworts, was compelling.

A community of concerned people had become essential to survival, according to the book. "In a society famous for dystopian visions," the authors wrote, of ours, "ecotopian visions present affirmations of our bonds with Earth."

I found one of the authors, Bill Devall, during the gathering for mass guerrilla theater. "The agencies that control the public lands are anthrocentric," he said. "It goes back to Gifford Pinchot, who linked them to development. Muir originally thought of the national forests as preserves. Any change at this point to biocentrism cannot be evolutionary." We were talking revolution.

I later saw him flapping his arms and cawing, taking part in a communal game, and asked if he was a crow.

"A raven," he said, "a very different proposition," and flapped off.

The homogenization of America has been postponed by the existence of public lands, where people can pursue lives truly different from those elsewhere, or at least pretend to. There were some play-actors here, but there were also people dedicated to slowing down the systematic diminishment of the West.

"We're a tribe," Foreman told the gathering that night. "We have our own rituals, demigods, shared language, and devils. We gather once a year to get to know each other, to plan events and exchange genetic material. Basically, we're Neanderthals. We've been in a ten-thousand-year eddy, but we're about to get back into the mainstream."

Earth First! was different, he said; it would fail in the end, but the battle was worth it. He cited Aldo Leopold's vision of the circular process of death and regeneration. "We shouldn't fear death, but welcome it when it comes. Only then will we have freedom. Modern man is obsessed with living forever."

He picked up a fistful of Uncompahgre dirt and trailed it on the breeze. "This is our immortality!"

▪ 4 ▪

IN THE BEGINNING, on the far side of the West, I had set out across roads where crews worked getting them ready for summer; the asphalt trucks were distinct and grimy in the abundant light, and girls in hard hats and sunglasses twirled stop signs visible for miles. Now the crews were all back, getting the roads ready for winter, and the shadows had lengthened.

I sometimes longed for the uneventful ribbon of the Interstate to pull me east again. I felt the suck of cities along it—haze-breathing bubbles of glass and concrete—but as soon as I got to one I couldn't wait to leave. Movement, and scenery, addict. The West may be a collection of remnants, but they are the most spectacular remnants on earth, full of the past, and of second chances.

Public lands are also an inadvertent refuge for the enduring notion of the West, and consequently for a significant piece of our collective unconscious. For six months I had contemplated the public domain through the windshield, or that narrow gap of window next to my hanging backpack, while eating hundreds of meals on a bunk made of plywood, between interviews. The West was a young land in the contradictory blush of geologic puberty, and biologic hiatus; that I had actually entered only a fraction of it was a source of some unhappiness to me.

Toward the end of the trip, on the edge of Nevada, I began to lose whatever it is that enables the person to distinguish himself from the land. The earth rose and fell before me, under a secondary highway perfectly straight and perfectly empty. In the middle of a reverie, I got up from the driver's seat and walked to the rear of the van. It seemed a logical thing to do, the landscape being deserted and the road a slip of concrete dwindling into mirage. After all, in the greater scheme of things, it made no difference where I drove, or at what velocity, since the country was endless.

I opened the ice chest and grasped the neck of a beer bottle—my first, I should add, in two days. Now, I do not believe in fate, but I do believe that revelation lies in peculiar circumstances, and for some reason this bottle would not budge. An entirely sane person would not have been back there to begin with, but one with at least a glimmer of reason would have, by then, been lunging for the steering wheel. Instead, I wrestled with the bottle.

Months later, a friend would remind me of a passage from *Moby-Dick* about the mesmerizing quality of the ocean, and its dangers: "There is no life in thee, now, except that rocking life imparted by a gentle rolling ship. . . . But while this sleep, this dream is on ye, move your foot or hand an inch; slip your hold at all; and your identity comes back in horror. . . . And perhaps, at mid-day, in the fairest weather, with one half-throttled shriek you drop through that transparent air into the summer sea, no more to rise for ever."

When finally the bottle relented and came out of the ice chest, I looked up and saw that I was indeed dropping through transparent air: the van had separated from the road. I rushed forward too late, and remember standing in the middle of the floor, gripping the bottle in one hand and the steering wheel in the other, shouting abuse at myself while a culvert materialized out of the glare. We—the van, the bottle, and I—sailed over it and came down with a tremendous crash on the far side. Doors flew open, half a ton of equipment rearranged itself behind me, and hubcaps leaped through the sage like chrome jack rabbits. The van rolled to a halt and I got out and looked back at a column of dust hanging in the air.

Miraculously, I was unhurt, and the van escaped with nothing more than an exploded shock absorber and a bent axle. I drove into a town where a mechanic—the modern medicine man—replaced the shock and straightened the wheel enough for me to drive on. I told him I had swerved to avoid a cow, a lie he recognized as such and listened to with perfect aplomb. He had been in that country long enough to know that people do strange things alone, and that the final justification is surviving.

Some time later, in southern California, my journey came to its end. Leaving El Centro heading east, Highway 8 dips close to the Mexican border, under the barren mountain, Pilot Knob. In its figurative shadow sits an isolated trailer camp and a BLM long-term visitor area. It is administered from El Centro, although Yuma is much closer—just a leap across the Arizona line—and reflects elemental concerns in transmission lines, metal homes on wheels, sway-backed fences, and aged machines that in the dry air are not allowed to die. Here George Patton trained his tank corps during World War II, and the tread marks from his imaginary battles can be seen after almost half a century.

No one stopped me as I turned in at the gate of the trailer park. I was looking for a secondhand thirty-two-foot Kencraft, the property of a retired Marine recently made a "host" by the BLM. He was responsible for recording the names of long-term visitors, a.k.a. snowbirds, and generally keeping an eye on this rocky bit of federal terrain. For this he had the privilege of staying longer than the two-week limit in the LTVA, and saved the twenty-five dollars he would have had to pay to park farther out in the wilderness. That doesn't sound like much of an incentive, but things are not always what they seem in the desert.

"Snowbird" has been in common usage for well over a century. It has roots in the army, from which deserters took off in the spring, when the snow began to melt and better climes and better existence beckoned. Now the word describes mostly older Americans who came south. The more recalcitrant ones refuse to pay to live on public land. Sometimes they draw their air-conditioned motor homes into circles, like covered wagons under attack.

Leslie Earl Derrington sat bare-chested at his kitchen table, an elbow resting next to his battered King James Bible. He wore military shoes, and socks rolled down to the leather—he was a dead ringer for General Westmoreland, with the same chiseled chin and white hair neatly grooved, except for the welts that ran from belt to biceps, stitching he said was left by a Japanese Hotchkiss submachine gun in the South Pacific, about the time I was born. "I was moving a piece of steel away from the muzzle of our howitzer," he told me, slipping easily into war stories, in a soft Southern accent, "when they started shooting. I could see the dust kick up. I turned, and the bullets hit me"—he touched himself gingerly—"one, two, three, four, five, six, seven . . ."

He had remained unconscious for seventeen days, and spent a year in a stateside hospital. He recovered, and taught artillery at Camp Pendleton; he became an ordnance technician, perfecting high-powered loads for tank destruction, and then left the Marines and headed west.

Derrington said he had top secret clearance. For twenty years he bounced among weapons systems manufacturers and bombing ranges—as a test site supervisor in Hollister, firing Maverick and FISK warheads, building "shape" charges at Lawrence Livermore's nuclear laboratory, designing explosive devices at White Sands.

He had retired three years before, and launched himself on a migration with no clear objective.

"What brought you to Pilot Knob?" I asked.

"My wife said I shouldn't build bombs. My family says a Christian shouldn't do that, shouldn't say things like 'son of a bitch.' Well, I do say 'son of a bitch' a lot. If somebody's a son of a bitch, I'll say so."

He had come here to be alone. He seldom saw his family, who disapproved of him. Leslie Earl Derrington had been raised a Methodist in Mississippi but had recently espoused a more evangelical form of the faith, which caused him more grief at home than building weapons. "They call me a Jesus freak."

He watched me, to see whose side I was on, his pale eyes watering in the harsh desert light.

"Some of them think I should give them money," he said,

producing a letter from a relative accusing him of doom-mongering and stinginess. "They say I'm a hypocrite, that a Christian wouldn't talk about the Third World War, the way I do. I don't know if you should write this, but . . ."

He leaned forward, hands clasped.

"Most people think we'll have bombs dropping, and a nuclear holocaust, but it won't be like that. The coastal areas of the United States will be flooded by dropping big bombs a few miles out. Three-hundred-megaton bombs will create tidal waves that'll wipe out San Diego, Los Angeles, Savannah, New York, Boston. One or two in the Gulf of Mexico would take care of everything up to Houston. They wouldn't have to be very precise with a subsurface burst. It would contaminate the water, you see. Alpha and beta rays aren't poisonous, but gamma rays would come in with the flood. Five bombs on a coast, and they'd have this son of a bitch beat."

His dog, a Doberman named Gideon—the Warrior—politely watched a stray kitten feed from a saucer under the table. Outside, the sun rebounded from every polished surface, and from the powdery white stretch between the highway and Mexico. Leslie smiled, and shrugged. The scenario was familiar to him, and also, I suspected, the look of horror on other people's faces. "I pulled in here one day, and met some snowbirds, and decided to stay and get healthy. I felt so depressed, and shot down, but after a few months the desert made me feel good. I fished in the canal, and ate under a tree I know of. I go for a walk every morning, just looking at things. Hell, it's real nice."

The dog woke him up every morning. He made a cup of coffee in the microwave and drank it as he walked on what amounted to an endless patio. "You meet nice people here, from different states. I show them how to camp in the desert. We pitch horseshoes and have a good ole time. They don't care if you're a good pitcher or not. The women get together for gabfests and knitting parties. People play instruments—guitars and fiddles."

Some drove to the Senior Citizen Center in Yuma every day for lunch, but not Leslie. He went to town once a week, to buy groceries and sell the aluminum soft drink cans he collected in the garbage bags that were left by what he called "the wetback people."

"They're the most interesting I've met, and a lot smarter than you'd think. They know when they come across the desert there"—he pointed to the south—"and see the transmission lines, to count four stanchions west of the big one, and there'll be a tunnel under the highway and the railroad tracks. They're out there now," he added, surveying the desert. "If you stood real still and watched one place for a while, you'd see them move."

He encountered illegal aliens often, he said. "I don't speak Spanish, but we communicate through sign language. One fella I ran into kept pointing to his stomach. I made him sit under a paloverde and went back for some water and a tomato. They like fresh vegetables, you know. Now when I bring them sandwiches, I stand there until they eat them, or the mayonnaise will spoil in the heat.

"I see the same people time and again. One group of five passed through and I fed them. Six months later I saw them hop off the train, in new clothes, and head south again. They waved. One group went into my trailer when I wasn't there and washed all my windows and dishes. They swept the place out. Later, one of the girls dislocated her shoulder. The border patrol got her, and some wetback people told me she was in the hospital down in San Luis Potosí. I went down there and paid the bill—it wasn't much—and the next time she came through she stopped by and thanked me."

We took a walk, led by Gideon. I put on sunglasses, but Leslie went unshaded, hatless, shirtless. A crane working on Pilot Knob raised a cloud of dust against the sky; a few seconds later I heard the clash of heavy machinery. The heat was brutal.

"Having a lot of money is a bunch of crap," Leslie said. "Why do you need it, as long as you've got a dog and a cat, and everybody's well fed?" The week before, he had given $170 to an itinerant Pentecostal minister who had been robbed in the San Francisco bus station. "I gave him forty dollars for food. I don't give money to anybody, only people who really need it."

He picked up a Diet Coke can from his BLM domain and dropped it into a plastic bag. "Some people might ask why a man with social security and two pension checks would sell empty cans in Yuma. Well, it's not the money—I give that away."

The discarded cans went into plastic bags left by people entering the country illegally. Leslie sold the cans and fed the aliens. The border patrol caught some, and recycled them, only to have them come back with new plastic bags. Those who made it through returned from the other direction in new clothes, with money, to recross the All American Canal. They too would return, with more plastic bags—a unique recycling operation, with Leslie as the eternal middleman.

We had left the trailer park far behind. Wispy tracks of a sidewinder lay across the desert floor, eerily congruent, as if drawn by a compass, each ellipse interrupted where the snake had lifted itself from the hot sand and moved on. "There aren't as many rattlesnakes around as people think," he said. "I've only seen four this year. One bit my dog, and cost me seventy-five dollars. The snake's still out there. I could have killed him, but they're not really so bad."

My head hurt; my mouth had turned to cotton. The broad expanse of no man's land between there and Mexico would not hold still.

Leslie stopped. He said, "This is where I spend my time."

I saw only a dry arroyo, and an ironwood tree.

He parted dense, drooping branches and led me into a room of latticework. "No one else has ever been in here," he said, a bit reluctantly, "except Gideon."

A milk crate against the trunk of the tree, with a board across, served as his chair. An old hibachi he had found somewhere provided the heat for his burgers. There was a water jug tucked neatly into a forked branch, and an old clasp knife stuck into a bole. The desert breeze cooled it all, scattering thermals out in a sea of aridity.

The dog lay down in the dappled shade.

"Does this remind you of the Marines?" I asked.

"No, it reminds me of camping on a hill outside of Houston, Miss'ippi, when I was eight."

He blinked, and looked at me with that funny grin, wondering if I saw the point of it all, not really caring if I didn't.

I asked how long he would stay.

"I don't really know. I like it here—it's handy. I can go straight into the desert. I ramble around. It ain't hot today, only ninety-five. On real hot days I wear a hat, and carry some water, mostly for Gideon. You have to be careful with dogs—they can't take the heat, you know."

He peered past the branches of the ironwood.

"In May, or June, I'll probably go over to Arizona for a while, to the mountains. It's nice up there—a little cooler. But I'll be back."

I imagine him sitting on the milk crate in that natural gazebo: a man on his throne, Gideon at his feet, reading his King James and meditating on the final, radioactive flood, while strangers move stealthily across his view and the ocotillo burns in the desert sunlight.

Acknowledgments and Sources

Many people helped with this book. Some showed me extraordinary country that did not find a place in the text but is still a valuable part of the kingdom, and of my perception of it. I want to acknowledge those places, and my gratitude to everyone who helped me, including those not mentioned.

In Washington, D.C., I received early assistance and encouragement from Jan Bedrosian at the BLM, and Lynn Engdahl, Billy Templeton, Candy Johnson, Bob Anderson, Dick Burch, Neil Morck, John Latz, Robert Ritsch, and Henri Bisson. David Prosperi, Barbara Maxfield, and the BLM's unofficial historian, Marion Clawson, later provided help and information about the agency.

At the Forest Service, Diane O'Connor put me in touch with essential members of the FS staff, among them Jerry Coutant, John Chambers, and Max Peterson, then chief of the FS. Diane answered an infinity of questions and helped me map out a rough itinerary of national forests in the West.

I found encouragement and good advice among professionals in Washington outside the federal agencies. They included Mike Scott, William Turnage, Tom Watkins, and Tom Robinson at the Wilderness Society; Tim Mahony at the Sierra Club; Ron Michieli at the National Cattlemen's Association; Tom Nelson of the American Mining Congress; and Keith Hayes at the American Petroleum Institute.

On the road, I was invariably offered assistance and hospitality. I particularly want to thank Pete and Sandy Tschel, who put me up in Pecos, New Mexico, and Mike O'Neill, who guided me through the paleontological mysteries of the Bisti Wilderness. Steve Service set me up in the Gila fire-fighting school, and George Grijalva, rodeo rider and fire boss, got me through the course and the hated step test.

Larry Soehlig and Ron Byers helped me find gold miners in the Tonto National Forest. For instruction in cowboying I want to thank Duane Blake, on the Arizona Strip, and his three sons; and Mark and Kim Nelson, of Boulder, Utah.

Billy Mahoney, John Stevens, and Art Goodtimes took the trouble to discuss history and life in Telluride. Staffers at the Western Colorado Congress offered valuable insights into the West Slope. Carl Bush, of the Rocky Mountain Sportsmen's Federation, explained the gentle art of opposing the bureaucracy. Ed Marston, publisher of *High Country News,* offered good companionship and advice.

Maurice Guerry, sheepman, kindly took me along on the official FS range tour south of the Snake River, in Idaho. Bert Webster opened my eyes to riparian upkeep and the life cycle of the wild trout. Several people at the annual Basque picnic in Gooding discussed Basque culture with enthusiasm.

In Jackson, Wyoming, Forest Supervisor Reid Jackson, environmentalist Mardi Muri, and Len Carlman of the Jackson Hole Alliance for Responsible Planning all graciously provided me time. I also want to thank Alice Frell, of the Rocky Mountain Oil and Gas Association, Dick Randall, of the Defenders of Wildlife, and John Balla of ASARCO.

Rick Dale was very accommodating with his coal mine in Colstrip, Montana, and Sonny and Anita Buckalew were extremely hospitable. So were Irv Alderson, Art Hayes, and Mark Nance, of Birney, Montana. The Northern Plains Resources Council provided good information, as always.

Jim Posewitz, of the Montana Department of Fish, Wildlife, and Parks, discoursed brilliantly on the grizzly. Further insights were provided by Tom France of the National Wildlife Federation and Bob Kiesling of the Nature Conservancy. Harold Yager and Burt Guthrie, ranchers near Choteau, were forthright with their views on the subject. So was Roy Jacobs, taxidermist.

Chuck Blixrud, an exemplary outfitter in the Bob Marshall Wilderness, and his wife, Sharon, kindly put me up in a difficult time. Doug Chadwick and Karen Reeves, of Polebridge, let me sleep on their place. Other Montanans I remember fondly include Paul Richards, Jasper Carlton, Steve McCoy, Susan Jan Rooj, Larry Campbell, and Gary Steele.

I want to thank the staff at the Missoula Aerial Fire Depot for telling me about the Okanogan fire over in Washington State, and Alan Gibbs for patiently describing what had taken place there. The people at the North Cascades Smokejumper Base were very helpful and candid.

Ralph Saperstein, of Douglas Timber Operators, explained the timber economy in Oregon, and Melvin Berg, the BLM district manager in Roseburg, eagerly discussed the government's role. Ray Doerner of the Association of O&C Counties also provided guidance.

Dick Wheeler, in Winnemucca, Nevada, was forthcoming on the subject of mustangs and the BLM. George High provided good stories about law enforcement on the Nevada range. The staff at Palomino Ranch was very helpful.

I talked long-distance several times to "Deep Root," a dissident Forest Service employee, after obtaining his number from Dave Foreman. His information and suggestions were all good. I never learned his real name.

Patrick Kidder and Carl Roundtree in Sacramento steered me toward contacts in the desert, as did Tony Staed. Ralph Hitchcock of Southern California Edison explained the economics of wind-generated electricity. Doug Evans, city planner, presented Palm Springs' case against windmills with feeling. Sean Hagerty, in El Centro, California's BLM office, explained the geology under the Imperial Sand Dunes, and water problems. Lillian Olech, wildlife specialist, eloquently discussed the plight of desert biota.

While the book was being written, and later, many people offered invaluable criticism of all or parts of the manuscript. I am indebted to Tracy Kidder, John Lang, Eleanor Dunn, Susan Todd, Ed Norton, Nancy Tartt, Bob Metcalf, my brothers, Frank and Dan Conaway, and particularly to my editor, Dick Todd. I couldn't have made the journey, nor made sense of it, without his constant encouragement, suggestions, and insight.

My family put up with the disruption caused by this project, and I'm grateful for that, and for the fact that they were able to share some of the experience with me. I particularly want to thank my wife, Penny, for single-handedly dealing with all the problems that arose at home, for an ever-loving response to calls from distant places, and for listening to the stories and reading every page.

What follows is not a formal bibliography, but a short list of useful and usually entertaining books for those interested in the American West:

Abbey, Edward, *Desert Solitaire.* New York: Ballantine, 1968.
Bartlett, Richard A., *Great Surveys of the American West.* Norman, Oklahoma: University of Oklahoma Press, 1962.

Clawson, Marion, *Uncle Sam's Acres.* Westport, Connecticut: Greenwood Press, 1951.

De Voto, Bernard, *The Course of Empire.* Lincoln, Nebraska: University of Nebraska Press, 1952.

Driver, Harold E., *Indians of North America.* Chicago: University of Chicago Press, 1961.

Ehrlich, Gretel, *The Solace of Open Spaces.* New York: Viking, 1985.

Garcia, Andrew, *Tough Trip Through Paradise: 1878–1879.* Bennett H. Stein, ed. Boston: Houghton Mifflin, 1967; Sausalito, California: Comstock, 1976.

Hine, Robert, *The American West.* 2nd ed. Boston: Little, Brown, 1984.

Holliday, J. S., *The World Rushed In.* New York: Simon & Schuster, 1981.

Krutch, Joseph Wood, *The Voice of the Desert.* New York: William Morrow, 1971.

Kues, Barry S., *Fossils of New Mexico.* Albuquerque: University of New Mexico Press, 1982.

Maclean, Norman, *A River Runs Through It & Other Stories.* Chicago: University of Chicago Press, 1976.

McPhee, John, *Basin and Range.* New York: Farrar, Straus & Giroux, 1981.

———, *Rising from the Plains.* New York: Farrar, Straus & Giroux, 1986.

Mohlenbrock, Robert H., *The Field Guide to U.S. National Forests.* New York: Congdon & Weed, 1984.

Peffer, E. Louise, *The Closing of the Public Domain.* Palo Alto, California: Stanford University Press, 1951.

Pinchot, Gifford, *Breaking New Ground.* New York: Harcourt, Brace, 1947.

Raphael, Ray, *Tree Talk.* Covelo, California: Island Press, 1981.

Ruess, Everett, *A Vagabond for Beauty.* Layton, Utah: Peregrine Smith, 1983.

Shulteis, Bud, *The Hidden West.* Berkeley, California: North Point Press, 1984.

Smith, Henry Nash, *Virgin Land.* Cambridge: Harvard University Press, 1950.

Stegner, Wallace, *Beyond the Hundredth Meridian.* Lincoln, Nebraska: University of Nebraska Press, 1953.

Twain, Mark, *Roughing It.* New York: Penguin, 1981.

Van Dyke, John C., *The Desert.* Layton, Utah: Peregrine Smith, 1980.

Webb, Walter Prescott, *The Great Plains.* Lincoln, Nebraska: University of Nebraska Press, 1931.

Wyant, William K., *Westward in Eden.* Berkeley: University of California Press, 1982.

Zaslowsky, Dan, and the Wilderness Society, *These American Lands.* New York: Henry Holt, 1986.

JAMES CONAWAY was born in Memphis, Tennessee. He is the author of two novels and several works of nonfiction. His articles have appeared in numerous publications, among them the *New York Times Magazine*, *Harper's* and the *Atlantic*. He has been a Wallace Stegner Creative Writing Fellow at Stanford University and a recipient of an Alicia Patterson Journalism Fellowship. From 1981 to 1985 he was a feature writer on the staff of the *Washington Post*. *Napa*, a book about the Napa Valley's wines and its social and political life, was published by Avon Books in 1992. Conaway teaches the writing of nonfiction at the University of Pittsburgh.